AFTER
APARTHEID

AFTER APARTHEID

THE FUTURE OF SOUTH AFRICA

SEBASTIAN MALLABY

TIMES BOOKS

Library of Congress Cataloging-in-Publication Data

Mallaby, Sebastian.
    After apartheid : the future of South Africa / Sebastian Mal-
laby. — 1st ed.
    p.   cm.
    Includes index.
    ISBN 0-8129-1938-6
    1. South Africa—Politics and government—1989–
2. Apartheid—South Africa.   3. South Africa—
Forecasting.   I. Title.
DT1970.M35   1992
968.06′4—dc20   91-50190

Manufactured in the United States of America

Designed by M 'N O Production Services, Inc.

9 8 7 6 5 4 3 2

First U.S. Edition

To Katty

CONTENTS

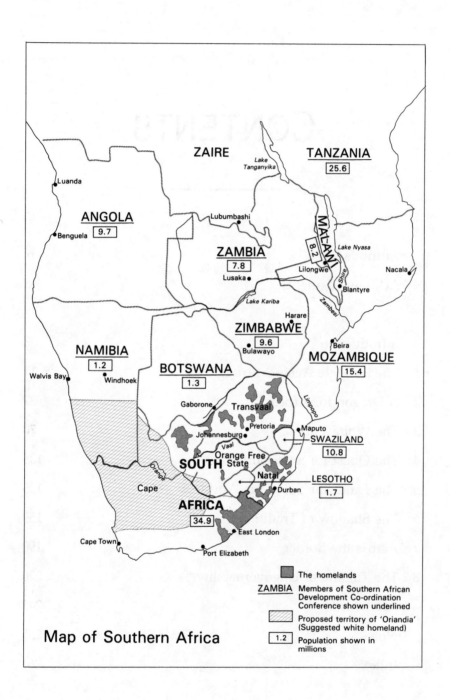

Map of Southern Africa

Legend:

The homelands

ZAMBIA — Members of Southern African Development Co-ordination Conference shown underlined

Proposed territory of 'Oriandia' (Suggested white homeland)

1.2 — Population shown in millions

Labels on map:

ZAIRE

TANZANIA 25.6

Lake Tanganyika

Luanda

ANGOLA 9.7

Benguela

Lubumbashi

MALAWI 8.2

Lake Nyasa

ZAMBIA 7.8

Lusaka

Lilongwe

Nacala

Blantyre

Shire

Lake Kariba

Zambesi

Harare

ZIMBABWE 9.6

Bulawayo

Beira

NAMIBIA 1.2

MOZAMBIQUE 15.4

Walvis Bay

Windhoek

BOTSWANA 1.3

Gaborone

Transvaal

Limpopo

Johannesburg

Pretoria

Maputo

SWAZILAND 10.8

Vaal

Orange Free State

SOUTH

Orange

Cape

Natal

LESOTHO 1.7

Durban

AFRICA 34.9

East London

Cape Town

Port Elizabeth

AUTHOR'S NOTE

———

Apartheid did violence to language, as well as to much else. It recognized four main racial categories: Africans, Whites, Coloreds, and Indians. "African," meaning South Africans with black skin, is a misleading term, since all South Africans are Africans. "Colored" is an artificial term: it throws together mixed-race people as well as a variety of racial groups, ranging from the brown-skinned Khoikhoi and San people (or Hottentots and Bushmen) to the descendants of Malay slaves brought to the Cape by Dutch settlers. It is impossible to ignore these terms, since their use has given them political significance. But at times I have also described "Indians" and "Coloreds" collectively as "brown." This is less ideological, and therefore ought to be less offensive.

South Africa's currency is the rand. The average exchange rate during the first nine months of 1991 was 2.74 rand to the dollar.

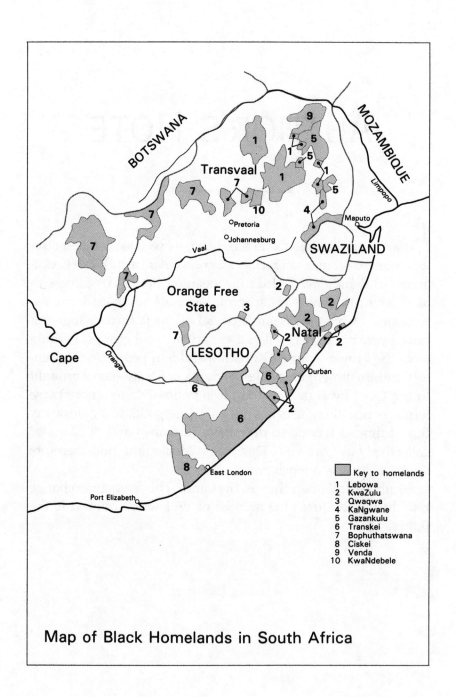

Map of Black Homelands in South Africa

Key to homelands
1 Lebowa
2 KwaZulu
3 Qwaqwa
4 KaNgwane
5 Gazankulu
6 Transkei
7 Bophuthatswana
8 Ciskei
9 Venda
10 KwaNdebele

ACKNOWLEDGMENTS

Many friends and fellow journalists have contributed to this book. I should like to thank in particular Philip Gawith, Bruce Robertson and Nick Harman, whose advice and friendship have been invaluable. Others have helped through their articles and newspaper columns, notably Patti Waldmeir, Nomavenda Mathiane, Denis Beckett and Allister Sparks. Anthony Sampson's *Black and Gold* and Joseph Lelyveld's *Move Your Shadow* have provided me with models of good writing to aspire to. Donald Horowitz's *A Democratic South Africa?* contributed greatly to my chapter on the constitution; the University of Wisconsin's land tenure center did as much for my chapter on land reform; Laurence Cockroft's *Africa's Way* confirmed my belief in the importance of African tradition. Patrick Laurence and John and Susan Peake gave me my first introductions in South Africa. Kathryn and Susan Gawith had me to stay frequently, and tolerated my endless use of their telephone. Friends at *The Economist* advised me on numerous subjects: Edward Carr on gold; Oliver Morton on AIDS; Gideon Rachman and Sophie Pedder on American race relations. Bill Hamilton, my parents, Katty Kay and Matt Frei plowed helpfully through the manuscript. Susanne McDadd, Julian Loose, Paul Golob and Melen Jeffrey went through it with fine-tooth combs. Thank you.

SEBASTIAN MALLABY
London, December 1991

AFTER
APARTHEID

INTRODUCTION

Africa began afresh in 1990. The collapse of communism in Eastern Europe sent a second wave of revolutions across the continent, with democrats rising against tired dictatorships in a dozen reenactments of the collapse of the Berlin Wall. From the Ivory Coast and Zambia to Mali and Benin, people demanded the political and economic freedoms that they had been promised at independence three decades earlier. On the tip of Africa, the last bastions of white rule gave way. Namibia gained its first sovereign black government. And South Africa's white rulers lifted the restrictions on black movements that had been banned for three decades; they released Nelson Mandela, the most famous prisoner in the world. South Africans are still struggling to replace white rule with something better. Nobody is sure what kind of country they will create.

This book is about South Africa's transition, and about its chances of success. It is written as the country bubbles with uncertainty and argument, conducted against a background of appalling political violence. On everything from constitutional theory to economic policy, South Africans are arguing from first principles. White tycoons and black revolutionaries spend weekends in hotel conference rooms, discussing land reform and labor law, education and exchange rates. In Europe or America debates on the relative merits of capitalism and communism hardly matter outside universities. In South Africa such arguments will determine the future. The country is possessed by the thrill and terror of a new beginning, in which almost no policy can be ruled out. Its people try to distill lessons from foreigners' experience: for industrial policy some look to South Korea, for constitutional models they look to Switzerland or the United States.

The success or failure of South Africa's transition will be felt beyond its borders. In the 1980s the country's white government fueled the wars in Mozambique and Angola, destroying those countries' economies and flooding their neighbors with hungry refugees. In the 1990s South Africa seems ready to play a more constructive role on the continent. Its big companies may bring fresh trade and investment to the region, building new railroads and power stations, perhaps digging new mines. The importance of such involvement is hard to overestimate. The democratic hopes newly kindled across Southern Africa will be disappointed without economic growth; and economic growth depends on foreign investment and aid. The rich world cannot be relied upon to provide enough of this. With the end of the Cold War, the big powers no longer see a strategic importance in Africa. After decades of unfruitful aid programs, donors are tempted to give up. Reborn Eastern Europe presents a rival claim on Western purses. Africa cannot count on the northern hemisphere; it needs South Africa's help.

In order to assist its neighbors, however, South Africa must be prosperous at home. That is quite a challenge. In the rest of Africa, the collapse of white rule was followed by instability and decline. If it is to do better, South Africa will have to reconcile its rival black movements, which set about attacking one another in 1990, as soon as all of them had been unbanned. It will have to tackle the huge backlogs in black education and housing bequeathed by the white government. At the same time, however, South Africa will have to persuade its 4.5 million white citizens to remain in the country with their money and skills, for without them the economy would halt. Throughout the region, the democratic experiment hangs in the balance. South Africans' skill in remaking their own country could tip it either way.

Before South Africa embarked on this adventure, most accounts of the country were obsessed with apartheid. That was quite right: racism exists everywhere, but no regime since Hitler's has espoused it quite so blatantly. Other societies have practiced discrimination on the basis of race, as in America's southern states; on the basis of tribe, as in Burundi; or on the basis of other criteria, as with India's castes. No other society has erected so complicated a legal scaffolding to support discrimination, and thereby appeared so universally offensive. South Africa's Population Registration Act, the keystone of apartheid, required that the race of each South African be registered at birth; but centuries of furtive miscegenation have blurred the tidy distinctions that the law implied. To determine borderline cases, bureaucrats scrutinized fingernails, peered at nostrils, and tested the curliness of people's hair by running pencils through it.

White South Africans built a vast edifice of privilege on these spurious distinctions. They reserved for themselves the best jobs, the best schools, nearly all the land and all political power. They bulldozed entire black suburbs, because they disliked having black communities living too near white ones. Those who resisted were treated viciously. Policemen gassed and whipped children at rally after rally in the black townships. Ordinary people continued to protest, even though they risked their lives.

Through all this, most blacks managed remarkably well to hang on to their humanity. In 1991 I asked Sampson Ndou, one of the older leaders of the mid-1980s township uprising, how his successive arrests and detention orders had affected his feelings toward whites. Did he feel pessimistic about the chances of racial reconciliation in the future? Did he look forward to the day when he could get his own back? He answered, "When you are looking at people who are torturing you, you don't know if they have feelings. Instead of being angry, you doubt their normality. At times you feel sorry for them. . . . Electrical shocks, beatings, all that funny stuff. I thought: we are physically oppressed; the whites through their education are mentally oppressed. They could not see what they were doing." There was no trace of recrimination in his voice. I had no doubt that the forgiveness was genuine.

With such heroes and villains, it was only natural that South Africa became the preeminent moral issue of international relations during the 1980s; and that the resistance to apartheid generated libraries of volumes. This book is different: apartheid has been defeated, and South Africa's leaders have a different battle on their hands. Whites have to learn to live without so many privileges; blacks have the even harder task of learning responsibility. In the decades of "the struggle," as the campaign against apartheid was known, blacks' main aim was to tear down white institutions; now they must learn to build new ones. During the struggle it was enough to demand economic sanctions; now black politicians have to think about getting the economy off the ground. It used to be easy to denounce black poverty; now black politicians will share responsibility for relieving it. Like other revolutionaries before them, black South Africans have to replace the attitudes of struggle with something more constructive. As much as anything, therefore, this is a book about the struggle against struggle.

National psychologies often lag behind political changes. In Latin America it has been easier to set up democratic institutions than to breed democratic values; even in the early 1990s some Argentines and Brazilians talk as though the solution to their countries' problems might be found in the return of military rule. Likewise, Eastern Europe's new governments have discovered that the most damaging legacy of communism is the attitudes that it bequeathed; people find it hard to make their own decisions rather than wait for instructions from party headquarters. For many black South Africans, blaming the white state was the equivalent of the communist practice of following party orders: both habits have corroded the willingness to take responsibility for oneself.

In South Africa this problem is likely to be especially hard to overcome, partly because black South Africans are less educated than Eastern Europeans, and partly because the struggle against apartheid bred a culture of indiscipline. Young blacks in the townships led boycotts and demonstrations, which they enforced by murdering people who refused to take part. These teenagers have little in common with responsible elders like Sampson Ndou; not all of them understand the need for restraint and reconciliation now that apartheid is gone. Apartheid was awful; the struggle was justified; but South Africa's new circumstances mean that yesterday's heroic resistance is in danger of becoming the damaging intolerance of today.

In March 1991 Archbishop Desmond Tutu, famous as a critic of apartheid during the 1980s, was so sickened by the township violence that he changed his focus of attack. There was something "desperately wrong" with the black community, he told his congregation in Cape Town. "We are becoming brutalized and almost anesthetized to accept what is totally unacceptable. . . . Political groups in the black community are fighting for turf and they do not seem to know, or certainly some of their followers don't seem to know, that a cardinal tenet of democracy is that people must be free to choose whom they want to support." He acknowledged the circumstances that had led black South Africans to violence: their dehumanizing poverty, the brutality of the white police. "But, ultimately, we must turn the spotlight on ourselves. We can't go on forever blaming apartheid."

The attitudes of the struggle sometimes obscure the challenges that lie ahead. To maintain morale in the fight against apartheid, blacks understandably assumed that victory would cure all their ills. They blamed apartheid for economic troubles, racial tension and the animosities among black tribes. They talked as if wealth redistribution could solve the problem of black poverty; as if land redistribution could provide everyone with land. Now these high expectations find expression in utopian policies that would do more harm than good. Activists want decent wages for everyone, so they call for a minimum wage; in fact this would push up unemployment (see chapter 2). Activists want land for everyone, so they favor communal tenure rather than private farms; in fact communal land ownership would probably ensure that South Africa's limited land was abused (see chapter 5). The truth is that it will be hard to provide for everyone in the new order. It will take a psychological shift for the struggle's more radical leaders to see that this is so.

To make sense of South Africa's transition, and to predict its likely outcome, this book draws on the experiences of other countries. As the Africa correspondent of *The Economist*, I lived in Zimbabwe in 1989 and 1990 and got to know a country that had shaken off white rule a decade earlier. Visiting South Africa frequently during that period, it seemed to me that some lessons from Zimbabwe would hold. South Africans often bristle at such comparisons. "No models hold for us," wrote Denis Beckett, an iconoclastic South African columnist, in 1991. "We're entirely on our own, and wherever we go is going to be a wholly new place." South Africa is richer and more sophisticated than the rest of Africa; white South Africans are not colonists; there are therefore no useful lessons from the history of decolonization in Africa or elsewhere. Yet although no single model holds the key to the future, neglecting lessons from abroad is surely as serious a mistake as swallowing them uncritically. Where comparison with Africa breaks down, it may be useful to look to Latin America, or to the experience of blacks in the United States since they were granted civil rights.

Commentators on South Africa sometimes do neglect lessons from abroad. Thus, for example, people play up the threat of a white backlash against reforms that favor blacks. Journalists adore grizzled Afrikaners who invoke their grandfathers' resistance to the British Empire in the Boer War and boast that they will defend their privileges with the same heroic obstinacy. English-speaking whites, anxious to blame the evils of apartheid on somebody else, are eager to believe in Boer extremism. Blacks like to have their stereotype of the white oppressor confirmed. But international experience suggests that there will be no white backlash. In Rhodesia whites held out against black rule as long as they militarily could; but today race relations in independent Zimbabwe are exemplary. In Namibia, independent since 1990, white anger was equally feared and equally overestimated. Modern Africa's whites have been too comfortable to fight their black governments. In chapter three I argue that South Africa's whites are no more likely to resort to armed resistance.

There are plenty more such lessons that often go unnoticed. Africa's hopes since independence have been frustrated partly by misunderstandings between traditional peasants and the modern people in the towns. In chapter six I suggest that this gulf threatens South Africa too; and yet this issue is not widely debated. Again, South Africans argue endlessly over which kind of economic policy the post-apartheid government will pursue. In other newly independent countries, however, the key problem has not been policy but the competence to implement it: bureaucratic inefficiency has done as much to stifle the economy as bad policies ever have. Anyone who has experienced the frustration of trying to contact the offices of the African National Congress knows that the movement is not very strong on administrative skills like answering the telephone.

I should explain one assumption which underpins this book. I do not take it for granted that the African National Congress will hold absolute power by the year 2000. Nor do I accept the opposite opinion: that South Africa's white rulers will find a way of holding on to power. Instead I have written this book in the expectation that the ANC will be an important partner, if not the senior partner, in any future coalition; and that at least one or two white politicians will remain in the cabinet. To predict the results of South Africa's transition, I have therefore concentrated on examining the policies of the ANC and the ruling white National Party, insofar as these are known, and on considering their likely impact. Some policies on both sides are pretty clearly impractical and are therefore likely to be discarded: I have suggested which these are. Others are more likely to survive the transition; whether they become government policy will depend on the future balance of power. At the minimum these policies will influence the tone of politics, and therefore the kind of place that South Africa will be.

1

THE STRUGGLE AGAINST STRUGGLE

The television camera crews had every reason to look pleased. The longer the crowd waited, the larger it grew. Bespectacled newspaper reporters and tough photographers were joined by tourists who had chanced to hear the news. After twenty-seven years in prison, Nelson Mandela was to be set free. A man jailed before television had even arrived in South Africa would be seen on millions of televisions all around the world. Young black activists with red armbands tried to keep the growing crowd behind a rope barrier some fifty yards from the prison. The newspaper reporters pressed up against it; the photographers elbowed them out of the way and stood in front of it; smug upon their various platforms, the television people had the best view of all. Then the din of a vast motor made everyone look up: another television crew, in a helicopter, was circling overhead.

That Sunday, February 11, 1990, ended the old South Africa and set the tone for the new. For years the release of Nelson Mandela had seemed the key to peace among South Africans, black, brown and white. In the dark days of the mid-1980s, when policemen shot at black protesters almost every month, many blacks longed for Mandela, the one leader who might talk sense into the white government and restraint into radical blacks. By the end of the decade, whites were pinning their hopes on Mandela too. After so much bitterness, the freeing of the world's most famous prisoner would demonstrate the government's openness to change. It would give South Africa a leader whose mythical status hoisted him above the dogmas that had bathed the country in violence. Editorial writers described Mandela as the father of the nation, not just as the leader of the antiapartheid cause. Mandela would address white politicians in their parliament in Cape Town, and forgive them the laws that they had passed to keep blacks down. Mandela would make peace in the province of Natal, where a political feud among rival black parties was killing an average of ten people a week. Nelson Mandela would emerge from prison to reconcile South Africans, like a priest absolving sins.

It was too much to hope for, and the rest of that Sunday gave a foretaste of the frustrations to come. The release was late and mismanaged. The world's television audiences watched and waited, some no doubt protesting at the interruption of their favorite programs. The television crews waited too, wilting under the midsummer sun. Their presenters strained for comments to fill the air time as, more than an hour after the appointed moment, Mandela still did not emerge. Surrounded by the hills of South Africa's wine-growing countryside, the South African Broadcasting Corporation's commentator, Clarence Keyter, was reduced to telling his audience, "Probably this is the most beautiful setting for any prison in the world." When the moment finally came, the crowd sprinted for the gate. The frail, gray-haired hero barely had time to raise his first into the air before ducking into a car to escape the onslaught of the world's press. Mandela's sedan made off for Cape Town, an hour's drive away. The journalists ran for their cars and set off in pursuit. The world's television audiences had no freedom speech to make up for their wait.

The speech eventually came in Cape Town, but not before yet more delays. Jammed hip to hip in a vast square outside

12

the city hall, thousands of people had spent the afternoon perspiring in the sun. I arrived from the prison at six o'clock, worrying that I might have missed the speech. The road into Cape Town had been blocked by crowds of celebrating blacks. White families returning from Sunday lunch in the countryside looked out of their cars in disbelief. The celebrators thrust their heads through windows and shouted, *"Amandla!"*, the black salute that means "power." White motorists grinned weakly and said, *"Ngawethu"* ("It is ours") in return, and in return for being let by.

I was certainly not late. Mandela's car had indeed arrived before me, but the driver had unwisely tried to force his way through the crowd to the steps of the city hall balcony, from which Mandela was to deliver his speech. The car tunneled through the mass of people, hot legs and bottoms squeezed against its sides. There was no hope of getting the doors opened in that crush, still less of getting a 71-year-old, full of the shock of release from a quarter-century's imprisonment, out of the car and safely through the crowd. The driver eventually realized his mistake, and slowly backed the car away from the balcony and out of the square.

It was another two hours before Mandela reappeared. The audience grew bad-tempered and thirsty; every so often an inanimate body was hauled onto the balcony from the crowd below. Looting started on the fringes of the square. Angry people hurled beer bottles at policemen, and got bird shot in return. Arriving in the square, I had seen a bleeding body lying in a pile of shopfront glass; I asked two onlookers how it had happened, but they seemed too shocked to say. Later, stuck in the middle of the mass of warm, soft bodies, I heard periodic cracks of gunfire and the shouts of fleeing men. During the first two days of Mandela's freedom, at least one hundred people were injured at welcoming rallies. A handful died. The violence, just as much as the disorganization of Mandela's release, was a sign of things to come.

Mandela finally entered the city hall from the back and appeared at the balcony overlooking the square. It was half-past seven, the sun was fading, and the huge yellow banner fixed above the balcony had been torn down by the wind. Television audiences around the world must have found it hard to make out the elderly figure behind the microphone, peering through spectacles at a prepared speech. For the crowd in the softening square, sunset enriched the honey color of the city hall's façade and made the address all the more moving.

"Amandla!"

"Ngawethu!" the crowd roared back.

"i-Afrika!"

"Mayibuye!"

Power is ours. Let Africa return to its people. Mandela continued as he had begun, playing on the stock hymns of the black cause. He was a man come among his people, not a grand stranger with foreign ideas. "I stand here before you not as a prophet but as a humble servant of you, the people," he went on. "Your tireless and heroic sacrifices have made it possible for me to be here today. I therefore place the remaining years of my life in your hands." Twenty-seven years of prison had done nothing to change Mandela's creed. He recalled his trial in 1964. His famous words from the dock were, he said, "as true today as they were then." And he quoted:

> I have fought against white domination, and I have fought against black domination. I have cherished the idea of a democratic and free society in which all persons live together in harmony and with equal opportunities. It is an ideal which I hope to live for and achieve. But if needs be, it is an ideal for which I am prepared to die.

Mandela was heroically unembittered. But to the dismay of those whites who had longed for the absolution of apartheid's sins, he also emphasized his loyalty to the African National Congress, the movement that had fought white privilege since its foundation in 1912. Mandela praised the ANC's allies and supporters: the guerrillas who had lost their lives waging its token armed struggle; the students, clergy and white liberals who had campaigned and protested inside the country; the foreigners who had supported them by imposing economic sanctions; even the Communist Party, whose alliance with the ANC was, according to Mandela, as strong as it had always been. The more radical the ally, the more loudly the crowd cheered; the biggest shouts greeted Mandela's praise for the armed struggle and for the communist contribution to the cause. The next day he told journalists that he still believed in the ANC's policy of nationalizing the mines and banks that form the backbone of South Africa's economy. The liberal editorialists were horrified. The myth was, after all, only a man— and a party politician at that.

Even South Africans who had never quite swallowed the myth had reason for concern. They understood that Mandela would be a party politician; and that, after so many years of imprisonment, his ideas on economics might have a 1950s feel. But they hoped that Mandela would be a statesman as well. Black South Africa cried out for strong leadership. In 1960 the white government had banned Mandela's ANC, as well as the smaller Pan-Africanist Congress, forcing their leaders into exile or hiding, and locking many of them up. In the decades that followed, new black leaders were silenced as soon as they emerged; the most famous of them, Steve Biko, died in detention in 1977. By the 1980s, therefore, black protest was uncontrolled by organized parties. Township spokesmen claimed that the riots and boycotts were being led and coordinated. The truth was that teenage gangs were often pursuing the struggle according to their whims.

Blacks' lack of leadership posed a problem for President F. W. de Klerk. From the day of his election in September 1989, he had acknowledged that the long battle to exclude black South Africans from government had failed. The white monopoly of power had yielded continuous black protest, which gradually undermined the white security that the monopoly was meant to protect. De Klerk was therefore convinced that it was time

15

to give blacks the vote and a real share in power. This would mean negotiating a new constitution: De Klerk needed coherent black organizations to talk to.

On February 2, 1990, in his speech before the opening of parliament, the president therefore ended the thirty-year ban on the African National Congress. The Communist Party and the Pan-Africanist Congress were unbanned too. The president also suspended the death penalty and abolished some restrictions on the press and on dozens of individuals and organizations whose politics had been considered troublesome. Detention without trial was now limited to six months. In the streets around the parliament, open-mouthed pedestrians stared at the banner headline on the front page of the afternoon newspaper. Young activists danced in Cape Town's stately squares. By releasing Mandela nine days later, De Klerk hoped to complete the process of giving muddled black politics a head.

The vast rallies, faintings and bird shot seemed in a way to serve the president's hope. They marked the importance of the occasion; they helped to convince South Africans that their country had changed. The sense of watershed was critical, because constitutional negotiation would be impossible unless black and white South Africans overcame the suspicions of the past. Whites had come to see blacks as dangerous revolutionaries, with whom it would be suicidal to share political power. Blacks had come to see whites as endlessly treacherous, a people who constantly invited blacks to negotiate, then refused to concede anything worthwhile.

President De Klerk's grand concessions, and the commotion that they caused, seemed to offer the hope of burying these memories. Even though soldiers still patrolled some townships, blacks were surely ready to be told that their old political tactics—in particular the refusal to negotiate with the white government—needed to change with the times. Hard-liners in the ANC, and in rival movements like the Pan-Africanist Congress, could surely not go on insisting that compromise was treachery, for President De Klerk had compromised first and in style.

Mandela's release not only gave blacks a leader; it helped to create circumstances in which he could lead.

Or so it seemed on that Sunday in Cape Town as Nelson Mandela started to speak. He declared, "The need to unite the people of our country is as important a task now as it always has been." But he quashed the idea that he could forge unity alone. "It is our task as leaders to place our views before our organization and to allow the democratic structures to decide on the way forward." People who had pinned their hopes on this hero found it extraordinary that he should merely offer a few views, particularly as the ones he did express were often qualified in his next breath. Mandela acknowledged that his release, as well as De Klerk's other concessions, distinguished the president from previous white leaders. But the president had not done enough; he had yet to lift the state of emergency, or to release people who had committed politically motivated crimes. The time might soon come when blacks should agree to negotiate, said Mandela; but it was not yet at hand. In fact, he told the thousands in Cape Town, "Now is the time to intensify the struggle on all fronts."

It soon became evident that Mandela had reason not to lead too boldly, for there were clear limits to his power. In a speech two days later outside his home in the township of Soweto, Mandela called on workers to return to their factories, on students to stop boycotting their schools. The audience cheered the gray-haired leader, but his moderate message seemed to pass them by. At the end of the speech, another speaker took the stage. There would be a march the next day to protest the state of black education: teachers should desert their classrooms to attend.

Discipline versus boycott. Mandela the leader versus Mandela the loyal party man. These themes dominated South Africa's transition from apartheid, dwarfing even the debates on future economic policy and the kind of constitution that the new country should have. Without discipline and leadership no society can hold together. Companies, government ministries and schools disintegrate, unable to produce or govern, unable to pass the wisdom of one generation on to the next. Sadly for South Africa, history has taught blacks the opposite of disciplined respect for leadership. The country's rulers and company managers have exploited black South Africans; its schools have been designed to impart a particular kind of wisdom—the wisdom to serve whites. In response to this manipulation, blacks have boycotted white institutions. As whites tried to stamp out black protest, black determination gathered force.

In 1936 the white government set up a Native Representative Council, to give blacks a token say in its affairs. Its members were black intellectuals, mostly members of the ANC. The council submitted its views to its white superiors, but the whites never seemed to hear. After ten years of frustration, the ANC denounced the council as a "toy telephone," and marched out. In 1952 the ANC extended the principle of boycott by launching the defiance campaign, which called upon black South Africans to disobey white laws. Blacks flouted the signs that reserved park benches and railway coaches for whites; they broke the curfew; they courted arrest.

The ANC's demonstrations continued until 1960, when the police shot and killed sixty-nine protesters at Sharpeville, a township fifty miles south of Johannesburg. They also shot at a crowd near Cape Town, provoking yet more demonstrations and strikes. The government declared a state of emergency; it detained nearly two thousand black activists; black parties were banned. This crackdown persuaded Nelson Mandela that peaceful protest would never rid his country of apartheid. In January 1962 he left the country to collect support for Umkhonto we Sizwe (Spear of the Nation), the ANC's new guerrilla wing. He returned six months later, and was soon caught by the police.

In 1976 black protest bubbled up again; this time the grievance was "Bantu education," the curriculum that trained blacks for menial work. "Natives will be taught from childhood to realize that equality with Europeans is not for them," said Hen-

drik Verwoerd when, as minister of native affairs, he introduced the system in 1953.[1] Verwoerd proceeded to spend five
times as much on each white pupil as on each black one; black
schools stressed tribal loyalty above subjects like mathematics.
The last straw came in 1974, when the government insisted that
black students be taught some subjects in Afrikaans. To blacks,
this was the language of the enemy; besides, many black teachers could not speak it very well. When in June 1976 students in
the township of Soweto rose up against the school system, the
police resorted to violence again. This time there were 575 dead
and some 4,000 wounded before the townships calmed.

In the 1980s the boycott of whites' institutions was dramati-
cally extended. In 1984, in an attempt to win over some of its
critics, the government invited Indian and colored (mixed-race)
South Africans to elect their own racially separate chambers
of parliament. These would give both groups representation
in the central government for the first time. But the offer still
left the black majority without any say in parliament; moreover,
the new Indian and colored parliamentary chambers offered
only token powers. This new "toy telephone" was boycotted
so furiously that only a quarter of the Indian and colored population chose to exercise its vote.

The campaign brought forth a new coalition of activists, the
United Democratic Front, which became the ally within South
Africa of the exiled ANC. Besides opposing the new chambers
of parliament, the Front called a boycott of black township
elections, which the government introduced in 1983 to replace
rule by white administrators. When polling day came, four in
five blacks declined to vote. Those elected on this sorry turnout
were branded stooges; some were killed; others were forced to
defend their houses with rolls of barbed wire. The campaign
branched out into boycotts of white-owned shops, white-
owned buses and township schools, even though by this stage
the worst aspects of the curriculum had gone. "Long live the
spirit of no compromise" became the slogan of the period. To
the young activists, oppression and martyrdom became badges
of heroism, strikes and boycotts the highest callings in life.

"When I am eighteen," said a fourteen-year-old to a *New York Times* reporter in 1985, "I will go to become a cadre in Lusaka. Then, instead of stones, I will have a bazooka."

In 1989, when I visited the ANC's headquarters in Lusaka, Zambia's capital, a small sign on the bulletin board proclaimed: "There is nothing more beautiful than a people in revolution." Not everyone inside South Africa shared this romantic view. Unrevolutionary blacks were stoned, hacked into pieces or subjected to "necklace murders," in which a tire full of gasoline was thrust around the victim and set alight. Some of this carnage was sanctioned by "people's courts," which handed out rough justice to enemies of the struggle; one such court in Alexandra, a township on the outskirts of Johannesburg, had two tires hung on the wall in place of the scales of justice.[2] The young activists who led the uprising called each other "comrade," and they terrified normal people as much as the zealous commissars of revolutions elsewhere. When the call came for blacks to stay away from work, people had to choose between the wrath of their employers and the wrath of their comrades; usually the comrades frightened them more. Housewives who went shopping in forbidden white-owned supermarkets risked ambush on their way home. The comrades forced some victims to swallow their purchases as punishment: flour, salt, cooking oil, the lot.

Nomavenda Mathiane, a black journalist who braved such repercussions, tells the story of a boycott in Chiawello, the part of Soweto where she lives. In 1987 the municipality cut off the electricity, and said it would stay cut off until people paid their bills. The residents' views differed: some believed it was only fair to pay for services; others believed that to resume payments would be to let all Soweto's boycotts down. Bit by bit, the desire for electricity got the better of some residents, who sneaked off to the electricity office to pay. Their lights came on again. Rather than see their boycott thwarted, the comrades broke open the power boxes and reconnected everyone. In response, the electricity board switched off the main supply: everyone was left in darkness, whether boycotter or not.[3] Not all Mathiane's neighbors thanked the comrades for that outcome, or for the result of the rent boycott that took place at the same time. To make up for unpaid rent, the police came and took televisions, refrigerators and sofas. Plenty of the victims had been prepared to pay their debts to the council, but the comrades' threats had made them afraid.

South Africa's antiapartheid boycotts disrupted just about every corner of national life. School boycotts ruined a generation of pupils. Rent boycotts ruined the townships' chances of being decently run. A Soweto pupil who started school in 1975 would have been prevented by boycotts from attending classes in five of the next twelve years. The boycotts of the mid-1980s left behind broken desks, overflowing lavatories and missing roofs where squatters had seized the chance of abandoned schoolrooms to steal some corrugated iron. By 1990 township residents around the country were more than one billion rands behind on their payments for services and rent. They lived under the threat of power and water cutoffs; unpaid garbage men and road crews periodically refused to work. As a result of the violence against representatives of the white system, more than one in three councilors' posts went unoccupied. The habit of boycott had become so ingrained that in the township of Munsieville, for example, people demonstrated for their council's resignation, forgetting that a previous demonstration had already achieved this end.

Boycotts poisoned industrial relations as well. In September 1990 the Congress of South African Trade Unions, the strongest union federation, called for a three-day national strike: not for better wages, not because of some national outrage, but because the government's progress in drafting amendments to the labor laws had been slow. Strikers were often not content with striking. Two months later, at the platinum mines in the homeland of Lebowa, strikers emerged from a shaft they had occupied to blow up a mine vehicle and damage a building. Elsewhere miners regularly attended union meetings in military uniforms, armed with wooden models of AK-47 assault rifles. Rumors circulated that white managers drank workers' blood samples

21

at meals. Production was disrupted by demonstrations that had nothing to do with wage claims and everything to do with the struggle. Managers objected to the disruption of work by politics. Unions asserted the right of free expression. Racial tensions flared. In the township of Tembisa a white chief matron accused of racism was attacked by a mob in August 1990; the rest of the white staff promptly called a strike.

Even the institution of the family was falling apart. Apartheid had long separated men from their families, allowing only workers to live in the towns. The relaxation of controls on black movement brought a new kind of dislocation: outside white South Africa's gleaming cities, shack settlements multiplied as peasants abandoned their overcultivated land. The crowding and poverty were bound to put pressure on family relations; with the added burden of the struggle, the family did not stand a chance. By 1990 possibly half of Soweto's children were not living with their parents. Teenage gangsters roamed the townships, accusing adults who objected to their behavior of siding with the state. Instead of parents disciplining children, children terrified parents with the violent discipline of the street.

In 1990 the South African police claimed to have confiscated 1,100 metric tons of marijuana, a quarter of the quantity confiscated in the entire world. Drugs, like strikes and demonstrations, were painted in the colors of the antiapartheid struggle. "Whites don't want us to smoke ganja because it makes us think brilliantly," said a Soweto smoker to a journalist from the newspaper *Weekly Mail*. "Ganja is behind the success of white professionals who smoke it like nobody's business." Small wonder that it was so hard to persuade black children to concentrate at school.

Perhaps the deadliest legacy of the struggle was the idea that politics, not self-help, held the solution to most things. It was not just that blacks were caught in the statist 1950s. By the time Nelson Mandela walked free, blacks had been trying for so long to win political power that they had forgotten other challenges. The struggle made blacks passive, said Aggrey Klaaste, editor of the *Sowetan* newspaper. They learned to wait for the miracle of political liberation to dissolve their troubles, rather than tack-ling at least some of their problems themselves. In the 1980s Klaaste began to campaign against this state of mind, calling on blacks to embrace self-improvement, pleading that business-men and scientists were models to be admired. Whites smoth-ered him with invitations to join their company boards. Blacks accused him of trying to make oppression look good. The mere idea of pursuing education smacked of playing down liberation. Klaaste endorsed the efforts of some Soweto residents to clear away refuse and plant gardens instead. "Garden politics," came the taunt.

Indeed the chaos of the townships was black politicians' proudest boast. At the beginning of 1985 Oliver Tambo, the ANC's exiled president, formally declared that destruction was now policy. His New Year's message called upon the ANC's supporters to "render South Africa ungovernable." The goal was to break whites' will to dominate, and in this sense ungov-ernability worked. The demonstrations and boycotts brought white policemen to the townships, armed with water cannon and whips. Foreign journalists came with them, armed with notebooks and cameras. For Americans, the sight of white po-licemen whipping black children recalled the trauma of the 1960s, when Martin Luther King, Jr., led the struggle for deseg-regation in the Southern states. For Europeans, it revived the old colonial guilt.

The result was economic sanctions, which made it harder for South Africa's government to keep the economy afloat. Factor-ies closed; whites grew poorer; and, as black unemployment spread, so did black riots. As in the 1960s and 1970s, whip and water cannon could impose the peace of exhaustion for a time. But President De Klerk, clearer-sighted than his predecessors, knew the respite would be limited, which is why he decided to release Mandela and declare that apartheid must go.

Ungovernability had achieved its object; it was time for black politicians to stop supporting it, and to join Aggrey Klaaste's campaign for a more constructive frame of mind. If untamed, the culture of strikes and boycotts would ruin South Africa's economy, with consequences for white and black alike. The political intolerance that came with it would reduce even the most democratic of constitutions to scrap. Ungovernability would add another dismal tragedy to Africa's long list. The ANC's leaders saw the danger all too clearly. But ungovernability, once embarked upon, is appallingly difficult to reverse.

Here was the challenge for Nelson Mandela, the one to which so many South Africans hoped he would rise on the day of his release. With his mythical status, Mandela would be able to instill discipline in the place of boycott; he could be a leader and a statesman, not just a loyal party man. In the early speeches after his release Mandela did appeal for discipline, telling workers to stay in their factories and children to stay in their schools. But he did not sound like a leader determined at all costs to make his view prevail. When he addressed the crowds in Cape Town, Mandela had declared himself not a prophet, but a servant of the people; and two days later, at the rally in Soweto to welcome him home, he once more affirmed, "It is not the kings and the generals that make history, but the masses of the people."

As 1990 wore on, those who feared ungovernability longed for an assertive general; for the first result of Mandela's release was that the violence grew worse. The government had freed the black nationalists whom it had once called terrorists. White conservatives cried traitor. In parliament, right-wingers referred to De Klerk as "comrade," and promised demonstrations that would make black protests look tame. One far-right leader, Robert van Tonder of the Boerestaat Party, warned of civil war. White extremists attacked the British embassy, invoking the defiance of their ancestors who took on the world's mightiest empire during the Boer War. In the mining town of Welkom, whites joined an organization called the Blanke Veiligheit, or White Security; hefty men, pistols on their hips, strutted the streets comparing Mandela to the pig on the farm who would not last until Christmas. Blacks retaliated with a boycott of white shops. When black miners gathered to protest the dismissal of some colleagues, white security guards let fire with rubber bullets. The miners pelted them with stones. By the time the fighting had stopped, two white managers were dead. Later, the police killed three blacks in a mining-hostel riot. The next day a white miner was murdered underground.

Mandela's release inflamed much more vicious violence among blacks. Since its election in 1948, De Klerk's National Party had ruled South Africa without interruption. This set a damaging precedent: as the era of black power drew closer, many South Africans believed that whoever emerged strongest from the transition would also rule for another four decades. As the crowds of journalists on foot and in helicopters chased after Mandela, rival black leaders worried that they would get left out. They declared that they too had fought apartheid, that they too deserved a role in the new order. Their insecurity bred violence, for in ungovernable townships any political disagreement, even a trivial one, was assumed to be a fight to the death. "The Pan-Africanist Congress represents African workers; the Azanian People's Organization represents black workers," AZAPO's general secretary once tried to explain to me. The two organizations had fought one another over this distinction. Both had fought the ANC's allies in the United Democratic Front as well.

The bloodiest fights, however, were between the Front and the Inkatha movement led by Chief Mangosuthu Buthelezi. Buthelezi's following among the country's 7.5 million Zulus made him a tougher challenge to the ANC camp than other black party heads; besides, the boycott leaders had a special reason to hold him in contempt. Buthelezi was chief minister of KwaZulu, one of the ten homelands established in the 1970s as a device to rid South Africa of blacks. In theory, all Zulus were to become citizens of KwaZulu, which would evolve from a self-governing territory into a full-fledged nation with a seat at the United Nations. Other tribes were assigned to other homelands, each a supposed reincarnation of a nineteenth-century tribal state. This process was intended to deprive all blacks of South African citizenship, and to leave whites the unchallenged majority in the land. The tribal states constituted just 14 percent of South African territory, though they were designed to house three-quarters of South Africa's people. It was the most ambitious injustice that apartheid ever devised.

At first the ANC did not resent Buthelezi's decision to become chief minister of KwaZulu, as he had taken the job to prevent the homeland from ever becoming independent. Thanks largely to his leadership, six out of ten homelands refused the government's blandishments, and the grand scheme to rid South Africa of its black majority failed. Buthelezi's prestige grew accordingly. In 1975 he founded Inkatha, the political party he described as a Zulu cultural movement, and started to recruit the 1.7 million members he would claim by the time of Mandela's release. His following among black South Africans in the 1970s extended far beyond his Zulu power base, for he had founded Inkatha with the ANC's approval and he posed as the chief ally of the Congress at home. At the same time his conservative policies—he supported capitalism, denounced economic sanctions and condemned armed resistance to apartheid—endeared him to liberal whites. He was a guest at the White House and at 10 Downing Street in London, for both Ronald Reagan and Margaret Thatcher were delighted to shake hands with a black leader who had no truck with communists or violence. And in 1986, together with local whites, Inkatha negotiated an imaginative constitutional blueprint for a multiracial government in the province of Natal.

The man the ANC had endorsed in the early 1970s had become a powerful alternative to the Congress's ideas. His opposition to the ANC's armed struggle, and also his denunciation of communism, galled the ANC, which eventually fell out with him in 1979. By the late 1980s the enmity had turned into full-blown war. The ANC painted Buthelezi as a puppet of the homeland system; and whatever the historical injustice of the accusation, it was clear that Buthelezi was using the white government's grants to KwaZulu to develop his power. Anyone wanting a KwaZulu pension, or a job in a KwaZulu school or clinic, was well advised to join Inkatha first. The KwaZulu police force worked closely with white policemen in hunting down their mutual enemies, the followers of the ANC.

The fight with the ANC did Buthelezi no good. He quickly lost his following among non-Zulus; and by 1990 his rivals had won over many Zulus too, particularly the younger ones in the towns. Villagers remained more sympathetic to Buthelezi's traditionalist appeal; but even in the countryside, Inkatha was beginning to lose ground. The release of Nelson Mandela threatened to cap this process by depriving Buthelezi of the international limelight as well. Now it was clearly Mandela's constitutional ideas that mattered; it was Mandela whom foreign leaders and journalists fell over themselves to meet.

In June 1990 Buthelezi's deputy, Oscar Dhlomo, resigned from Inkatha, heightening the sense of a movement in decline. Buthelezi had to do something decisive to recapture the initiative. He condemned the notion that South Africa would follow other countries of the region, where exiled guerrilla movements took over when white regimes fell. He claimed that his personal demands for Mandela's freedom had brought about the release. He railed against the prospect of the ANC's exercising a "revolutionary veto" over constitutional negotiations, by threatening to resume its armed struggle if it did not like the result. At the same time, however, Buthelezi seemed to be resorting to a violent veto of his own.

In the late 1980s the ANC-Inkatha fighting in the province of Natal consumed lives at the rate of ten a week. Immediately after Mandela's release in February 1990, fifty people died in three days. In March an army of Inkatha warriors trooped into a valley of ANC-aligned villages and laid waste dozens of homes. Then in July Buthelezi formally gave his Zulu cultural movement national ambitions; the new Inkatha Freedom Party would seek white and black members all over the country, rather than being confined to Zulus in Natal. The carnage promptly spilled out of Natal into the polyglot townships around Johannesburg. About five hundred people died in ten days. Altogether some three thousand people died in politically related violence during 1990, the highest toll South Africa had ever seen. As the killing gathered momentum, some South Africans wondered how it could ever be stopped. Local politicians on all sides used the violence as an excuse to extinguish opponents. Determined businessmen used it as a cover to send children to burn a rival's shop. Tenants attacked landlords, who hired thugs to fight back. Both marched on squatter settlements that threatened to use up their water or grazing land. In a township called Khutsong (meaning "peace" in the Sotho language), pro-ANC comrades boycotted the shop of an unpopular local landlord. The landlord's son formed a rival gang; some of its members also claimed to belong to the ANC. Soon the "Gadaffis" (comrades) were fighting the "Zim-Zims" (landlords), meanwhile killing plenty of neutrals. In one attack in a school, the Gadaffis cornered a group of children they regarded as enemies, cut off pieces of their ears, and forced the victims to eat the pieces.

When I visited Natal in 1990, I met an Inkatha politician, a stalwart of his local party branch. The valley below us was dotted with the husks of homesteads, burned and looted during fighting earlier that year. The chairman stood outside a shop that had mysteriously escaped, wearing a gold-buttoned blazer over his prosperous stomach. A man smoking a cigarette rolled out of a scrap of newspaper arrived to buy a bottle of spirits, which was what the shop mainly sold. The chairman discussed his local rival, a pro-ANC chief. The only way to deal with Chief Maphumulo, he smiled, was "to beat him out." He clearly liked this phrase of his, and repeated it several times. That month the chief's car had been ambushed, Mafia-style, as it slowed for a bend on the dust road to his house. He was not in it, but the gunmen killed two passengers who were. In 1991 Chief Maphumulo was attacked again, and the assassins hit their mark.

The legacy of ungovernability, the threat of racial violence and the feud between the ANC and Inkatha in Natal: all three problems cried out for Mandela the leader to emerge. Without peace in the townships, constitutional negotiations would be all but impossible; and South Africa's hopes of a new beginning would be disappointed yet again. Beyond politics and constitutions, however, lay another problem, one that would provide as urgent a test of leadership as any in South Africa. That problem was AIDS.

By the time of Mandela's release, it was already too late to prevent disaster in much of Africa. Roughly one in two of the world's people with AIDS were thought to be African; the World Health Organization reckoned that one in forty people in central Africa carried the HIV virus. The Futures Group, a firm of American demographers, predicted that by the year 2015 Uganda's population would be around 20 million, rather than the 32 million it might have been without AIDS. Even the country's president, Yoweri Museveni, admitted to his people that millions of children would be orphaned by the plague.

In South Africa, however, there was still time to avert this calamity. The HIV virus evolved early in Central Africa; it took a while to spread as far as the continent's southern tip. Whereas in 1991 Uganda's AIDS control program estimated that 1.2 million people might already carry the HIV virus, South African experts were guessing that nearer eighty thousand of their people carried it; and South Africans outnumbered Ugandans by more than two to one. Besides the advantage of starting later than the rest of Africa, South Africa had the benefit of better health care. Clean water and disposable syringes are a luxury on the continent; doctors have to advise each other on which type of disposable surgical glove copes best with reuse. However overstretched South Africa's hospitals, they are better equipped than this. Moreover, South Africa's government can reach most of its people through pamphlets and radio broadcasts; one of the great difficulties of AIDS control in black Africa is explaining the disease to illiterate peasants scattered through the bush.

Yet South Africa's plight is worrying enough. Workers from neighboring countries bring in the disease, which spreads especially quickly among miners living in single-sex hostels far from their wives. Doctors think that, failing a change in behavior or the discovery of a cure, the number of HIV carriers may double every year or so in the epidemic's early stages, before some sort of saturation sets in. By the year 2000, says an actuary for South Africa's biggest life insurer, 10 million South Africans will be HIV positive. Others put the figure at 7.5 million. Either number signals the flooding of clinics and hospitals, and disaster for the companies whose employees sicken and die. Besides babies who catch the virus from their mothers, the people most at risk are in the prime of their lives—precisely those whom the economy most needs. Indeed evidence from some other African countries suggests that AIDS is most likely to strike down skilled and successful adults: the better paid the man about town, the more bedmates he attracts.

To escape disaster, South Africans need to take the AIDS threat seriously. Both white and black communities present barriers to this. The white government's puritanism keeps it from providing sex education to teenagers; it has outlawed homosexuality and prostitution, making both difficult to control. Where white doctors have tried to warn their patients, they have found blacks suspicious of white men's medical advice. The same goes for advice on family planning. A black musician by the name of Patrick Dooms calls the government's promotion of condoms "a policy based on voodoo logic reeking with an aura of genocide." Put less flamboyantly, whites promote condoms because they fear being overrun by blacks.

Since it became evident by 1990 that white advice could not change such attitudes, the responsibility to speak out rested with blacks. It would take straight language to get people in the townships to reform their behavior; otherwise the AIDS epidemic in South Africa would reach the proportions it had already done in Central Africa. Here was yet another test of leadership. As with so many others, South Africans looked to Nelson Mandela and his senior colleagues in the ANC.

AIDS, boycotts and violence in Natal: on all these issues, the first challenge of leadership was to get blacks to recognize that a solution was their responsibility, and to defeat the passivity of which Aggrey Klaaste complained. Instead of blaming all their ills on apartheid, blacks needed to take charge of their own lives. The culture of ungovernability, with its passion for breaking down the white system, had to be replaced by a different culture: one that would encourage black South Africans to build a new country for themselves.

This would involve a profound change of outlook. If you do not fear AIDS, you will catch it, explained white doctors. "A lot of black youths, gay and straight," said a black spokesman to a newspaper, "still think AIDS stands for American Idea to Discourage Sex." Big families mean prolonged poverty, goes the family-planning message on South African radio. No, say black activists: the real cause of poverty is apartheid. Education is a ladder to a better future. Nonsense, comes the answer: schools form part of "the system" and all its evil ways. Without law and order, the country is doomed. But for blacks the law is a white conjurer who deprives them of rights and takes all their land.

Some activists also considered the violence in Natal the responsibility of the state. During the late 1980s, when the ANC was still illegal, the police force had supported the conservative Buthelezi in his fight against ANC followers. The question was how far this police bias had survived despite the ANC's unbanning. A partial answer came in July 1991, with a scandal that was soon dubbed "Inkathagate." Undeniable leaks forced senior government ministers to admit that they had instructed the police to finance large Inkatha rallies in November 1989 and March 1990; both were followed by anti-ANC violence. These payments amounted to 250,000 rand; another 1.5 million rand was found to have gone to the pro-Inkatha United Workers' Union of South Africa.

Inkathagate went some way to vindicate those who blamed the government for Natal's violence. Indeed the scandal raised the possibility that the good faith of President De Klerk, acknowledged repeatedly by Nelson Mandela in the year after his release, had all along been a sham. The president declared that he had known nothing of the secret financing of Inkatha; but some South Africans suggested that he had deliberately unbanned the ANC and professed his commitment to peaceful and fair political competition, while at the same time being prepared to allow Inkatha to undermine the ANC by violence. This was conceivable—but not more than that. The president might have hoped by such duplicity to weaken his strongest political opponents. But as well as hurting the ANC, the violence affected De Klerk's efforts to persuade his people to accept power-sharing with blacks; for many whites saw the violence as a warning of the greater devastation that a black government would bring. In June 1990 a whites-only by-election in Natal confirmed these fears: the antinegotiation Conservative Party doubled its vote, and De Klerk's Nationalists almost lost the seat. The violence hardened attitudes among blacks as well. During 1990 and 1991 Natal's fighting delayed the start of constitutional negotiations. De Klerk had staked his career on black-white reconciliation. Bloodshed threatened it.

The president therefore appeared to do what he could to pacify Natal. In April 1990 he raised the number of troops assigned to policing Pietermaritzburg, Natal's capital, from 200 to 1,500; the monthly death toll fell from 180 to 116. At the same time he promised to do something about the poverty which fueled the violence, and to tackle the backlog of murder cases in the courts. He even promised to clamp down on bias in the police. The Inkathagate scandal showed that De Klerk—and certainly his ministers—had not done enough to deliver on that promise. It revealed that his foreign minister, Pik Botha, had sought to bolster Inkatha as a counterweight to the ANC—and that he had lied to cover this up. But it still seemed too much to blame Natal's grisly violence on President De Klerk.

This did not deter Harry Gwala, the ANC leader in Pietermaritzburg, from doing just that. As chief minister of one of apartheid's homelands, Buthelezi was seen by some as a creature of the white government; so instead of pressing for ANC-Inkatha peace talks, Gwala thought it enough in 1990 to call upon De Klerk to tighten the grip on his puppet's strings. And despite the army's success in curbing the violence, the ANC stuck to its old slogan that the troops should leave the townships. To some black commentators, this was too much: the slogans of the struggle, once entirely appropriate, were now an excuse for people who disliked accepting responsibility themselves. "We have sat smugly on our oppressed backsides," wrote Jon Qwelane during the ANC-Inkatha fighting, "and meted out our own brand of inhumanity to our fellow men."

All over the world, the habit of blaming the authorities has proved very hard to break. It survives in some circles in the United States, a quarter-century after blacks won the right to vote. In 1988 Steve Cokely, an adviser to Chicago's mayor, attributed the AIDS epidemic, which affected blacks disproportionately, to "doctors, especially Jewish ones, who inject the AIDS virus in the blacks." This opinion was dismissed as outrageous by most people, but in June 1990 an opinion poll commissioned by the *New York Times* and WCBS-TV News found considerable support for Cokely's views: 29 percent of black New Yorkers were willing to countenance the idea that AIDS was created by whites deliberately to infect blacks.

Just as in South Africa, American blacks' sense of oppression breeds intolerance of criticism: the critic is quickly accused of taking the oppressor's side. If a white journalist investigates a black mayor's corruption, he or she risks being called a racist; a black journalist who does so may well be called disloyal. In 1986 a columnist in the *Washington Post*'s Sunday magazine defended shopkeepers who barred black youths from their shops because they were likely to be violent. Infuriated readers dumped thousands of copies of the magazine on the *Post*'s front steps; the columnist protested that he had been hoping to provoke a debate, not a brick through his window. In 1990 an American journalist named Carlos Alberto Montaner said on television that the Puerto Rican ghettos were full of single mothers. For this the television station was—shades of South Africa—boycotted by advertisers.

This sort of intolerance exasperates black intellectuals. Like Aggrey Klaaste in South Africa, they denounce the idea that past injustice should put blacks above criticism; they rail against the tendency to blame racism for all black woes. At the same time the intolerance causes American liberals to tiptoe around racial issues; in the nation that prides itself on freedom of expression, some things are simply not worth saying. It will be years before this changes. American blacks have a century of slavery to remember; even today they are abused by a police force run mainly by whites. In 1989 a hidden news camera caught two Long Beach police officers shoving the head of a black activist through a broken window. Two years later a Los Angeles man testing out a new camera taped something even worse. As Rodney King lay on the ground, police officers administered shocks to his body with a stun gun, clubbed him at least forty times, kicked him and stamped on his head. This videotape was shown over and over on television. "It looked," said the head of the CBS News office in Los Angeles, "like something that came out of South Africa."

Black intolerance of criticism; black criticism of intolerance; white guilt: if America has not shaken off these mindsets, it will certainly be hard for South Africa to do so. Black South Africans grow up on the history of white perfidy, which fuels their paranoia about white doctors and AIDS. In the nineteenth century whites spread north from the South African coastline, legitimizing their land grabs with treaties that blacks could not read. African resistance met with a mixture of violence and deceit. In 1835, when the British colonists were fighting one of their many frontier wars against the natives, they invited Hintsa, king of the Xhosa people, to peace negotiations in the British camp. The moment Hintsa arrived for the peace talks, he was declared a hostage. He tried to escape and was wounded as he ran. As he lay slumped in a watercourse, a British scout blew off the top of his head. Then the British soldiers "cut off his ears as keepsakes to show around the military camps."[4]

White behavior did not improve much with time. In 1960, at the height of the Sharpeville protests, another black leader was persuaded to abandon confrontation for peace talks. A crowd of thirty thousand protesters marched on parliament in Cape Town. South Africa's destiny seemed for a moment to hang in the balance; to this day, some people look back on that moment in 1960 when a black "people's power" revolution nearly toppled the white state. But the man at the head of the crowd, a young Pan-Africanist named Philip Kgosana, was persuaded to turn away from parliament and head for the police station instead. There he agreed to send his followers home in return for a meeting with the minister of justice later in the day. When he arrived for the meeting, the police locked him up.

Even in President De Klerk's brave new order, squatter camps get bulldozed and blacks get abused. The tear-gassing of five hundred people in central Johannesburg warrants a couple of paragraphs on page three of the newspaper. South Africa is one of the few nations in the world to retain corporal punishment; in the late 1980s an average of about one hundred South Africans were sentenced to such punishment each day. Capital punishment was also widespread. Although President De Klerk suspended the death penalty in 1990, he restored it the following year; as in the United States, the death penalty is almost always enforced by a white judiciary against offenders who are black. Most seriously of all, blacks went on dying at the hands of shady gangs of killers, widely believed to be supported by extremist members of the police. These murders continued even after the Inkathagate scandal, which brought solemn promises from the government that it would stop its dirty tricks. In one particularly vicious bout of killing in September 1991, a hundred people died in four days.

Visiting a refugee camp during Natal's violence in 1990, I caught a glimpse of the way the law appears to blacks. The refugees were ANC supporters, who claimed to have fled their homes for fear of Inkatha raids. They lived in lines of dirty tents, each one stuffed with three times as many people as it was meant to hold. There were mothers and children and a week-old baby; and a gang of teenagers who knew that they supported the ANC in Natal's warfare, but who could not find the words to say why. I squatted in a circle with some other visitors, and talked to an elder in a blue jacket that said "Auto Carriers" on the back. The elder was explaining that the police force was biased in favor of Inkatha, but that the army did its best to be fair. Then four white soldiers and two policemen arrived. They walked into the camp and arrested a ten-year-old, who was marched off, looking terrified, glancing back over his shoulder, trying to catch his mother's eye. South African soldiers are supposed to wear their names stitched onto their uniforms. These did not, and got angry when asked who they were. Perhaps the ten-year-old had really stolen something. But the manner of his arrest, on top of his refugee people's hardships, made the gray-bearded elder wonder whether soldiers were really fairer than policemen after all.

Whites gave blacks "toy telephones" for institutions, so boycott was the sensible response. Whites shot black protesters, so blacks came to see themselves as victims. Black leaders who preach discipline and self-improvement are preaching against history; and yet there is little choice but to confront that history. South Africa is part of Africa, a continent whose misery hardly counsels leaving history to itself.

2

A DRAGON FOR AFRICA

Africa's frustrations and failed hopes crowd into Nigeria, the continent's one aspirant to the status of big power. Nigeria accounts for about a fifth of black Africa's population and a third of its exports; its army looms over the neighbors in its West African backyard. Yet Nigeria stands for all the things that South Africa must avoid. Though the country is blessed with generous oil reserves, natural gas and agricultural potential, Nigeria's people are among the poorest in the world.

My story of travel in Nigeria takes place in December 1988, but a visitor any time in the late 1980s might have come home with tales similar or worse. A smart London travel agent had booked my route: I would fly from Ghana to the Nigerian capital, Lagos; I would spend three days there; then I would fly on to Kaduna, another city to the north. People in England had warned me about Lagos; when I asked an experienced businessman which hotel was best to stay at, he named the one closest to the airport "so that you can get out fast." White travelers often exaggerate; but during the week I spent in Ghana I collected even more warnings from locals about how vicious Nigerians were. Taxi drivers will speed you to some godforsaken

37

ghetto, relieve you of everything but your underwear and drive off; and it is a long walk from the ghetto to most consulates. Or, if by chance you should fall in with an honest taxi driver, doubtless you and he will be held up at gunpoint in one of Lagos's notorious traffic jams; in one such incident in 1987, Lynda Obasanjo, the wife of a former president, was killed. Lagos bubbles with energy and insults; even Nigerians cheerfully admit it. "This is an impossible country," said one of the country's leaders during a particularly trying phase of his country's long transition to civilian rule. "It is too hot. Then you put on the air conditioner and people say it is too cold."

My trip revealed the country in all its impossibility. In central Lagos I fought my way to the national airline office and asked to have my nine o'clock flight to Kaduna confirmed. My request untactfully woke the attendant; Nigeria's energy does not preclude people's sleeping at their desks. She stretched and blinked and looked up in amazement. I repeated that I had come to get my ticket confirmed. The attendant considered. Then: "We operate on a first come, first served basis." I should go to the airport and take my turn.

At seven o'clock the check-in counter was deserted but for a plump Lebanese businessman looking as bewildered as me. "The plane is full," said a voice beside me. "You are too late"— I looked crestfallen—"but I could help you if you like." The Lebanese seemed interested and, since he had clearly been in Nigeria longer than me, I thought it wise to be interested as well. I paid the man about three dollars. He led me out of the airport building, around the side past the discarded beer cans and dead cats, and onto the tarmac where half a dozen aircraft were waiting. "That is your one," he said, pointing. "When they call it, you run."

And so I did. The plane was eventually called at about eleven o'clock. Not having much to carry, I arrived near the front of the line. Soon latecomers formed a rival line in parallel, and the line became a scrimmage. The airport officials, who profit from this rare variety of the first come, first served system, feigned extreme indignation at the passengers' bad manners. They shouted and waved and refused to open the aircraft doors until a proper line was formed.

Meanwhile they shook hands with other officials, touts and wandering policemen. The handshake meant that all was well: a particular bribe had been paid and remembered, a particular somebody was assured of a seat. The scrimmage continued. Tempers boiled under the sun. More people arrived, dressed in glorious gold-embroidered robes. This breed of passenger disdained the line entirely, standing elegantly to the side until, when the official thought he saw an opportunity, the aircraft door was opened for a moment to let these gilded people in. This was the signal for the crowd to charge the entrance. Heads were lowered, voices raised; weak or old or pregnant passengers risked being trampled under foot.

It turned out that I had been conned. My agent had not had the power to get me on the plane, so I was left standing on the tarmac with the Lebanese businessman, large wet patches stretching from his armpits down the sides of his shirt. It took me the rest of the day to discover when the next plane was leaving and to find the right person to bribe. Throughout, the Lebanese regaled me with his life story; his family owned various mills in Nigeria, which had made a handsome living in the days when Nigeria's oil exports had boomed. Now, he lamented, the country was growing more and more chaotic. "Sometimes I have to get out of here. I just have to go back to Lebanon and relax."

All across Africa, a vast amount of energy is wasted getting trivial things done. An experienced briber would have got on a flight more quickly than I, though the absence of a timetable condemns everyone to spend at least half a day catching a plane. The time-wasting extends into dozens of other areas. It can take a Tunisian household five years to get a telephone installed, a Ghanaian household as long as thirty. In Zaire only the two biggest cities have any working telephones at all.[1] When I lived in Zimbabwe, I got used to picking up the telephone and hearing nothing: no dial tone, no out-of-order tone, not even a strange voice on a crossed line. Just emptiness. Some-

39

times I would wedge the receiver between shoulder and chin and open a newspaper. Five minutes and a stiff neck later, there would be a crackle and the precious tone would start. I would drop my newspaper and start dialing. Halfway through the number, a busy signal would interrupt.

Offices cannot work without telephones; some kinds of offices, such as financial brokerages, depend on plugging each employee into a dozen different lines. Erratic electricity supplies; first come, first served aircraft; broken roads and dangerous water supplies—all weigh down companies, obliging them to pay for private generators, private jets, water purifiers and so on. A World Bank study of Lagos found that large manufacturing companies are burdened by costs 30 percent higher than they would be if water, electricity, transport and postal services were reliable. For smaller companies the burden is still heavier.

The inefficiencies reinforce each other. In Mozambique's capital, Maputo, the post office lines are full of former civil servants who have given up their jobs to become messengers for foreign aid agencies. The messengers get paid more than they received from the government; the aid agencies get people efficient enough to pick their way through Mozambique's bureaucracies. But the Mozambique government loses good employees, ensuring that the ministries and post offices will go on requiring deft messengers to cope. Mozambique is particularly wretched, for its Portuguese colonizers trained no Africans to do skilled jobs. Yet next-door Zimbabwe also suffers, even though its people are among Africa's best trained. Arriving there in 1989, I spent a month pleading with officials in three different ministries to let my computer through customs. Eventually I vented my frustrations in an article for *The Economist*. My next visit to customs was different. "Ah! Mr. Mallaby! You are from *The Economist*! We have your computer ready for you now."

These Zimbabwean officials had the very considerable merit of being uncorrupt, not least because they were paid more or less enough to live on. In Uganda, by contrast, a middle-ranking civil servant is paid a bit less than $10 a month; it is hardly surprising that even President Yoweri Museveni's vigorous government cannot squeeze corruption out. In next-door Kenya the government is not even trying to discourage corruption. Local businessmen complain that whenever someone is successful, he gets approached by a well-connected rival who wants to buy him out. If he refuses, the law mysteriously changes to end his business's success; in the end, the victim is obliged to sell to the well-connected suitor, though at a lower price.

One such story concerned Nairobi's main casino, which lost its license for gambling in Kenyan shillings. It therefore started losing money until (so local rumor had it) the owner gave up and sold out cheap—and his successor had the license restored. Of course nobody could prove such stories, which were never aired in public—Kenya's high and mighty do not take criticism well. But there was enough evidence around in 1990 for a Western diplomat (he too declined to be identified in public) to tell businessmen from his country to invest their money elsewhere.

When grandees behave this way, so does everybody else. Once as I rounded the bend of a Kenyan road I heard something crunch under the wheel of my truck. The bend had prevented me from seeing it; besides, it was five in the morning and still dark. I stopped at a police checkpoint 100 yards ahead. A face appeared at my window and stared at me gravely. "You have run over an official sign," said the policeman. "Government property. You must come with me to Nairobi where we will sort this out." It was an easy choice. I could spend the day in a police station. Or I could ask politely how much the fine was likely to be, and whether the policeman would be so good as to take the money, please, and give it to whichever police department supposedly wanted it.

Black Africa served as a warning to South Africa of how bad things could get. To escape the corruption and collapsing infrastructure, foreign investors bailed out of the continent in the 1980s, depriving its economies of new technologies and skilled expatriate managers, depriving its people of jobs. By the end of the decade, nearly a third of the British companies with industrial investments in English-speaking black Africa had pulled out.[2] Africa's population was growing by some 3 percent a year, so the mass of job-seekers swelled as the number of jobs stagnated: by the end of the 1980s, the average African was 40 percent poorer than he had been at the start. This kind of decline would make it impossible for South Africa's future rulers to conquer ungovernability, since unemployed teenagers have little to lose from riots. As South Africa approached its transition, and as the township violence worsened, the precedents from black Africa made some people despair.

Most South Africans found such pessimism too alarmist. South Africa is the most developed country in sub-Saharan Africa; it has the highest gross domestic product per person except for tiny, oil-blessed Gabon. The roads are immaculate, the telephones work, the bureaucrats are not bad by the standards of their kind. Far from dwelling on African precedents, some optimistic businessmen and economists held out the miracle of East Asia's economic dragons, and suggested that South Africa could re-create the miracle if it tried. The East Asians had proved it was possible to recover from war and poverty remarkably quickly. South Korea's economy, for example, had racked up an average growth per year of 10 percent between 1965 and 1980, meaning that the average Korean nearly trebled his income in the intervening years. Perhaps this was too much to aspire to; but the optimists recalled the boom time of the 1960s, when South Africa's economy had grown by an entirely respectable 5.5 percent a year. They suggested that, without apartheid and the scourge of economic sanctions, South Africa's economy might have gone on flourishing through the 1970s and 1980s. Now that apartheid was to be dismantled, surely the 1960s would return?

When Nelson Mandela walked free, both black Africa and South Korea seemed a world away from South Africa. In the ensuing months, as the arguments over South Africa's prospects gathered steam in the conference rooms and newspaper columns, many South Africans dismissed both the gloom and the optimism, doubting that South Africa's middling performance could ever change so much. Yet a generation is long enough for a country to rise from poverty to riches, or to fall the other way. Half a century ago, Argentina was one of the world's richest economies; Africa was less developed, but its prospects were considered brighter than those of Asia's densely populated states. Now Argentina is a byword for hyperinflation; Asia is a model of development; Africa is at the bottom of the pile.

Despite its gleaming infrastructure, South Africa suffered from very African troubles in the early 1990s: slow growth, big families, low investment and AIDS. With 60 percent of its export revenues coming from gold and other forms of mining, South Africa, like many of its African neighbors, was hostage to fickle commodity prices. In the 1970s annual real growth fell to 3.4 percent; in the 1980s it fell again to 1.5 percent; in the year of Mandela's release, South Africa's economy actually shrank. Meanwhile the population was swelling by 2.5 percent a year, adding around one thousand newcomers to the work force each day. According to the best available estimates, more than one in three workers had no formal job, and half the unemployed did not even have unofficial work in the subsistence economy. AIDS threatened to change that, but then AIDS would bring still worse problems—soaring health bills, falling productivity—in its turn. This kind of economy was in no position to support the huge expansion of welfare that black South Africans expected. On the contrary, the swelling population and stagnant economy meant that South Africans, like most Africans, were getting poorer all the time.

As the newspapers reported more and more killings in the townships, South Africans longed for economic recovery to defuse the anger of the unemployed. To support their hope that political reform would revive the economy, the optimists stressed the burdens that had come with the old order. Apartheid had conjured up a vast bureaucracy that weighed down the economy. Apartheid had repressed the talents of black and brown South Africans, who were given poor education and forbidden to own property or perform various skilled jobs.

Apartheid had poisoned industrial relations and fostered anarchy in the black townships, so that businesses were crippled by absenteeism and strikes. Worst of all, apartheid had saddled South Africa with Western governments' economic sanctions, and with the even more debilitating flight of private businesses and banks.

The siege of sanctions began in earnest during the 1980s, but there had been rehearsals earlier. After the shooting of sixty-nine protesters at Sharpeville in 1960, investors pulled £48 million (the equivalent of $800 million in 1990) out of the country. A similar reaction followed the Soweto riots of 1976; for two years afterward, even Switzerland's famously apolitical bankers were reluctant to lend, fearing that political instability might damage South Africa's ability to repay. Apartheid was already hurting the economy; but the repercussions of Sharpeville and Soweto were nothing compared with the panic that accompanied the countrywide revolt of the 1980s. Goaded by television pictures of white policemen beating blacks, America, the Commonwealth and the European Community declared restrictions on South African trade. Foreign companies began to disinvest: between 1984 and 1990 nearly four hundred left the country.[3] And on July 31, 1985, Chase Manhattan Bank decided to call in its South African loans as they fell due, and to freeze all further credit.

Other lenders followed: during August American banks withdrew some $400 million from South Africa, about a tenth of all their loans. By the close of trading on August 27 the rand was worth half what it had been (measured in sterling) a year earlier. The government felt obliged to close the market for four days, to freeze repayments on its debt, and to reintroduce exchange controls. White South Africans dubbed Willard Butcher, Chase Manhattan's chairman, the Butcher of the Rand.

For a time, President P. W. Botha's government sneered at its high-minded foreign critics. Had not Australia persecuted aborigines? Had not the United States massacred Native Americans? Did not India practice apartheid under the name of the caste system? Besides, the foreigners seemed self-interested as well as hypocritical. The Australians pressed for the cutting of air links; their national airline had scrapped its South Africa flights anyway. The Americans banned fruit imports, which pleased their home producers. The Indians wanted all trade banned, which would cost them nothing since India had officially stopped trading with South Africa long ago. Britain was the one consistent opponent of sanctions, which was natural since it was the biggest investor in South Africa by far.[4]

President Botha, a cantankerous old autocrat who struck fear into his colleagues, was not the kind of man to give in easily to this chorus of double standards. In August 1985, in a speech widely expected to announce the crossing of the Rubicon into a new era of reform, Botha instead told the world to keep its views about apartheid to itself. "I am not prepared to lead white South Africans and other minority groups on a road to abdication and suicide," he said. "Don't push us too far! Don't push us too far!" Botha's speech accelerated the collapse of the rand; but it took more than that to break South Africa's defiance. In March 1988 South Africa's ambassador to the United Nations stalked out of a Security Council debate on sanctions after challenging the world to "do its damnedest": it was said with the relish of a melodrama villain.

Throughout the late 1980s visiting journalists were lectured on how sanctions would never work; how they would hurt blacks more than whites; how they would only make Afrikaners more stubborn. Yet the lectures merely served to betray the government's obsession with foreign opinion, and its awareness that sanctions did hurt. The truth was that South Africa's economy was more than usually dependent on trade, since it imported most of the machinery it needed for its factories. To pay for that equipment, and to repay the country's foreign lenders, South Africa needed healthy exports.

In 1986 the United States decided to shut out South African agricultural produce, coal, iron, steel, uranium, sugar and gold coins; the following year its imports from South Africa fell by 40 percent. In 1987 the European Community imposed a softer set of sanctions; fruit imports, for example, were still allowed, though in certain European circles good hosts stopped offering Cape oranges to their guests. South African exporters sought out new markets in Japan and East Asia. They got around the European and American bans by having their goods packaged and labeled in neighboring countries; at one time Swaziland's fruit exports apparently exceeded the country's entire production. But the transshipment and relabeling were expensive. Worse, South Africans often found that they could only get foreigners to accept their goods if they offered a "political discount."

One way or another South Africa managed to run a healthy trade surplus throughout the sanctions period, healthy enough to keep on repaying the foreign bankers who were still clamoring to get their money out. But there was no doubt that exporters would have done much better without the handicap of sanctions, especially given the advantage of the dramatic devaluation of the rand. In 1989 the economics team at Bankorp, one of the country's largest banking groups, reckoned that trade sanctions had cost South Africa 8 billion rand. Meanwhile the flight of capital was even more serious, as foreign companies departed, bankers demanded repayment, and stockbrokers moved money out of South African shares.

Assuming that, in the absence of politics, money might have flowed into the country at the rate it had before 1985, Bankorp's economists calculated that South Africa had forgone some 32 billion rand in loans and direct investment over the past five years; and they added that, without this flight of money, the economy's 2 percent annual growth in the late 1980s might have been nearer 4 percent. Other calculations confirmed the cost of sanctions. The American Investor Responsibility Research Center reckoned that, without the direct and indirect effects of sanctions, the country's gross domestic product "would be 20 to 35 percent higher today than it actually is."[5]

The desire to stop the siege of sanctions almost certainly encouraged President De Klerk to do away with apartheid. His predecessor had tried to defy the world during the second half of the 1980s; but the defiance had not worked. South Africa's government had discovered, in the words of the finance minister, Barend du Plessis, that running a pariah economy was like trying to run a business without the services of a banker. Growth was all but impossible; vast sums of energy had to be concentrated on paying off debts. Looking back on the sanctions years, Gavin Relly, chairman of the giant Anglo American Corporation, commented, "One might almost say that we have lived through the modern economic equivalent of the seven plagues of Egypt." Nobody presiding over South Africa's angry townships could afford policies that hamstrung the economy. Du Plessis himself admitted that without economic growth, "By the mid-1990s it will be virtually impossible for any government to govern this country because of the number of unemployed."

The cost of isolation had been enormous, and South Africans rejoiced as they felt it begin to lift. After the release of Nelson Mandela more tourists started arriving; European supermarkets became less shy of South African fruit; Northern Ireland Electricity bought a consignment of South African coal, shunned by British power companies for twenty years. In December 1990 a group of sixty-five black businessmen visited the United States to investigate the post-sanctions possibilities; they carried with them a letter of support from Mandela. South Africans looked back upon a year in which they had made new trading contacts in most of Eastern Europe; black Africa, which had shunned formal links during the era of apartheid, was also opening up. Foreign financiers were loosening the vise. International goodwill made it easier to roll over the country's debt. The third quarter of 1990 was the first for three years in which South Africa enjoyed a net capital inflow: foreigners blessed South Africa with 820 million rand of long-term capital, plus another 700 million rand in short-term loans. Eskom, the state electricity company, found it could raise modest sums from overseas investors. And in September 1991 South Africa's government launched a public bond issue on Europe's capital markets, its first since Chase Manhattan pulled the plug on the country in 1985.

*   *   *

The prospect of South Africa without sanctions excited outsiders too. Hundreds of foreign firms had invested in the country in its economic heyday, attracted by its natural resources and efficient infrastructure, and by the sense of opportunity that comes with economic growth. In the 1980s political pressures had helped to drive some four hundred of these companies out again; just over five hundred remained behind. The disinvestors included many household names: there was Barclays Bank from Britain, Kodak and Coca-Cola from the United States. The passing of apartheid would free these companies to return to South Africa; and Nelson Mandela's release prompted a string of visits from executives, all wondering whether they should reinvest. Before doing so, however, they would take a hard look at South Africa's prospects. The view was not altogether good.

Alongside the easing of sanctions came much gloomier news about gold, the metal which had made South Africa. The first small gold finds had been reported in the 1850s, though for the next two decades diamonds caused more excitement. In 1886, however, came the discovery of the gold reef known as the Witwatersrand, which was to transform the country. Corrugated-iron cities sprang up in the interior, pulling the country's center of gravity firmly away from the original white settlements in the Cape. Financiers, engineers and adventurers arrived from America and Europe; black workers came from villages in every corner of South Africa and beyond. A century later South Africa produced nearly 80 percent of the non-communist world's gold. The corrugated-iron shacks had partly given way to buildings of steel and glass. South Africa had come to rely upon the gold industry, at once its biggest taxpayer, biggest foreign exchange earner and biggest employer.

By 1990, however, the industry was running down; that year it sent forty thousand unwanted workers back to their villages. The *Weekly Mail* carried a heartrending story of a former miner who found that the only means of supporting his family in the Transkei was to deal in marijuana.[6] The proceeds were not enough to feed four children. "One day after fetching the cows, I came home and found my wife has gone with the six-month-old baby," said the dealer. "She left the others behind. I think she couldn't stand to see the small one starve." On the next page the *Mail*, like just about every other South African newspaper, carried an article about the prospects for the gold mines, which seemed certain to create many more redundancies and broken homes.

Gold still accounted for a quarter of South Africa's exports. But the shafts were getting deeper, the ore poorer, and during the course of the 1970s and 1980s South Africa's output had fallen by two-fifths.[7] Meanwhile gold production in the rest of the world had undergone a revolution. A new technology made it possible to extract gold profitably from low-grade deposits near the surface. As a result, the world's output rose by 60 percent during the 1980s, while South Africa's contribution declined from 50 to less than 30 percent.

The cost of South African production made it hard to believe that the country would ever regain its old market share. The new method of "leaching" oxidized surface deposits enabled South Africa's competitors to produce gold at a cost of around $150 an ounce, compared with an average of more than $300 an ounce for South Africa's old-style mines. Many of the potential new mines planned in South Africa lay at depths of 11,500 feet or more, and would cost around 3 billion rand each to develop. Apart from the depths, costs had been pushed up by inflation, particularly in wages. Better pay for black miners since the legalization of black trade unions in 1980 had eroded some of the disparities with whites. But better wages had also pushed some mines to the brink of closure. At the start of the 1980s South Africa's gold mines had been the world's cheapest producers; by the end of the decade they were the most expensive. Kennedy Maxwell, the president of South Africa's Chamber of Mines, himself conceded dryly that "the 1980s were something of a disaster for gold mining".

The rising costs of production would have mattered less if the gold price had been higher. At the time of Mandela's release, the finance ministry was expecting a price of $450 an ounce. In fact the price stayed doggedly below $400. South Africans talked hopefully of a recovery. By the end of the year war was looming in the Persian Gulf; the Soviet Union was in turmoil; the West was in recession; banks were failing in New England; and in Geneva there was a breakdown in talks on freeing world trade. Things had not looked so gloomy since the legendary recession of the 1930s; things had never looked so bright for gold, traditionally a safe haven in troubled times. South African commentators thought the time for a recovery had finally come. They recalled the leap in the price of gold from $470 to $850 an ounce within a month after Russia's invasion of Afghanistan at the end of 1979; another jump like that would save the country's poorer mines from closure.

But this time gold refused to jump. The price jittered briefly above the $400 mark after Iraq invaded Kuwait on August 2, 1990, but by October it was back to around $370. When the allies' counterinvasion began, in January 1991, the price actually fell; even the spectacle of a dozen countries beating up two of the world's biggest oil producers failed to make gold twitch. The new generation of traders had forgotten that gold was meant to be a safe haven. When the fighting finished, South Africans had to face the glum truth that 190,000 people, or 45 percent of the country's gold miners, were working on unprofitable shafts. The dull gold price was denting the gains from the fading of sanctions; every $10 it shed cost the economy $200 million in foreign exchange over the course of a year.

South Africa's gold spokespeople did not give up hope. They declared that the shallow mines in other countries would soon be exhausted; that recession in the West would drive investors back to gold; that affluence in East Asia would boost demand for gold jewelry. Yet this preoccupation with the gold price reminded South Africans that their economy depended on primary products, whose seesawing prices were beyond their control. It was a familiar African predicament. In the 1970s Zambia collapsed along with copper prices; West Africa's cocoa producers rise and fall with the price of their beans. South Africa's smart telephones and factories set it apart, to be sure. But as the chaos continued in the townships, this tide of African misery threatened to drown South Africa's modern side. Would the lifting of sanctions really work a miracle? Pessimists, dismissing the dreams of copying East Asia's dragons, saw plenty of room for doubt.

It seemed clear that the easing of sanctions would bring some immediate benefits. South Africa would again enjoy the services of a banker. The barriers to exporters would go. A sudden spate of lending, together with some development aid, might well produce a burst of prosperity in the first years after apartheid. After that, however, the outlook seemed less sure. Some of the legacies of apartheid would prove more persistent; and yet it was crucial that they be overcome. If the first spurt of post-apartheid growth was to be followed by steady improvement, South Africa would need more than aid and bank loans. It would need investors to build factories and create jobs.

In June 1986 Archbishop Desmond Tutu had used the *New York Times* to tell American businesses, "Please do us a favor: get out and come back when we have a democratic and just South Africa." Unfortunately investment cannot be turned on and off like a faucet. Businesses had quit the country for more than just political reasons; they had sound financial motives too. General Motors, the biggest American employer in South Africa, had lost money for four years in a row by the time it pulled out in 1986. South Africa did not seem attractive even to local companies: in the first half of the 1980s they doubled the real value of their investments outside the country, at a time when they had all but ceased to invest at home.[8] With the gold industry depressing the economy, the financial cause of underinvestment threatened to persist even after the political one had gone.

Kent Durr, then minister for trade and industry, boasted privately on the afternoon of the ANC's unbanning that a representative of a disinvested company had called on him to discuss the possibility of coming back. Other government spokespeople pointed out that, unlike Eastern Europe, South Africa had the advantage of speaking the world's international language; and that it was well stocked with the financiers and commercial lawyers whom foreign investors need. Yet the multinational executives who visited South Africa in ensuing months seemed in no hurry to invest. Some South Africans wondered whether the visitors were more interested in their climate than their economy. Meyer Kahn, the executive chairman of South African Breweries, reckoned that the average prospective investor packed five pairs of swimming trunks and only one suit.[9] There would be no flood of new investment capital without the prospect of a flood of profits to match.

The dearth of investment was one legacy of sanctions that would be hard to get rid of. Protectionism might prove equally hard to undo. The sharp devaluation of the rand in 1985 had made foreign goods expensive for South Africans. On top of that, the government responded to sanctions by raising tariffs, making it even harder for foreigners to sell their goods competitively in South African shops. In one estimate, the average effective tariff on imports to South Africa rose from 30 percent in 1984 to 70 percent in 1988.[10]

The country's industrialists therefore enjoyed a captive home market; outselling their foreign rivals did not involve any special efficiency. If tariffs were lifted, some complacent South African manufacturers would come down to earth with a bump. And sooner or later tariffs would have to be relaxed, for devaluation and protectionism were rusting the economy. Machinery had become so expensive to replace that factory managers and farmers made do with old equipment; according to South Africa's Reserve Bank, in the second half of the 1980s the average age of machinery in private manufacturing increased by almost a third. As the machines ran down, the factories grew less and less efficient. South African consumers had to make do with poor quality and higher prices; and the chances of exporting manufactured products shrank.

To make the most of the end of sanctions, and to lessen its

dependence on exports of primary products, South Africa had to open its economy as much as possible. It would have to lift all tariffs on machinery; and it would have to shake companies out of their complacency by lifting other tariffs too, thereby allowing foreign producers to compete with South Africans in their home market. It was bound to be unpleasant. Already in 1990 the easing of tariffs on textiles had cost six thousand jobs, according to the Textile Federation. A trade deal with Turkey, apparently a reward for Turkish help in busting sanctions, included the near-scrapping of tariffs on imported Turkish blankets. Local industry suffered again. Easing protectionism was painful; but in the long term sticking to protection would hurt a lot more.

As sanctions eased, it was only natural that Western businesspeople should consider South Africa's potential; and that South Africans themselves should heave a sigh of relief. Yet the optimism had its limits. Sanctions had actually strengthened some aspects of the economy. They had forced exporters to seek new markets; they had forced the government to reduce its foreign debt. But sanctions had also left a legacy of thin investment and trade protectionism that would not be quickly undone. Foreign loans were set to flow again; but then there was the gloomy state of gold. South Africa seemed poised in the balance; and the nature of the new government's economic policies could tip it either way.

The thought of so much responsibility resting on the shoulders of the African National Congress filled some South Africans with dread. The Congress was ill prepared for government by its years of exile and underground resistance. Its leaders knew little about economics or government. In fact they often seemed incapable of organizing themselves; ANC stood for "African National Chaos," according to one unkind joke. Besides, the white government's propaganda had long painted the ANC as a communist movement, ready to nationalize white land and companies, to suppress the market in the name of the state.

The collapse of communism in Eastern Europe made the

adoption of such policies barely conceivable. Nearer home, the disasters of African socialism reinforced the point. The flight of foreign companies from the continent had helped to persuade most African governments to change their policies: by the time of the ANC's unbanning, deregulation was well under way, supervised by the International Monetary Fund and the World Bank. In South Africa De Klerk himself was promising to tackle the budget deficit, curb inflation and cut back red tape. Regulations on everything from transport to building would be abolished or simplified; and in November 1989 the government privatized Iscor, the state iron and steel company. The gospel of the free market seemed to have swept the world, which encouraged President De Klerk to unban the ANC despite its attachment to socialist ideas. Surely, by 1990, the ANC appreciated the virtues of the market? On his second day of freedom Nelson Mandela declared that he still believed in nationalization. The stock market shivered; white editorialists grew shrill.

Communism's failure had indeed left African socialists in confusion; but it had not persuaded them to jettison their old ideas all at once. Before Gorbachev began to change things, African left-wingers had paid fraternal visits to Cuba or Eastern Europe, where they were shown model hospitals and pig farms and given a nice time. They were not introduced to communism's weaknesses, so they later found it hard to understand its demise. In Zimbabwe the foreign minister, Nathan Shamuyarira, summoned the resident Eastern European ambassadors and assured them that he deplored the rumors of communist collapse: the ambassadors had to say that the rumors were true. In South Africa ANC leaders were also caught off balance. One black journalist recalls talking to a senior figure from the Congress as the first wave of East Germans was flooding through the Iron Curtain: the two of them marveled at how people could run from a people's state.

The sense of disorientation showed through in the Africans' policies. In Zimbabwe President Robert Mugabe urged more foreign investment and a stricter adherence to Marxism, all in the same speech. Likewise, the ANC and its trade union allies insisted that they saw a role for the private sector, while adding that they saw a bigger role for the state. During the sanctions era black activists had argued that apartheid could not survive without the tacit support of business. Now they seemed close to believing that they themselves would be able to govern successfully without business sympathy.

The disorientation was particularly acute in South Africa, because most blacks had come to equate capitalism with apartheid. The association of the two systems went back to Cecil Rhodes, who in the late nineteenth century doubled as mining magnate and prime minister of the Cape Colony. His diamond company, De Beers, helped to found South African capitalism; his government in the Cape helped to plant the racial discrimination that flowered as apartheid. A mixture of greed and white supremacism drove Rhodes to spread the British Empire northward; he called the new colony Rhodesia, in honor of himself. Rhodes delighted Marxists: he provided a textbook case of capital's hold on the bourgeois state.

A century later, however, the alliance between business and apartheid had disintegrated, because businesspeople had found that apartheid was getting in their way. Lacking skilled white workers, business lobbied successfully against laws that reserved skilled jobs for whites. Plagued by strikes organized by illegal black trade unions, business insisted on legalization so that orderly industrial relations could emerge. When racial discrimination brought sanctions, businesspeople began to denounce apartheid in public speeches, quiet interviews and advertisements in the press. They started to house black executives in suburbs that the apartheid laws had reserved for whites. At the same time the business establishment was starting to include a minority of blacks. The most flamboyant example was Richard Maponya, whose retailing empire employed twenty-five hundred people. Maponya decorated his BMWs with statuettes of racehorses; their jockeys wore black, green and gold, the colors of the ANC.

The belief that business and apartheid were inseparable persisted nonetheless. In the 1960s black South Africans chanted "Apartheid has a friend in Chase Manhattan," because Chase had started lending to South Africa in the wake of the Sharpeville shootings of 1960. After Chase called in its loans in 1985, it received a letter of thanks from a black political prisoner in South Africa, written on toilet paper. The sheets were pieced together and photocopied for circulation around the bank.[11] But in general blacks did not think much of business's contribution to their cause. Blacks called upon corporations to withhold taxes. Executives laughed at the idea of defying the law on that scale. Some activists, who had been locked up and tortured for their convictions, found this insultingly complacent; they wanted business to confront apartheid with as much self-sacrifice as the township youths. During one of South Africa's negotiations with its foreign creditors, three leading antiapartheid clergymen declared that the bankers should demand "not only the white government's resignation, but the seizing of South Africa's assets abroad, including aircraft and ships."[12] The financiers were more interested in salvaging their money. Blacks' suspicions of capitalism remained.

In 1989 Pieter le Roux, a politically moderate economics lecturer at the black and mixed-race University of the Western Cape, asked his third-year students which school of economic thought they espoused. One in three said they were social democrats. One in three said they were Marxists. And one in three described themselves as Trotskyists. In 1990 lecturers at the University of the Witwatersrand, Johannesburg's (mainly white) English-speaking campus, tried to expunge the words "commerce" and "business" from the names of the faculties that taught those subjects, because both terms smacked of oppression. The ANC's advisers called the stock exchange a casino, deregulation an attack on the trade unions. They observed declining investment, and concluded that businesspeople were unpatriotic. They mistrusted the profit motive; an economist with the miners' union demanded "the productive use of our country's mineral heritage for people and not just profits." Demonstrators outside the stock exchange demanded an end to privatization, which they said was a ruse to impoverish a future black government. The Communist Party described multinational companies as "the shock force of neo-colonialism." The ANC and its allies simply did not like capitalism.

With gold mines closing, and with township violence continuing, South Africa's businesspeople and economists prayed that the ANC's attitudes would change before it gained a share of power. But despite Eastern Europe's revolutions and the disasters of planners' economics nearer home, the ANC's leaders were under immense pressure to make the same mistakes. Activists wanted jobs in the new bureaucracy; peasants wanted whites' farmland; trade unions wanted a minimum wage. The country's 7 million squatters wanted legal homes, and those who did have houses wanted electricity and water. Some had been told how, starting in the 1920s, the white government had wiped out malnutrition and unemployment among Afrikaners by paying for school meal programs and by accepting the role of employer of last resort. Unskilled Afrikaners sat behind post office counters, punched railroad tickets or found jobs in the army or police. During the long fight for political rights, black South Africans naturally supposed that after apartheid their own government would do as much for them. ANC spokesmen repeatedly declared that liberation would mean nothing if it did not bring redistribution in its wake.

Yet it was impossible to escape the need to promote growth as well. The Afrikaner governments had plundered the majority to help their small tribe; but plundering the minority could never generate enough money to cure the poverty of 27 million blacks. In 1990 it was estimated that it would cost 56 billion rand (about a fifth of the country's gross domestic product) to bring black housing, health, education and pensions up to the standards enjoyed by whites; and each year the bill grew in line with the population. Without fast economic growth, there would be no hope of satisfying black expectations. The ANC therefore devised a slogan that promised growth while satisfying its sense of past injustice. "Growth through redistribution" became the refrain.

Was this possible? In some respects the ANC's mistrust of business did seem compatible with faster economic growth. South Africa's giant conglomerates were too powerful for the economy's good. By some measures, the four leaders controlled some 80 percent of the capitalization of Johannesburg's stock exchange. Even Gavin Relly, chairman of the vast Anglo American Corporation until he stepped down in 1990, admitted that this degree of concentration was damaging. The power of the big conglomerates inhibited free competition. Besides, Anglo's breadth of businesses—ranging from gold to farms to dog food—made it unwieldy; it was the kind of unfocused conglomerate that a British or American corporate raider would delight in breaking up. South Africa has nobody rich enough to buy control of the big companies, whose ownership structure is in any case designed to make takeover bids hard. But the ANC's instinct to curtail the power of the big companies was by no means unhealthy. The question was how.

Nationalization was not the obvious answer, for it would replace private concentration of ownership with even greater concentration in the hands of the state. Moreover, nationalization, if it involved compensating private owners, would leave the state too poor to provide better schools, health care and homes. Soon after his release, Nelson Mandela therefore toned down his talk of nationalization, declaring that he would welcome other strategies for correcting past wrongs. Moderate ANC advisers started to suggest less drastic measures. They proposed stiff rules against monopolies, like the antitrust legislation in the United States. They talked of directing big companies' investment decisions, either through government appointees in the boardrooms, or through control of investment finance. Why, asked the ANC's advisers, were South Africans piling their money into the stock exchange, rather than investing in projects that created jobs? Surely they could put their cash into township housing instead?

The urge to direct investment took different forms. Sometimes the ANC seemed to want to direct the investments of the mining and manufacturing companies. This was unlikely to assist the economy. However sluggish the big-company bureaucrats, they were almost certainly better at appraising investment opportunities than bureaucrats from the state. The second variant was more promising. The ANC proposed to force the big savings institutions to put a fixed percentage of their money into socially useful projects. In 1990 the assets of South Africa's life insurance and pension funds came to around 130 billion rand, and they were expected to rise to 180 billion rand by the century's end. If the government were to require 10 percent of this money to be spent on housing, it would find a decent chunk of the 24 billion rand needed to make good the backlog. The life insurers did not reject this sort of thinking out of hand, though they did say that too much forced investment in marginally profitable ventures would chase savers away.

In the first months after its unbanning, the ANC's next wish seemed to be a minimum wage. Both the trade unions and the ANC's Department of Economics and Planning (note the "Planning") backed the idea. Both were reluctant to acknowledge the trade-off between higher wages and unemployment: as the cost of labor rises, the demand for it falls. The ANC's economists retorted that a minimum wage would make workers mass consumers, which would in turn boost the economy and create more jobs: "growth through redistribution," as the slogan said.

It was true that redistributing buying power from rich to poor would reduce demand for fancy imports and increase demand for things produced at home—especially those cheap goods and services produced by labor-intensive outfits operating out of township yards. Of course, redistribution might also encourage skilled people to leave the country; and the extra demand would probably produce extra inflation as well as extra growth.

But these were not the main objections to the minimum wage. The idea's biggest failing was that it redistributed money to workers rather than to the unemployed; for it was the jobless who really needed help. Since the legalization of black trade unions in 1980, wages for blacks had risen faster than wages for whites. By some international measures, black wages had actually risen too much; South African workers cost more and produced less than those in competing countries. Meanwhile black unemployment was growing ever worse. South Africa's big economic divide was no longer racial. It was between those with jobs and those without. By raising workers' pay and discouraging new employment, the minimum wage was likely to widen this gap.

The influence of trade unions on the ANC's policies explained part of its enthusiasm for that trade-off. But the explanation also lay in the influence of foreign, white advisers. Africa's dearth of graduates makes it vulnerable to experts from outside. The continent's universities and ministries are peppered with imported technocrats; the budgets and development plans announced by government ministers have often been written by an *éminence blanche*. The white hand behind the scenes is usually benign; but there is always a danger that economists and planners, imported from another country, will tell others how to live without considering whether they would like to live that way themselves. Breyten Breytenbach, an Afrikaans writer who was jailed in the 1970s for taking up arms against the white state, had something to say about these imported planners in West Africa, in a novel called *Memory of Snow and of Dust*: foreign idealists are attracted to African revolutions "like flies to honey. . . . And when the house of cards tumbles, they will not be the ones facing the firing squads."[13]

In 1980, when Zimbabwe won its independence, an American economist named Ann Seidman arrived at the country's only university. She made friends with the new government ministers, who had little experience of economic management. She suggested that they could contain inflation by means of price controls. Since firms' costs were rising, the rules against putting up prices made life all but impossible for them. Some companies went under. Others went to next-door Botswana. Zimbabwe's price controls went on scaring off investment for the rest of the decade.

South Africa, with its more educated black people, ought to be less susceptible to outside advisers. Yet in March 1991 I attended an economics discussion group in Johannesburg at which the speakers for both the ANC and the Inkatha Freedom Party were white. The ANC line was put by Niva Makgetla, daughter of Ann Seidman. At home in the United States, Makgetla was unknown as an economist; in South Africa, she had endeared herself to the right people and was therefore speaking for a party that represented a large chunk of the country. Much better economists had offered to help the ANC, but had been turned down. As in political parties all over the world, being in the right place at the right time mattered more than quality of advice.

In London earlier that month I had had lunch with Laurence Harris, an economist from the School of Oriental and African Studies who had advised the ANC's economics department for several years. I sat in a restaurant near the British Museum, watching this polite, bespectacled man eat his pasta. Harris spoke softly, avoiding provocative comment, deflecting my questions with questions of his own. His manner reminded me of a recent paper he had written,[14] a good deal of which was devoted to pleading that the ANC had considered every side of every question and was far more reasonable than its critics supposed.

Harris admitted the troubles of central planning: bureaucrats are often incompetent; state intervention can distort the price signals that businesses need. But at each turn he challenged me not to give up hope. Intervention was difficult, to be sure; but should governments abandon all effort to change the economy for the good? A minimum wage might push up unemployment, yes; but surely the ANC should try to influence the kind of jobs its people performed. If higher wages meant fewer jobs for domestic servants, for example, so be it: the ANC had no desire to build an economy on labor of that kind. Yet Harris did not explain how putting domestic servants out of work would help to generate more dignified jobs. His determination not to give up hoping seemed likely to cause suffering, without necessarily bringing South Africa closer to the dignified new order he challenged me to want.

As the months passed, however, the ANC's ideas seemed less and less fixed. The movement's trade union allies began to doubt the wisdom of a minimum wage, realizing that when the state sets pay levels the unions are in danger of losing their role. ANC spokespeople underwent a siege of lecture invitations, and were constantly asked to justify their ideas to economists, visiting dignitaries and a hostile white press. The ANC's economics department was soon convinced of its own limitations. At weekend seminars economists from banks and businesses would arrive armed with facts and figures displayed in multicolored graphs. In response, the ANC's representative would offer moral indignation at the injustices of the past. Questioners would often be told that the ANC was still researching such and such an issue, or that there was still no formal policy because the movement needed its supporters' approval first. In private, ANC economists sometimes gave up trying to fend off criticism and asked their critics for advice. The two most senior figures in the economics department, Max Sisulu and Tito Mboweni, both sought to escape the responsibilities of policy-making by taking sabbaticals at the University of the Western Cape.

The ANC's lack of self-confidence gave the powerful companies their chance. The sanctions debate had taught them how to talk politics, for they were forever having to fend off the accusation that they were apartheid's friends. Company reports discussed national politics nearly as much as production targets; as early as 1988 the Premier Group, South Africa's largest food company, went so far as to declare: "Negotiations with the ANC are an historic inevitability." In 1990 Anglo American, which with its sister company, De Beers, is comfortably South Africa's biggest conglomerate, published a short book on constitution-writing. The Federated Chamber of Industries put forward a bill of rights.

Business's top political priority was to charm the ANC. The captains of industry first visited the exiled ANC in 1985; both sides fell over each other to make friends. The tycoons arrived in open-necked shirts; the revolutionaries wore suits and ties. "One of the nicest days I've ever spent," said Gavin Relly of Anglo American afterward. "A marvelous meeting," said Oliver Tambo, the ANC's president.[15] With the ANC's unbanning, such meetings proliferated. After visiting the ANC in March 1990, Peter Wrighton, chairman of the Premier Group, stated, "We were most impressed by the pragmatism of the ANC executive and found, in the final analysis, that the things which unite us are far stronger than those which divide us."

As the ANC's leaders came home from exile, they were invited to meet business leaders, and occasionally accepted a weekend in the country or a flight in a corporate jet. Thabo Mbeki, the ANC's director of foreign affairs, stayed with Peter Wrighton at his vacation home in the Cape; and he signed his name on the wall of the wine cellar at Wrighton's Johannesburg house. It was hardly surprising that, soon after its unbanning, the ANC muted its early talk of nationalization, saying that it would be glad to consider alternative ways of addressing black needs. Joe Slovo, who was the leader of the South African Communist Party as well as a senior ANC figure, said he wanted a middle ground between the failures of socialism and the ravages of capitalism.

Some South Africans, though nervous about the ANC's economic policies, had reservations about the success of the big business lobby. They were not sure what the corporate chairmen would do with their influence. Publicly, the captains of industry professed to believe in the free market, and some of their policies were designed to spread this creed. In the late 1980s several large companies started to foster black entrepre-

neurs. Anglo American began to buy overalls, signs and clean-
ing equipment from one-man workshops, rather than making
everything itself.

Anglo American assigned Gareth Penny, a determined
young product of Eton and of Oxford, to oversee this scheme.
Penny took me to see his "entrepreneurs" at a set of workshops
coincidentally called Pennyville. There was a deafening noise
of metal-bashing and welding. Penny clapped a strong hand
on the shoulder of a man making squeegees such as you might
use to wash windows. "You see!" shouted Penny in my ear.
"He makes these for our mines." Penny beamed at the man,
who nodded in acquiescence. "We get his raw materials for
him, the rubber and so on, because we know how to get good
prices. Then he makes them, we pay him, and we have our
truck collect the finished product." Since Anglo American had
also found the squeegee man his workshop, and helped him
with his accounts, it seemed doubtful whether he was independent enough to merit the title of "entrepreneur." As time
passed, however, there seemed a decent chance that some of
Penny's protégés would stand on their own feet.

Anglo American's Oxford-educated bosses were also trying
to spread a taste for capitalism among their own employees. In
1988 they started to offer free shares in the company, hoping
this would make workers identify with the company's health.
The scheme meant inventing words for "share" in several African languages, and fending off union hostility to "token" ownership. By 1990 one hundred and sixty thousand Anglo
employees had shrugged off the unions' objections, and held
more than 200 million rand in shares. The company eagerly
pointed out that blacks' interest in the stock market was also
growing rapidly through pension and insurance funds. The
mining union's pension fund boasted more members than any
other such fund in South Africa, and was growing at a rate of
100 million rand a year. As blacks' stake in the stock exchange
expanded, white managers hoped that their hostility to private
ownership of companies would fade.

One-man workshops that supplied cheap squeegees, together with worker ownership of a few thousand shares, suited big companies' interests. In some respects, however, free-market capitalism did not suit them at all. They seemed certain, for example, to oppose tough antitrust laws, which would conjure up teams of investigators to question their pricing policies and restrict their choice of lines of business to pursue. The captains of industry would also lobby the new government for subsidies on their products, even if subsidies damaged the hope of balancing the budget and keeping inflation down. And South Africa's companies would resist the lifting of tariffs, even though there was nothing that the rusting economy needed more. For all their talk of competition and free markets, few businesspeople wanted to see foreign goods competing fairly with their products in the shops.

Utopian theorists seduced the ANC by promising jobs and decent wages for all. Industrialists seduced the movement with the glamour of their power. With these conflicting influences, it was not clear how ANC policies would eventually turn out; yet the confusion itself made one thing seem sure. Whatever the policy, it would be implemented falteringly. Ideas would change according to which lobbyist held the initiative. Decisions would not necessarily be consistent. Decisions would be reversed. Most of all, decisions would take time, as the ANC struggled to make up its mind on everything from exchange-rate policy to a new investment code. Questioners would continue to be told that such and such a dilemma required a decision from the people, or that a certain tricky issue required further research.

A look at neighboring Zimbabwe suggested that muddled policies could do nearly as much damage as consistently bad ones. After coming to power in 1980, President Mugabe's government half forgot its radical promises to the guerrillas who had fought the war for independence. At the same time, the government started to listen to the arguments of white businesspeople. The result was confusion. The supposedly Marxist government nationalized nothing outright; but it was not at all shy about buying shares in businesses ranging from a coal mine to a newspaper. The state's share of the gross domestic product rose during the first decade of independence from less than a quarter to more than a third. Inevitably the government favored the companies it owned shares in. To balance the favoritism, private companies recruited government friends: senior civil servants slotted comfortably into even more senior company jobs. Businesspeople wasted their energies on lobbying for special favors, rather than competing on the prices of their products. To those who knew Zimbabwe, South Africa's fuss about nationalization seemed beside the point. In the words of Tony Hawkins, professor of business studies at the University of Zimbabwe, "There are many more ways of killing the golden goose than expropriating it."

The Zimbabwe government's most damaging interventions had nothing to do with state ownership. At independence the new government shared the ANC's suspicion of the mining companies, which were said to be manipulating prices so as to smuggle money abroad. It therefore set up the Minerals Marketing Corporation, to sell the miners' produce for them. Politicians told the corporation where to sell and whom to hire; mineral exports stagnated. The government, which was being advised by Ann Seidman, also made the mistake of supposing that it could manage prices better than the market.

But the price freeze had the effect of freezing the economy. The government was caught between an electorate that wanted cheap food and companies that wanted decent profits; the country's top business executives complained that they produced controlled goods like beer and sugar purely as a social service. There were no clear criteria to determine who deserved a price increase, so Zimbabwe's managers had to lobby the government almost constantly. Sometimes an increase would be so delayed that desperate companies stopped production; shelves stood empty in Zimbabwe's shops.

South Africans never tire of debating the merits of socialism and capitalism, redistribution and economic growth. Zimbabwe shows that this is only half the argument. Red tape and muddle have stifled Zimbabwe without much help from ideology. To be sure, South Africa has a bigger reserve of educated people to operate its civil service; but it would be too much to expect that all will be well. The country's bureaucracy will inevitably lose cohesion as it ceases to be the monopoly of Afrikaners. That is a fair price for democracy; only an unrepresentative civil service would not reflect the country's conflict and diversity. But the dislocation will be made worse by blacks' inexperience of government. The ANC's offices in Zambia—hidden down Lusaka's back alleys, guarded by dozy youths—were hardly a preparation for government. Communication between the different buildings was uncertain. The education department had no telephone; other departments did not always answer theirs. Inside the dingy offices there was little sign of work. During the long years of exile, most ANC people became masters of inactivity: they chatted and waited while the youths in the townships led the antiapartheid fight. The Congress was entirely unready for the shock of its unbanning in 1990, which thrust it into the middle of South Africa's fast-moving debates. With that unbanning, the ANC could at last be quoted in the South African press. A Johannesburg journalist duly phoned an ANC spokesman and asked him what he felt. The spokesman could think of nothing better to say than "No comment."

African liberation movements can hardly be blamed for lacking the money to run smart offices full of cheery staff, especially when they operate in countries where no office is smart. The ANC certainly outclassed its rivals in the Pan-Africanist Congress, whose main achievement in exile recently has been to smuggle drugs. But however relatively impressive the ANC, and however understandable its shortcomings, the fact was that in the first year of its unbanning it did not look capable of running an economy well. The Johannesburg offices were better equipped than the Lusaka ones; at least the telephones worked. But people continued to make jokes about African National Chaos. "Since 1970," complained Ameen Akhalwaya, a columnist sympathetic to the ANC's cause, "not one extra-

parliamentary meeting I've attended started within thirty minutes of the advertised time." In the days when activists had
to dodge the police and stand in line for coughing buses, their
lateness was forgivable. By 1990, however, many black politicians had cars and even drivers, and the police were no longer
a problem. If black politicians behaved unpunctually in government, said Akhalwaya, wouldn't their followers start to wish
back the whites who, like Mussolini in another era, at least had
a reputation for making the trains run on time? Which
prompted Ken Owen, a much more critical commentator, to
say of the ANC, "Not even its supporters claim for it the competence to run a railroad, much less a country."

In the end, the quality of management makes or breaks a country. It explains much more about Africa's economic failures than
any of the other theories: poor prices for its commodity exports,
tribal tensions, too much intervention by the state. All economies have to cope with changing prices; most countries are
divided by regional feelings not so very different from Africans'
loyalty to tribe. State intervention has indeed been disastrous
in Africa, but that does not mean state intervention is always
bad. South Korea, the model that South Africans longed to
follow, intervened considerably during the 1960s and 1970s,
and achieved miraculous growth. South Korea's success depended less on its economic philosophy than on the fact that it
was implemented well.

Sound economic management, in government and in private
firms, depends on sound education. Here South Korea spared
no cost. Virtually all children have attended primary school
since the 1960s. Secondary-school enrolment has risen since
1965 from 35 percent to around 90 percent. Education in South
Africa does not bear comparison. In 1990 researchers at Standard Bank reported that, of South Africa's 11 million workers,
just 31 percent had had secondary schooling. Another 36 percent had been only to primary school. And 30 percent had no
education at all.

It would be hard to expand the educational system fast

enough to improve these figures because of the phenomenal growth in the number of would-be pupils. Between 1982 and 1988 enrolment at township schools doubled; but the number being turned away remained alarming. According to the ANC's education committee in Soweto, something like one in five of the township's children were refused places at the start of the school year. Those who were admitted received at best a patchy education. When the examination results came in for 1990, it turned out that hardly more than a third of blacks had passed their secondary-school final exam, as against 97 percent for white pupils. Only 7 percent of blacks had done well enough to go on to college. Black education is especially awful in the subjects that industry wants. In 1988 only 734 black high school seniors in the whole country passed the final exam in mathematics.

Standard Bank also reported that South Africa's ratio of managers to workers was among the world's lowest. It stood at 1 to 42, compared with between 1 to 3 and 7 to 10 in most developed economies. This, said the bank, "is the inevitable outcome of endeavouring to build a modern economy of 36 million people on the skills and talents of only about 13 per cent of its population".[16] As South Africa watched sanctions lift and the gold price fall, as its people debated the future of their economy, the most serious of all problems was the shortage of skilled people. Whether it liked it or not, the ANC knew it could not afford an exodus of whites.

3

THE WHITE TRIBES

A casual visitor to South Africa, surveying the sun and the landscape and the barbecues, could be forgiven for dismissing the danger of an exodus of whites. White South Africans are born in fine hospitals, as smart and as subsidized as most in the West. As children the majority attend gleaming state schools, equipped with laboratories and endless playing fields. After school there is a good chance of college, later a near-guarantee of work. Whites look forward to big houses with space for the family; perhaps even a swimming pool, a tennis court, a maid. But something else happens to white South African men along the way. One day I met a businessman with a white shirt and a gray suit who told me:

> I was based on a hill above a township with a platoon of twenty-eight men. Every day the township people would come and tell me there was going to be an attack somewhere that night: they needed my men's protection. I couldn't respond to all of them. I didn't know if all of them were telling the truth. One of them might have been planning an ambush. I mean maybe the guy wanted my men at a certain place that evening so that he could kill them. But every night we would go into the township. . . .
>
> I was trained for bush warfare. The bush is open. It calms

70

you. You know where the enemy might be. When you go into the township, the enemy is everywhere. He could be anyone. And you can't see him. Some nights I would go in. It would be raining. You could see nothing. And they would play tricks on you. Dig holes with broken glass in them. People would fall and get cut all the time. And then if you're a white South African, it could be the first time you see how the other half lives. You begin to question what you're fighting for. Your discipline goes.

One night, when I was leading my guys in, I cracked. We were going along, and a bottle broke somewhere. We got down. There was nothing; maybe it was just a dog. We got up, walked a bit further, and there was another bottle. And I thought: I don't want to do this any more. I don't want to risk my life because these people are hacking each other up. And I took my guys out, we went and had a *braai* [barbecue], lots of beers, and the next morning the township people launched a complaint against me. My men had been seen drunk, and I had to answer to my senior officer.

During the 1980s thousands of national servicemen were sent to police the violent townships. Sometimes they simply repressed black rebellion in the name of white authority; sometimes they tried to control feuds within the black community, such as the one between Chief Buthelezi's Inkatha movement and the ANC. Other national servicemen were sent into Angola, where they fought full-scale conventional battles against Angolan and Cuban troops. Any nineteen-year-old would find that traumatic; but the South African national serviceman had an extra burden on his mind. This was not a war like the one against Hitler, from which you came home a hero with history on your side. This was a war like the one the French fought in Algeria. You went out and patrolled unfamiliar ghettos, where the enemy could be anyone and could not be seen. You came home as much villain as hero, with cousins and newspapers protesting that you had risked your life for a shameful cause. And in the end the government that sent you out said sorry, it was a mistake, the war is unwinnable and not even right.

The French national servicemen shrugged off Algeria. They

crossed the Mediterranean back to Europe; they returned to Paris or Lyons and picked up their lives. White South Africans cannot go home across an ocean; they will live with the townships for the rest of their years. Like Israelis, they have fought enemies internal as well as external. Like Israelis, white South Africans have learned from national service the cost of their citizenship, the cost of being a small embattled people surrounded and outnumbered by a hostile race. A thoughtful minority is driven to the hardest questions. Is it worth being a white South African? Why hang on in Africa, this continent of alien people where survival depends upon the gun?

These questions will outlive national service and the white government that created it, for throughout their lives white South Africans are teased by the dilemmas of living in an alien land. The majority of whites do not speak any of the country's various African languages. They seldom go into a black township. They know blacks as servants or office colleagues, but rarely as friends. White South Africans live among poorer people whom they do not understand. Small wonder that they fear the anger of the underprivileged; or that long after national service many still keep guns. As the townships swelled with immigrants from the countryside, pushing up rates of unemployment and crime, whites worried that the misery of the majority would pull their own living standards down. While there was still a white government to protect their interests, most put up with Africa's uncertainties. Was it just the swimming pools that kept them? Or did they, despite everything, identify with this land?

The doubts about staying on in Africa were most marked among the English-speakers, who made up some 2 million of South Africa's 4.5 million whites. They were richer and better educated than the Afrikaners; with their international language, they would find it easier to work in Britain or Australia, Canada or the United States. Besides, the British had come to Africa later. The first British settlers landed in the Cape in 1820; the first Afrikaners had arrived from Holland in 1652. The British opened trade and cultural links with Europe; the Afrikaners were a very different type of settler, quickly losing touch with their Dutch roots. The British settlers developed a slightly accented English; the Afrikaners evolved a new language of their own.

The first Dutch settlers were sent to the Cape by the Dutch East India Company, to grow fresh food to restock the trading ships as they passed between Asia and Holland. It was a modest role in the grand drama of Dutch empire; and it is hardly surprising that the settlers at the victualing station were an unambitious lot. They had little in common with America's pilgrim fathers, who aspired to a new and purer order than the Europe they had left behind; nor with the adventurer-colonists, who sought fast fortunes in the New World; nor with the self-righteous civilizers of Victorian Britain. These were simpler settlers, who soon lost their memories of Europe, and seemed to visiting travelers to have adopted the natives' idle ways. They were becoming Afrikaners—which means simply Africans— and they were evolving their new language, a Dutch with words borrowed from French and German that later became known as Afrikaans.

In the nineteenth century the British brought the industrial revolution to South Africa. They set up factories and practiced new kinds of agriculture. They campaigned against slavery, enforced new labor laws, and lobbied for a free press. This tide of European influence infuriated the Dutch settlers who lived in the Cape: between 1835 and 1837 some fourteen thousand of them packed their belongings onto ox-wagons and embarked upon the Great Trek, the centerpiece of Afrikaner folklore to this day. The trekkers led their families a thousand miles into the African interior, where they founded their own republics, proudly independent of the colonial power. At the end of the century these mini-states—the Orange Free State and the Transvaal—took on the might of the British Empire in the Boer War. The Afrikaners proved so determined that the British invented concentration camps in order to subdue them: they herded women and children into such unsanitary prison camps that some twenty-six thousand died. The experience completed Afrikaners' pride in being white Africans, a tough people who embraced the dark continent, who resisted colonial European intervention to the last.

In their briefer stay in Africa; English-speakers grappled inconclusively with the continent, never identifying with it to the full. Travelers from the England of Gainsborough and Constable, searching for meadows and peaceful streams, were appalled by the dry monotony of the veld, a "Ragged brown carpet, vast and bare."[1] Africa's people were even more bewildering. In 1870, as a young man newly arrived in Africa, Cecil Rhodes wrote to his mother: "I don't think anything equals the smell of a party of kaffir women on a hot day if you pass on the lee side of them."[2] Rhodes and his fellow Englishmen resolved to keep the subject races at arm's length—much as British colonists did in the rest of the Empire. Wherever they went the British preferred to rule the natives indirectly, bribing chiefs or maharajas to keep their people calm. The emblem of the British Empire was the gentlemen's club, a haven from the foreign world outside. There were British rules and British menus; the natives intruded only as waiters, usually dressed in British clothes.

The distance between white and native found expression in the fear of miscegenation, which violated the boundary between races, creating half-caste children with no natural home. The novels of Sarah Gertrude Millin, an English-speaking South African active between the 1920s and the 1950s, are full of the preoccupation with mixed blood. In *God's Stepchildren* a mixed-race family tries in vain to live the life of whites. Barry, whose skin is pale enough to conceal his background, goes to Oxford and marries an Englishwoman. On his return to South Africa, however, his secret is betrayed. His wife deserts him, pregnant with his child. In the end Barry goes home to live with his poor family, accepting the futility of aspiring to a life above his race, accepting even that he was wrong to marry a white bride. "For my sin in begetting him, I am not to see my child." Miscegenation tainted a family indelibly; future generations might deny it successfully for brief periods, but the taint would always come back to give them away.

By refusing to mix with Africans, the English settlers were admitting that they did not belong to the continent; the logic of their position was that one day they would return home. That was just what happened at independence in most of Africa: the colonizers packed their belongings into tea-chests rather than stay on under African rule. South Africa was different. Its white community was more firmly established than those of other British colonies. The Afrikaners were most firmly rooted in the continent; but even the British presence in South Africa predated the settlement of Kenya or Rhodesia by seventy years. From the 1870s the diamond and gold mines gave South Africa an importance beyond any other part of Africa. By 1882 the diamond town of Kimberley had electric streetlights; London did not yet have them. South Africa also attracted more settlers. By the time of the 1911 census it boasted a million and a quarter whites; Rhodesia's white community never exceeded two hundred and fifty thousand. In 1910 South Africa's importance was rewarded with virtual independence. The British colony in the Cape joined with the former Boer republics under the Act of Union, and modern South Africa was born.

In the 1960s, when decolonization came to the rest of Africa, South Africa's English-speaking whites were sufficiently established to stay on. They did not identify with Africans; yet they had been in Africa long enough to build a white community with solid roots. Moreover, by the middle of the twentieth century the differences between English and Afrikaner were starting to fade. The Afrikaners were shaking off their grandfathers' backwardness. Many had left the farms for the cities; a few became educated and sophisticated, identifying less with Africa and more with the developed world.

And so it was an Afrikaner government which, in the 1950s, enacted apartheid, a system designed to allow white South Africans to hang on to their patch of Africa without mixing with its people. The new laws were cruder than any an English-speaking government would have implemented; but they suited well the English fear of racial mixing. Apartheid forbade blacks to share white schools, hospitals, suburbs, buses and electoral rolls. Apartheid outlawed miscegenation: mixed marriages and interracial sex were banned. Apartheid separated whites from Africans, but it also strengthened whites' hold on Africa's land. The Land Acts of the early twentieth century had already restricted black rights of ownership; but in the 1960s Hendrik Verwoerd, prime minister and philosopher of grand apartheid, set out to complete blacks' dispossession by taking their rights of citizenship too. Blacks were given ten impoverished "homelands" to live in; the rest of South Africa was declared the home of whites.

This vision of Africa without Africans was supported by a web of myth. The Dutch Reformed Church, to which most Afrikaners belonged, produced biblical support for segregation. Anthropologists pretended that the homelands were reincarnations of ancient tribal kingdoms that blacks yearned to revive. As Africa's independent countries fell on hard times, South African broadcasters played up the chaos of black rule; denied visas by most African countries, white audiences were not in a position to test the propaganda against observations of their own. Isolated on the tip of Africa, whites identified more and more with the developed world. They sometimes referred to themselves as Europeans; a typical television documentary about the Ivory Coast reassured the viewer that "such customs may seem alien to the Western mind, but to the African they are normal."

The mad scheme of segregation was never going to work. South Africa's economy was built on black labor, so it was impossible to banish blacks to the homelands and keep South Africa for whites. Besides, there was no way that so many people could be squashed onto so little land. As the black population grew, this became ever more obvious; by the 1980s the townships that ringed whites' gleaming cities were absorbing thousands of newcomers from the homelands every day. Squatters sprang up everywhere, building villages of corrugated iron and cardboard as quickly as the police chased them away. In

1980 blacks had accounted for just over half of South Africa's urban population. By the year 2000 they are expected to out-number whites by nearly five to one.

As the 1980s wore on, it was not just the black underclass that spilled over apartheid's fences; the black middle class was spreading too. The economy had outgrown the settler popula-tion; it needed more lawyers and accountants and managers than could be found from white ranks. The new opportunities were grasped disproportionately by South Africa's million-strong Indian community, but some also went to colored people and blacks. Whites were no longer the only people in suits and BMWs. By 1990 they accounted for less than half the country's total spending power; advertisers designed multiracial posters and commercials to capture both markets, black and white. Demography and economics were breaking apartheid down.

Whites faced up to apartheid's failure reluctantly. They did their best not to see it. They discussed the soaring growth of the black population and unemployment rather as Britons discussed their chaotic schools, or Americans the threat of drugs: serious problems, certainly, but not ones likely to result in the collapse of the political order. They seized on chinks in the wall of sanctions and pretended they were windows. Margaret Thatcher's opposition to sanctions won her torrents of applause; favorable articles in the British press were gleefully reported in South Africa's newspapers the next day.

For all the bravado, white confidence was faltering. The long tide of immigration from Europe was ebbing: according to offi-cial statistics, thirty-two thousand whites emigrated between 1986 and 1988; many more left the country without filling out forms. Young men got out to avoid the unwinnable battles in the ghettos; families packed up to avoid raising children in a hopeless land.

White disorientation was summed up in the style of P. W. Botha, who became prime minister in 1978 and ruled until 1989. Botha began as a reformer, a brave leader who saw which way the wind was blowing and sought to manage change. He recognized the power of black labor by legalizing black trade unions. He repealed the pass laws and abolished influx control, which had checked the tide of migration from countryside to town. He accepted that migration would be permanent, by allowing blacks to buy their township houses. The laws against miscegenation were scrapped as well, and racial mixing was accepted in shopping centers and offices.

Botha did away with most of "petty apartheid"; but he shrank from tackling the problem at apartheid's core. Blacks wanted more than the end of petty discrimination; they wanted the vote. Botha wriggled and dodged around this problem, producing a string of half-promises to share power. In 1983 a new constitution promoted Botha from prime minister to president and created two new chambers of parliament: a House of Representatives for coloreds and a House of Delegates for Indians. Both chambers were junior to the white one, which Botha justified on the ground that Indian and colored South Africans were less numerous than whites. The same argument could not be made for black South Africans, so Botha offered them no chamber at all. This insult sparked the riots of the mid-1980s, which prompted sanctions in their turn. In his last years in office, P. W. Botha had become a bitter old autocrat who refused to listen to what blacks wanted and who had no idea of what to offer them instead.

It took the change from P. W. to F. W. for reform to resume. President De Klerk accepted the full implications of apartheid's failure: he unbanned blacks' political organizations and acknowledged that they must have a real share in government. De Klerk had finally abandoned whites' hopes of extending their privileges beyond the colonial age. On what basis would whites stay in Africa now?

A few optimistic liberals declared that they could see no problem. They had always opposed apartheid; they professed nothing but happiness now that it was almost gone. Apartheid had torn whites and blacks apart, frustrating the interracial friendships that would otherwise have been natural. Under the ANC's color-blind leadership, the old tensions would give way to a new racial harmony. After all, the ANC had whites on its National Executive; white marshals frisked people for weapons at its rallies; white researchers wrote its policy pamphlets. When Molly Blackburn, a white civil-rights campaigner, died in a car accident in 1986, twenty thousand blacks turned out for her funeral.

The liberal optimists were right that the ANC was remarkably free of racism. Several senior Congress leaders were influenced by Christian teachings; they believed in brotherhood and disapproved of revenge. Albert Luthuli, president of the ANC during the defiance campaign of the 1950s, was a Methodist lay preacher. Oliver Tambo, the ANC's exiled president, had once hoped to become an Anglican priest. Inside the country, the ANC's most prominent sympathizers included clerics such as Desmond Tutu, the Anglican archbishop of Cape Town who won a Nobel prize in 1984.

Alongside Christianity came the influence of courageous whites. Black clergy, for example, were confirmed in their nonracism by Beyers Naudé, who spoke out against apartheid even though it meant losing his ministry in the Dutch Reformed Church. Black activists looked up to Joe Slovo, who had abandoned his legal career to join the ANC, who lost his wife to a parcel bomb, who eventually came home in 1990 with grandfatherly white hair. These were the famous cases; but a host of smaller gestures reinforced the ANC's nonracist tone. In the midst of Natal's violence, a group of middle-class women found that a white presence in a township had the effect of deterring an attack. It was a risky business: attacks, when they happened, involved setting fire to homesteads and slicing up the occupants as they emerged. The women from suburbia took the risk all the same. They spent the nights in threatened houses, proving that not all whites were insensitive to black pain.

At times South Africans did seem to defy racial barriers; and a liberal visitor from Europe might well have concluded that, in the post-apartheid future, race would be more or less ignored. I thought as much myself when, after several brief visits to the region, I arrived to live in Zimbabwe in 1989. I brought with me the usual liberal suppositions about race: that it matters only in the eyes of bigots; that bigotry alone prevented black and white Zimbabweans from getting along, intermarrying, and eventually merging. By all accounts, Zimbabwe had made a fair start. The whites who ruled the country when it was called Rhodesia had held on through a war for independence that cost more than thirty thousand lives. But in 1979 they gave up their resistance, and since then blacks and whites had got along remarkably well. They were still some way from intermarrying, admittedly; and whites still shivered at dinner-party stories of witch doctors who told AIDS patients to cure themselves by raping white virgins. But the fears and stereotypes would surely fade with time. As I arrived in Africa, I felt hopeful that an unprejudiced outsider would find little difficulty in making black friends.

As soon as I saw the city of Harare, I realized it would be hard to cross the racial boundary, whether it was the result of bigotry or not. Separation is written into the city's geography. The townships (since independence renamed "high-density suburbs") are off to the south of the city; the smarter suburbs lie to the north. Kenneth Kaunda Avenue is the frontier. As you cross southward, the jacaranda blossoms stop; the city hunches its shoulders; elbows stick out; female necks support astonishing piles of shopping. The shopfronts are lower and darker and more crowded. There are no whites on the pavement. A few swish by in cars, with power at their toe-tips. It is rather like Johannesburg on a smaller, more provincial scale.

The longer I spent in Harare, the more numerous seemed the barriers to friendship across Kenneth Kaunda Avenue. The most obvious one was economic. Like nearly all whites in the country, I was embarrassingly rich. The Jeep I brought out with me attracted the sorts of reactions that a Rolls-Royce might get in London. South of K. K. Avenue, few people had any sort of car. Each morning they waited in bus lines for as much as two hours. Crushed hip to hip with their fellow commuters and unable to move, they gave pickpockets an easy time. When the weekend arrived, the last thing they wanted was a foreigner's invitation to dinner, and another battle with the bus.

Making friends with successful blacks who had moved into the northern suburbs proved almost as hard. At first I thought this might reflect hostility to anyone white and British, bequeathed by blacks' memories of Rhodesia and reinforced by the common view that Margaret Thatcher had sided against blacks in South Africa. I abandoned this notion after talking to a white Zimbabwean, who had established her pro-black credentials by falling foul of the Rhodesian government during the 1970s. She taught at Harare's university, where most of her colleagues were black. Not one, she said, had become a close friend.

So what made befriending blacks so hard? One obstacle was the deference blacks still showed to whites. A white who visits a slum in Lagos or Nairobi is probably asking for trouble. But in Mbare, just south of K. K. Avenue, people practically stood to attention when I asked them the way. ("Yes, please, baas!" "You don't have to call me boss." "Okay, baas!") Middle-class blacks, of course, were altogether more self-confident. But even they were generally too polite to say what they were thinking, which made building friendships hard. They were inhibited, even prim; they found foreigners' relaxed confidence off-putting. Besides, their social and financial energies went mainly to their extended families, who took priority over meeting an acquaintance in a restaurant for lunch. Successful people in Harare were often called upon to spend their weekends and their money on the weddings and funerals of country cousins, or to have relatives to stay when they came to town.

As the months passed, however, I came to the conclusion that there was more to it than this. Zimbabweans appeared to be less short of time than of inclination to get to know outsiders. They seemed to approach whites as they would a business contact: conversation might be agreeable, but one could not expect to relax. Nor would one choose to mix business with pleasure: on the two occasions I was invited to supper by a black family, the other guests were white. The discomfort at mixed socializing was reflected in people's command of English. Zimbabweans who discussed their work or politics with perfect fluency would suddenly seem strained if conversation lightened. English was the language of the office; Shona was for gossiping with friends.

Blacks in Zimbabwe were not just estranged from whites; they seemed to have only half accepted the city and the modern values that whites represent. People who had lived for years in Harare would tell me that their "home" was the village of their birth. Even sophisticated blacks felt as much for the countryside, with its wealth of African tradition, as for the modern city. One Zimbabwean who had lived in the United States for years told me that when her son died prematurely, she brought his body all the way back from Washington, D.C., to her village to bury him.

Zimbabwe's better writers were full of the agony of transition from the village. In Charles Mungoshi's short stories, the modern manners of the city bring more trouble than good. The schoolroom casts doubt upon traditional beliefs and sows impatience with the peasant's life; it encourages children to desert their families and the graves of their ancestors for the glitter of the town. But education provides no guarantee of a city job. "Education is a western thing and we throw away brother and sister for it but when it fails we are lost," laments one of Mungoshi's characters. "The city is like the throat of a crocodile," says the peasant-heroine in *Bones*, a novel by Chenjerai Hove; "it swallows both the dirty and the clean." At the end of my year in Zimbabwe I concluded that the half-acceptance of the city had a lot to do with the half-acceptance of whites.

Would race relations in South Africa turn out any easier, as the liberal optimists hoped? South Africa's black middle class had lived in cities longer than that of Zimbabwe, where industrialization came later and on a smaller scale. Black South Africans were also richer. Many more had been to college. They were more sophisticated than black Zimbabweans; multiracial friendships therefore seemed to stand a better chance. Indeed the ANC's mixed membership proved the difference from Zimbabwe, where until independence President Robert Mugabe's ZANU party had almost nothing to do with whites. In South Africa the Pan-Africanist Congress, which shared ZANU's hostility to white involvement, had never rivaled the ANC in size.

And yet it was hard to believe those optimists who maintained that in the new South Africa blacks and whites would have no difficulty getting along. Among left-wing white students it was de rigueur to make black friends, but five years later the same left-wingers could be found socializing almost entirely with whites. At a fashionable wedding of a white couple in Johannesburg the guests thought it an excellent idea to sing the hymn of black resistance. 'Nkosi sikelel'i-Afrika,' they began, then discovered that half of them did not know the second verse. In 1990 Rian Malan, an unknown Afrikaner, published a book about the distances between white and black South Africans. He immediately became the toast of Johannesburg's parties. Malan's theme had clearly touched his countrymen's hearts.

Malan's book was largely about himself, a white who had been sixteen years old in 1970 and was very much a child of his time. Che Guevara's crusade to liberate Bolivian Indians inspired Malan to try the same for oppressed black South Africans. He declared teenage war on rockspiders, crunchies, hairybacks and ropes—as his fellow Afrikaners were variously called. He perceived a sinister link between the state's racial repression and his school's ruthless outlawing of long hair. The rockspiders had banned the Beatles from the radio after John Lennon claimed more popularity than Jesus: that was why they had to be overthrown.

Malan therefore turned against his people; he called his book *My Traitor's Heart*. Yet he found as he grew older that he felt uneasy among blacks too. He yearned to help them; but he seldom met blacks except when buying dope in back alleys. After he finished school he worked as a reporter for the *Johan-*

nesburg Star. He did his best to befriend his black colleagues. When he invited one home, his mother addressed the guest in pidgin English.

Though he longed to, Malan could never discuss politics with the *Star*'s black journalists: he feared their bitterness and his own patronizing sympathy. The township riots of 1976 left him wondering whether whites could ever win black acceptance. A white sociologist devoted to the black cause had been working in Soweto when the riots began: the mob killed him. Shortly afterward a black man went on the rampage with an ax in a white shopping center. Blacks sympathized with the murderer's frustration. But Malan could not help reflecting that, whatever his own political views, he might have been among the victims. That evening the newsroom drinking bout was scarred by silences. Malan felt that he and his supposed friends were meeting "like soldiers in no-man's land, exchanging cigarettes and handshakes on Christmas day."

To escape this agony of polarization, Malan left South Africa. Like many political exiles, he soon pined for lost dilemmas. He returned home to decide whether whites had a future in South Africa; his book seemed to suggest that they did not. It sneered at the contortions of white liberals who tried to be part of black liberation: decorating their rooms with Kenyan textiles, dancing to black music, and speaking reverently of AAH-free-kah. They pronounced South Africa's conflict political rather than racial, and made it clear which side they were on by espousing socialism—"the opium of the élite," in Malan's cruel phrase. But these whites were not on the barricades in the townships: their black brothers might have killed them.

Malan's book finished with the story of Neil Alcock, a secular saint who lived only to help blacks. He spoke fluent Zulu and lived in a Zulu hut. When he tried to arrange peace talks between Natal's warring clans, one faction killed him. His wife lived on in his hut: her Zulu foster sons stole most of her belongings. She hung on anyway, determined that her identification with Africa would not be broken, even by the most horrible misfortune that could be put in her way. " 'Love is worth nothing,' " she told the author, " 'until it has been tested by its own defeat.' "[3] To live in Africa, Malan seemed to conclude, you must accept that it may kill you.

Some whites remained committed to South Africa without pretending that racial harmony would come easily. They acknowledged that it would be hard to live in Africa but declared the effort worthwhile. Their upbringing and childhood memories tied them to the country. They knew that taxes would rise and wealth would be redistributed, and they welcomed it. Peter Wrighton, chairman of the Premier Group, stated, "We must accept that those who have benefited materially in the past will be called on to make material sacrifices in the future. The long-term safety and prosperity of the few are in the hands of the many, and individuals will only progress if the community does so as well."

Besides, transition was exciting. Clem Sunter, a British executive who worked for Anglo American, told me that there had been a time during the riots of the mid-1980s when he worried about his future in South Africa. Then Anglo's bright managers put together a short book about the country's options: there was a low road down which the country would descend if it pursued statist economic policies, and a free-market high road which would take South Africa in the direction of Japan. Clem Sunter was chosen to take this futurology around the country, addressing meetings in endless provincial towns. There were 230 such gatherings; at each one Sunter and his audience debated the merits of capitalism versus socialism, federalism versus a unitary state. In what other country would ordinary people have discussed these issues with such passion? Sunter had no desire to leave again.

In Europe or America an educated philanthropist gets lost in the crowd; in South Africa he or she can make a difference. Whites still in their twenties and thirties had a big hand in setting up the black trade union movement. They sat on ANC think tanks, wrote newspaper columns and managed factories. In 1990 I telephoned Chief Buthelezi's office to request an interview. The white secretary who answered put me through to the office of Buthelezi's white aide. The aide was away, so the secretary gave me his deputy; he was white as well. Buthelezi also retained a white ex-journalist to manage his public relations in Johannesburg, and a white academic to head the Inkatha Institute, which produced pro-Buthelezi research. Apartheid not only distributed wealth unequally; it reserved for whites the privilege of influence too.

There is no analogy for this in developed countries, where democracy ensures that education and influence are more widely spread. South Africa's privileged campaigners against privilege recall instead the Britons or Americans of a former era. In 1893 Beatrice Webb, who spent a life campaigning for social reform in Britain, recorded in her diary her glee at breaking with the main body of the Royal Commission on Labor and signing a dissenting socialist report. She had struck a blow against class privilege, but she had been in a position to do so because of her own wealth. "Certainly," she concluded, "persons with brains and independent means may have a rare good time."[4] White South Africans, opposing apartheid and living in their garden suburbs, could easily say the same.

Yet not all whites relished the opportunity to be part of a political campaign. The thrill of transition, which kept Sunter in South Africa, encouraged other whites to leave. They resented having to apologize for not being involved in politics; they left the country in search of uncomplicated yuppie lives. Others found transition frightening. In 1990 an anonymous pamphlet painted black rule in the colors of the apocalypse, expressing whites' most extreme terror at the loss of control. The pamphlet was faxed around South Africa; it exhorted blacks to rise up and kill the white oppressors on a particular day.[5] The message began with "*Amandla!*" and was subtitled "Views and news of blacks fighting for freedom in South Africa." It declared:

> We will kill all the white racists and we will be free in Azania, free from oppression and discrimination!
> . . . The police are our enemy, we MUST rise up and take

what belongs to us! Comrade Nelson told us to. We will attack the white racists in their houses built on the ruins of our ancestors' huts. FREE SOUTH AFRICA!

. . . Go and choose your house in a white area today, when we win that house will be yours! WE MUST STRIKE ON THE 10TH OF APRIL!

The pamphlet was obviously a fake. Azania is the name for South Africa used by black-consciousness parties such as the Pan-Africanist Congress, not by Nelson Mandela or the ANC. Both Mandela and the police declared the pamphlet bogus: "an amateurish effort aimed at creating uncertainty and panic," sniffed a spokesman for the police. The pamphlet's authors were trying to turn whites against the idea of negotiation between government and the ANC; April 10 was the day before the first talks about talks were expected.

Perhaps not many whites were worried by this pamphlet. Less apocalyptic rumors were taken more seriously. Arthur Goldstuck, a South African journalist who in 1990 published a book about his country's "urban legends," reported the persistence of stories about servants plotting to take over their employers' houses. Dinner parties buzzed with anecdotes about somebody's second cousin whose maid one day announced that she was paying the ANC 10 rand a month, so that when the Congress took over the country she would take over the house. This story made the rounds with minor variations, until a spate of these supposed incidents was written up in the *Johannesburg Star*. The article did not include any interviews with servants claiming to have paid subscriptions to the "Mandela Fund." According to Goldstuck, similar stories circulated in the last months of Rhodesia in 1979.

Whites felt alien Africa invading. By 1990 the shops in central Johannesburg already sold more to blacks than whites, which meant that they were as likely to stock crude hot plates as fancy stoves. Just to the north, white suburbs had given way to bohemia: multiracial, honky-tonk, full of cut-price shops and cut-price prostitutes. Most whites did their shopping and aerobics in the politer suburbs further north. The nightmare, laughed one white Johannesburger, was that even the arty cinemas in the rich northern suburbs would start showing kung fu films in Zulu. The jokes masked more serious fears: whether there would be decent education for their children, decent hospitals to cushion their old age. It was not just a question of race; whites were obsessed with "standards." When in 1991 ANC leaders declared that South Africa's universities should admit more black students, an indignant C. Zaverdinos of Pietermaritzburg wrote to the *Johannesburg Star*: "In no country is 'mass education' the responsibility of the university, if it deserves the name, and forcing the increase in numbers of whatever the colour can only lead to its destruction."

Most worrying of all was the violence, which spilled from the townships more and more. Newspapers trumped each other with car hijack stories: the gang that shot a motorist and drove off with his corpse still in the car; the woman who, held up at gunpoint, tried to surrender her keys but was refused—the assailants wanted to abduct her, not just her car. Gunmen held up restaurants: customers surrendered watches, wallets, occasionally their shoes. One victim, a liberal member of parliament, joked (or was he joking?) that the experience had left him torn between emigrating and joining the far-right Conservative Party. Thieves patrolled traffic jams, breaking car windows and grabbing handbags or anything else within reach. One incident that particularly delighted editors involved a businessman who gave two employees a lift home to Soweto; after dropping them off he stopped at a traffic light and was shot dead.

In December 1990 a gang with an AK-47 assault rifle turned up in the middle of Johannesburg's white suburbs and murdered a housewife in front of her two children. This encouraged Adriaan Vlok, then minister of law and order, to offer a vast ransom for illegal weapons. By March a mere seventy AK-47s had been handed in. That month André Jacobs, the head of the National Association of Private Transport Operators, gravely told a conference that if current trends continued, South Africa's car thieves would soon be stealing more cars per year than the country produced. Already in 1990 6 billion rand worth of vehicles had been stolen. Cape Town, said the newspapers, was the most violent place on earth; in 1990 it suffered 64.6 murders per 100,000 people. Johannesburg's annual murder rate was 20 per 100,000 residents, which comfortably outdid New York's 13 per 100,000 and London's 2.5.

Whites spoke fearfully of Lebanon. They defended their gardens with big fences and dogs. Alsatians were particularly popular; so were Staffordshire bull terriers, known affectionately as crocodiles-on-leash. Security firms multiplied, not least because insurance companies refused claims from people who had not invested properly in self-defense. Classy people equipped their houses with alarm buttons that summoned "rapid-response armed units"; but the manager of one established outfit complained that "any fool with a gun and a dog can set himself up." The chairman of another security company estimated that fifteen hundred firms had sprung up in his sector, employing around three hundred thousand people. Other boom businesses included weapons shops (smart ones offered everything from guns to eye-blinding sprays to crossbows), shooting ranges and courses that taught family dogs to assault unknown visitors. By the end of 1990, a year in which political violence had tripled, an entrepreneur who specialized in barbed-wire installations had become a millionaire.

Nearly 3 million South Africans were said to hold firearm licenses. At one nightclub guests were politely asked to hand in their weapons along with their coats. The vice-chancellor of the University of the Witwatersrand, Johannesburg's English-speaking campus, felt obliged to rule that students should not carry guns on campus. The police warned women that they "should carry a firearm at all times to ensure safety," and women and old people were advised not to live alone. The violence naturally made whites apprehensive about life after apartheid, when policemen might no longer be so attentive to their worries, when courts might be more lenient on black crime. The violence breathed truth into Archbishop Tutu's gibe, "In this country we have so many people who want to change so long as things remain the same."

Some whites still sought refuge in the old self-delusion, believing that political change could be postponed. In March 1991, more than a year after the release of Nelson Mandela, I took a ride in a Johannesburg taxi, a spluttering old Peugeot with a spluttering old Afrikaner slumped behind the wheel. I asked what he felt about the prospect of a black president. "There won't be one! Not for another ten or twenty years," came the reply.

Whites who expected blacks to dominate government sooner did not necessarily accept that it would be dominated by Nelson Mandela. They put their faith in the conservative Chief Buthelezi, who had comfortingly denounced communism and the armed struggle of the ANC. At *The Economist* I received several letters attacking my articles for assuming that the ANC would loom large in the next government. "The biggest and most powerful internal political group in South Africa among the black community is not the ANC but Inkatha," explained a Mr. Branscombe of Rivonia in the province of Transvaal. "The ANC is basically Xhosa, who are about 10 per cent of the population of this country, whereas Inkatha is basically Zulu, who total about 24 per cent of South Africa's people. The ANC is the product of very cleverly orchestrated overseas controlled propaganda, whereas Inkatha is based on the grass-roots support of the biggest single nation in South Africa."

Actually Mr. Branscombe had his figures wrong: counting the homelands, South Africa had something like 7 million Xhosas in 1990, or 19 percent of the population. The Zulus, of whom there were around 7.5 million, did not have the overwhelming numerical advantage that Mr. Branscombe claimed. Besides, it was difficult to see Buthelezi's Inkatha Freedom Party as the victim of the ANC's superior propaganda, organized by powerful whites. After all, Buthelezi had been received by Ronald Reagan and Margaret Thatcher; he had received secret grants from the South African government; he had been invited to the seventieth-birthday party of Harry Oppenheimer, the richest of South Africa's tycoons. Buthelezi's conservatism had won him grants from all around the world; he was the one who had been puffed up by propaganda, not the ANC. In one poll of urban blacks in April 1990, Inkatha scored an approval rating of just 1 percent, compared with 64 percent for the ANC and 8 percent for De Klerk's National Party.[6]

The ANC did its best to calm white worries; on the occasion of his first negotiations with the government, Mandela addressed the television cameras in Afrikaans, assuring his audience that the ANC understood their fears. But whites could not help noticing that Mandela had spoken kindly of Fidel Castro and Moammar Qaddafi as well. Businessmen fretted over the threat of nationalization; intellectuals feared the ANC's alliance with the communists. Where else in the world, sighed a liberal sympathizer at an ANC rally, would you still see the hammer and sickle so proudly displayed?

In the first months after the ANC's unbanning, few whites took the plunge and left; fewer, certainly, than in the mid-1980s, when ungovernability had first reared its head. The crime figures were still low compared with the toll in the black townships: out of 11,750 murders reported in 1990, only 305 victims were white. Besides, whites' fears of a decline in "standards" were often so exaggerated that they could be easily assuaged. Many whites had dreaded the thought of black neighbors who would keep them awake all night with music and send down the value of their property. But well before the ANC's unbanning they had begun to discover that black, Indian and colored South Africans who could afford to live in white areas would not harm their precious "standards" at all. Indeed the opposite was true. In Mayfair, a Johannesburg suburb that turned "gray" in the mid-1980s, a 1988 survey found that just a third of the white residents had passed the secondary-school final exam, compared with two-thirds of the Indian newcomers. That year a Conservative town council was elected in Boksburg and tried to reimpose segregation. When it threatened to cut off the water and electricity of ten Indian families, white residents rallied to the Indians' support. Their neighbors, they protested, were cultured and educated, and paid good money for their homes.

In 1991, when the Group Areas Act was finally repealed, whites continued to be pleased by the results. The new residents of well-to-do suburbs were well-to-do themselves. It did not matter if they were Indian; they could even be black. This may sound obvious to outsiders; to some white South Africans it came as a wonderful surprise. On the first day after the abolition of group areas newspaper editors thought it worth carrying reports like this one, from the *Sunday Times*:

> The influx of middle-class buyers had upgraded former white areas, and initial resentment to the newcomers changed as whites discovered "their darker-skinned neighbours were people just like them."
>
> Some whites even found themselves envious of the shiny BMWs parked in their black neighbours' driveways, said Mr. McKee [an estate agent from Cape Town]. . . .
>
> Typical of last Sunday's house-hunters were a middle-aged churchman and his family, who looked like any other prospective home-buyers in Durban's Westville suburb.[7]

And, farther on in the same article, a black house-hunter was quoted:

> I want a modern house with a beautiful garden and, most important, a two-car garage for my Mercedes and Cressida.

Fifteen years earlier, this would have caused a sensation. Lekgau Mathabathe, who went on to become the first black director of the Premier Group, remembers a business trip in the 1970s to Pietersburg, a conservative Afrikaner town in the northern Transvaal. His colleagues, who were all white, had reserved rooms in a nice hotel just outside town; because of apartheid, Mathabathe had registered somewhere else. When the group arrived at the hotel, one of the whites asked whether Mathabathe could stay there too. Certainly, came the answer;

there were servants' quarters in the yard. The white colleague persisted. This black was not a servant; he was (and here he took poetic license) the white man's boss. If the boss was told to sleep in servants' quarters, all hell would break loose; indeed, the white deputy might even lose his job. The receptionist considered, and eyed the burly Afrikaners around the hotel bar. Then he made an announcement. Please could the regular guests very kindly make an exception for once: a distinguished cabinet minister from a homeland was visiting, sent by the white government itself. Mathabathe was allowed to stay the night, though he judged it wise not to linger in the bar.

By 1990 whites had spent more than a decade getting used to the idea of affluent blacks. Homeland politicians spoke on television; black executives shopped in smart stores. Whites had watched the rest of Africa acquire black rulers; and though apartheid's propaganda had told them that black rule had brought communism, Eastern Europe's revolutions had soothed communism's sting. In the week of the ANC's unbanning I sat in a gentlemen's club in Cape Town, and had lunch with a businessman who had deserted Yorkshire in favor of the African sun. As a young man he had been a police officer in the colony of Nyasaland. When Nyasaland became Malawi, he decided it was time to leave. He went to Bechuanaland, which soon became Botswana; he went to Rhodesia, which became Zimbabwe in its turn. Now he was sitting on a balcony in Cape Town; to the south lay nothing but the sea. This time, he admitted quite cheerfully, he would stay despite black rule. After all, the whites in next-door Namibia had recently allowed a black guerrilla movement to contest and win a fair election; and the one-time "terrorists" were behaving remarkably well.

Whites were not deserting, but they were certainly hedging their bets. Money seeped out of the country. Johannesburg lawyers took American bar exams. Embassies received more visa applications. People in the tree-lined suburbs wrote more frequently to their cousins in England and Australia. If the country returned to the instability of the mid-1980s these waverers might leave; for the sad truth is that a society short of skills always has difficulty keeping what skills it has. Even in peaceful England, plenty of clever youngsters have deserted the economically depressed north for the brighter prospects in London. When violence or political uncertainty is added to depression, the exodus swells: the West is increasingly familiar with qualified Russians desperate for a job.

South Africa is no different: its clever, mobile people have their eyes on brighter prospects overseas. By 1990 just five of a class of forty-seven M.B.A. students who had been at the University of the Witwatersrand in 1982 still lived in South Africa. In 1986 almost twice as many engineers emigrated from the country as immigrated. The health service was already importing doctors in large numbers, many of them from Israel. Medical students at Soweto's hospital have been known to complain that to learn anything from their superiors they must first learn Hebrew. The National Manpower Commission talked of a shortage of two hundred and twenty-eight thousand graduates by the turn of the century.

Many of these voluntary exiles miss their country; they sit in London and curse the weather and scour the papers for South African news. If South Africa's transition goes well, some may return; if it goes badly, the exodus will grow like a big white snowball. In 1991 Denis Beckett, one of South Africa's best journalists, confessed in his Sunday column that, for the first time, he accepted that one day he might leave. There had been a time when he resented friends who quit the country, shrinking the stock of skills and liberal values that made South Africa a decent place. Now the shrinking had reached a point at which Beckett doubted his own permanence. "We sort our Christmas cards in two piles for posting, foreign and local," he wrote. "If you go back far enough they were nearly all local. This year the piles are the same size."

One category of white South African certainly will not be leaving. Many young Afrikaners, who have been to college and speak perfect English, are as mobile as their British counterparts. But outside the big cities there still survives another kind of Afrikaner, much closer to the stubborn forefathers who fought the British in the Boer War. These are the people who celebrate the Great Trek into the African interior, who recall that the British Empire invented concentration camps to subdue their great-grandparents, and who still feel beleaguered by the big forces of the world. For years the Afrikaners held out against the black nationalism that swept Africa; against communism, which took the blacks' side; and against the liberalism of former colonial powers, which protested all the more shrilly at Afrikaner behavior because it was not so different from what theirs once had been. Surely survival against all these enemies was a divine signal; with their roots in Calvinist Holland, Afrikaners were quite ready to see themselves as God's elect. In the aftermath of the Boer War they had been a broken people, with starving children and landless farmers begging in the towns. By 1948 they had recovered; that year their National Party won the general election against an Anglo-Afrikaner coalition led by Jan Smuts. The new prime minister, Daniel Malan, declared, "Afrikanerdom is not the work of man but the creation of God." Thereafter schoolbooks taught young Afrikaners that they were a chosen people, who had overcome a host of mightier enemies with help from on high.

In the eyes of diehard Afrikaners, the new enemy in 1990 was President De Klerk. His reforms defied the myths that had sustained apartheid: that whites alone were made in God's image; that whites had been divinely chosen to rule South Africa; that Afrikaners' culture and religion would be swamped if they relinquished political control. Even the lesser reforms of P. W. Botha had been enough to provoke a right-wing backlash. In 1982 seventeen Nationalist members of parliament deserted to found the Conservative Party, which stood for maintaining apartheid in full. Outside parliament there emerged a handful of neo-Nazi parties, with military uniforms and the language of revolt. The biggest of these was the Afrikaanse Weerstandsbeweging (AWB), or Afrikaner Resistance Movement, which adopted a swastika-like emblem made up of three sevens: sevens, said the movement, occurred frequently in the Bible, and the triple seven was a counterpoise to the Antichrist's triple six. With its sense of biblical self-righteousness, the AWB tried after the ANC's unbanning to present De Klerk with thirty pieces of silver in a child's coffin. Then it took to spraying National Party meetings with tear gas. The worst South Africa's English-speakers threatened was a drain of capital and skills; these Afrikaner extremists promised something more dramatic. They promised to meet De Klerk with force.

A remarkable number of people believed the promise. It was as if Afrikaners, blacks, English-speakers and even foreigners were conspiring to exaggerate the right-wing threat. Afrikaners were so impressed by their stubborn ancestors that they believed the Boer people might resort to arms again. Blacks were so impressed by the evil of apartheid that they believed its creators were capable of anything. English-speakers found it convenient to be impressed as well. When apartheid drew the world's hostility, the myth of the stubborn Afrikaner removed the blame from English shoulders, even though the foundation of apartheid had been laid by the proudly English Cecil Rhodes. When the world's hostility brought sanctions, the stubborn Afrikaner suited English-speakers still better. Sanctions would provoke this stiff-necked people into tougher policies, said the English, not mentioning that sanctions would hurt their businesses as well. This argument played extremely well with Margaret Thatcher's Conservative government in London, which was delighted to find a reason not to damage British–South African trade. As it turned out, sanctions worked; but when right-wingers threatened civil war against De Klerk, plenty of English-speakers seemed set on exaggerating Afrikaner stubbornness again.

Journalists egged them on. Reporters loved interviewing grizzled Afrikaners, who breathed fire and slaughter and wore neo-Nazi garb. The favorite fire-breather was Eugene Terre'-Blanche, founder and leader of the AWB. Terre'Blanche knew how to move his people at the hustings. "If the blacks start a revolution to destroy our property, rape our women, even our children, there will be a white force under the leadership of the

Afrikaanse Weerstandsbeweging that will fight back."[8] Terre'Blanche mixed such tub-thumping with sentimental folk poems, and he was blessed with charismatic eyes. Reporters would journey for miles to meet him; Jani Allen, a model turned columnist, was particularly impressed. She described their first encounter in detail: "Right now I've got to remind myself to breathe. I'm impaled on the blue flames of his blow-torch eyes." Later there were rumors that she and Terre'Blanche were having an affair.

In April 1991 London's Channel Four showed a documentary about Terre'Blanche and his party. Terre'Blanche's driver declared that the AWB might have to resort to political assassinations. He invited the camera into his kitchen, where the ingredients of tear gas were displayed. He even mixed a little for the benefit of the interviewer, who had to retreat into the backyard. Terre'Blanche himself was shown telling a supporter not to surrender his weapons, whatever the government said. The camera crew was allowed to visit an AWB training camp, where the movement's khaki-clad followers were taught to handle guns. They made such marvelous footage, these wild-eyed bully boys staring into the camera, swearing that they would fight De Klerk.

Yet the far right had been preaching assassination and civil war for a year already; so far its actions had been less terrible than its words. It had bombed the offices of two Afrikaans newspapers. It had attacked a trade union office, two National Party buildings and, in the spirit of past Boer resistance, the British embassy. There had been rumors in the press of a scheme to poison Soweto's water. The most notorious daredevil was Piet 'Skiet" Rudolph; Skiet (which means "shoot") had stolen arms from the air force headquarters in Pretoria, then gone underground. He carried out five bombings; his success in eluding the police earned him the title of Boer Pimpernel, and he issued a bold promise that he would never be taken alive.

In September 1990 that is just what happened. Skiet was arrested. He manfully went on a hunger strike. After two days he caved in and called on his followers to hand back the weapons they had stolen from the airbase. By January Skiet had been persuaded to call on his Orde Boerevolk (Order of Boer People) to renounce violence in favor of negotiation. He later went on a second hunger strike; but he was released in March looking perfectly healthy, and he told journalists that he had meant to negotiate all along. "I am not a violent man," he protested; the bombs had been intended merely to strengthen his negotiating position, and he had made sure that none of the explosions hurt anyone. As soon as other right-wing detainees were released, he said, the Orde Boerevolk would be disbanded.

After Skiet's capture, the far right was not cowed. In November thugs from the Blanke Bevrydingsburo (White Freedom Bureau) took on a group of four hundred black children picnicking in the northern town of Louis Trichardt. They set to with whips and fan belts from cars. Nine black children were treated at a hospital. Thirteen whites were arrested and charged. The police also dealt promptly with thugs who attacked other groups of black children, as well as with a more bloodthirsty extremist called Eugene Marais. In October 1990 he and two accomplices opened fire on a bus outside Durban, killing seven blacks. This was supposed to avenge the stabbing a few hours earlier of some whites on a beach. If Marais had carried out this murder on the orders of the AWB, Terre'Blanche's threatening language would have been proved serious. But when the case came to trial the following year, it transpired that the killer's chief inspiration was something called the Israel Vision Church. Karel Liebenberg, one of the church's senior members, told the court that black people were wild animals and did not have souls. Marais duly received seven death sentences, as well as a jail term of 329 years. But he seemed an isolated lunatic swayed by a wild preacher, not a member of an organized right-wing backlash.

In fact the far right was anything but organized. It consisted of innumerable splinters that never came together to form a single plank. Besides Terre'Blanche's AWB and Skiet's Orde

Boerevolk and the Blanke Bevrydingsburo that attacked school-children, there was the Afrikaner Volkswag, the White Wolves, the Boere Weerstandsbeweging and the Boerestaat Party. A group called the Order of Death was said to be planning the assassinations of Mandela and De Klerk. Within the AWB there was a bodyguard corps called Aquila (meaning "Eagle," a name borrowed from the elite soldiers who guarded the military mascots of ancient Rome), a militia called the Stormvalke (meaning "Stormtroopers"—this term came from Nazi Germany) and a peppering of armed groups called *brandwagte* ("vanguards")— or so the AWB's leaders claimed. Like most splinter movements that collect around charismatic leaders, these were forever declaring alliances, quarreling, dividing or disappearing altogether. On his release from prison, Piet "Skiet" Rudolph forgot about the Orde Boerevolk of which he was supposedly the leader and accepted the job of press secretary for the AWB. But this was nothing compared with the realignment that had occurred in 1989, when the news emerged of Terre'Blanche's supposed affair. It was not just that the leader was spending a suspicious amount of time with a dubious female journalist. The real scandal was that Terre'Blanche was caught one night with Jani Allen breaking into the Paardekraal Monument, a revered Afrikaner shrine. Virtually the AWB's entire leadership resigned.

The myth of a right-wing backlash persisted nonetheless. Whatever the farce among the leaders, right-wing ideas were said to enjoy formidable support among two powerful types of Afrikaner, the farmers and the police. In January 1991 these two groups were at each other's throats. A group of farmers arrived in Pretoria to protest the scrapping of the Land Acts, which reserved most land for whites. They blocked the streets with their tractors and refused to go anywhere until President De Klerk granted them an audience. That evening, at a reception at the South African embassy in London, diplomats rehearsed their usual line. Reform in South Africa was up against some tough opponents . . . these Afrikaners, you know . . . it's a different world out there in the depths of the Transvaal. But the police proved tougher than the farmers. They evicted them from Pretoria within twenty-four hours.

Even the most extreme provocation drew a relatively mild reaction from the right wing. In August 1991 De Klerk decided to visit Ventersdorp, a small Afrikaner farming town and a stronghold of Terre'Blanche's AWB. The timing as well as the location made the visit risky, for De Klerk had demoted the two leading hard-liners in his cabinet after the Inkathagate scandal the previous week. The demotions came in response to ANC pressure, and made De Klerk look more treacherous than ever in the eyes of the white right. Sure enough, the Ventersdorp visit provoked protest. White toughs took to the streets. Shooting broke out between them and the police. By the time the violence finished, three right-wingers lay dead; and the AWB's sympathizers were comparing the incident to the 1960 police shooting at Sharpeville. But the truth was that two of the three martyrs had been accidentally run over by minibuses. The third had been shot; but the police suggested that he might have been killed by his own side's bullets. The incident showed once again that despite the secret backing of Inkatha's attacks on the ANC, there was little evidence of right-wing mutiny within the police force. And, by South Africa's standards, it was trivial. The same night a fresh bout of fighting broke out between the ANC and Inkatha in Alexandra township: twenty-four people died.

The parliamentary right wing was no more formidable than the extraparliamentary thugs. When De Klerk unbanned the ANC, the Conservative Party vowed to make his job impossible. It pointed out, correctly, that the president had far exceeded the reformist promises he had made during the election campaign five months earlier. It declared that the Nationalists no longer had the support of their people. It resolved to force a fresh election; but the question was how. At first the Conservatives promised all manner of disruption. Yet they soon thought better of their threats to call white workers out on strike. They shrank from an open alliance with Terre'Blanche's wild gunmen. They did not even have the guts to precipitate a mini-general election by resigning en masse from parliament. No Nationalist members crossed the floor to join them. More than a year after Mandela's release, the Conservative Party was still issuing dire threats and failing to deliver on them. When De Klerk promised to scrap the Land Acts, the Conservatives' leader, Andries Treurnicht, vowed that his party would "rise up in the struggle" to defend land and freedom, using all "necessary means." Did those means include violence? Treurnicht would not say.

The worst the Conservatives could manage was to delay reform. In 1990 the Separate Amenities Act was repealed, removing the legal basis for the segregation of parks, buses, swimming pools and so on. Conservative town councils around the country refused to open their pools to blacks; in the small town of Springs the council resisted integration by closing two swimming pools entirely. After the white thugs attacked black children picnicking in Louis Trichardt, a Conservative parliamentarian commented that people who used newly desegregated facilities ought to have expected trouble. The foot-dragging was damaging, for it made blacks wonder when the fine reformist promises would mean change on the ground. But the foot-dragging fell far short of the promised armed revolt.

Afrikaners had lost the old spirit of resistance. The overwhelming majority had become comfortable people with life-insurance policies, not the redneck trekkers of old. Many of their children went to college, where they were more likely to join left- than right-wing groups. On May 26, 1990, the day the Conservative Party organized a grand demonstration against De Klerk's reforms, a rival gathering of Afrikaners commemorated *Houtstok*, as the Woodstock rock festival is locally known. Even in the northern Transvaal, supposedly the heart of redneck country, white families went to steak houses on Sundays, where they got balloons and soft drinks for the kids. The last connection with their pioneer past was the piped-in country-and-western music.

Afrikaners who attended meetings of the National Party were

more likely to admire displays of model airplanes than of ox-wagons. At the party's Transvaal congress in October 1990 the Afrikaans folk songs were gone; instead there was Danie Nie-haus, a long-haired pop singer. Despite the policies of the far-right Conservative Party, its culture was not very different. In August 1990 the leader of the party addressed his people in Pretoria's city hall, from a stage decorated with pot plants. The high point of antireform militancy came when another speaker asked the delegates to stop paying their television licenses be-cause the ANC was getting too much air time; he had to assure his audience that it was still OK to watch videos. Like the ANC's left-wing fringe, right-wingers were fond of historical comparison. They likened De Klerk to Kerensky, who ruled briefly between Russia's two revolutions in 1917. Soon De Klerk–Kerensky would be pushed aside by Mandela-Lenin. The Republic of South Africa would become a different kind of RSA—the Republic of Socialist Azania. But the Conservatives did not compare their own party with the impotent (white) Russian aristocracy.

Of course many whites sympathized with the Conservatives. In early 1991 South Africa's political pundits were putting their support at around 40 percent, and after a by-election victory in November some put the Conservative following at 50 percent of the white electorate. But it was not the sort of support that extended to the barricades; for, deep down, Afrikaners knew that the Conservatives had no workable alternatives to De Klerk's reforms. The wise men of their tribe had been telling them for years that apartheid was doomed. In the mid-1980s the Broederbond, a semisecret club of influential Afrikaners, put about the controversial view that black rule did not threaten Afrikaner identity, which it said depended on language and religion rather than the exercise of government. At the same time, Afrikaner academics, once the speechwriters and counsel-ors of cabinet ministers, broke with the National Party and demanded faster reform. The Dutch Reformed Church, some-times described as the National Party at prayer, declared that racial discrimination could not be justified, and called upon government and the ANC to talk; *Beeld*, a pro-government newspaper, supported this call. Privately, government ministers admitted that negotiation was inevitable. Academics and businesspeople preempted them by visiting the ANC with increasing regularity after 1985.

Besides, the Conservatives had tried and failed to reverse the tide of desegregation. In October 1988 the party won control of some ninety town councils, and restored the "whites only" signs to the parks, swimming pools and bus stops. Blacks from the local townships responded by boycotting white-owned shops and fast-food restaurants. Some of these businesses folded; the rest attacked the council for depriving them of their customers. By the time F. W. de Klerk embarked upon his revolution, Conservative supporters had learned for themselves that the flood of blacks into the towns could not be reversed. Despite white worries at the ANC's unbanning, the Conservatives' support was not going to outstrip De Klerk's— especially once the benefits of the president's reforms became apparent. When, in July 1991, it was announced that sporting sanctions would at last be lifted, white spirits lifted too. "The best news in 31 years," said the huge headline in *Beeld*. White South Africans are passionate about sports. If their cricket and rugby heroes could compete internationally once more, perhaps all the political uncertainty had been worth it.

The threat of white backlash has worried other countries; it has never turned out to be as bad as was feared. In the Southern United States whites still grumble about black laziness and lack of patriotism. But they are not angry enough to take up guns; and since the 1960s all but a handful of white leaders have been eager to win black votes. In Namibia, next door to South Africa, the pre-independence election in 1989 was rife with predictions of white terrorism; attending a rally of the main white-backed party, I was tempted to believe the worst. Hefty men surrounded me, pulling at my notebook and demanding to know what I had written down. Being white and foreign, I was able to beat a tactful retreat. Had I been black, I might have had my

jaw broken. White· officers from Namibia's South African–backed army regaled journalists with statistics of how
many black "terrorists" they had killed during the war for independence; and they were not above admitting that—to hell
with independence—they would not be handing in their guns.
Yet the white backlash never materialized. The terrorists won
the election, and all remained calm. There was talk of white
mischief at independence in Zimbabwe too. Its liberation war
had cost more than thirty thousand lives; an avowed Marxist
had been elected; there were almost no liberals among the country's whites. Although whites and blacks remain distant socially, black rule has been accepted peacefully by whites.

Part of the reason for white acquiescence in these countries
is that whites have kept their jobs. Few Afrikaners are still
faithful to the ideas of Hendrik Verwoerd, prime minister in
the 1960s and prime mover of grand apartheid. But his legacy
lives on in the huge Afrikaner civil service: in its offices in the
Verwoerd Building in Cape Town, and in the civil servants'
homes in Verwoerdburg just south of Pretoria. In the months
after Mandela's release, Verwoerd's extended family still felt
secure; it trusted De Klerk to negotiate restraint into the ANC.
An ANC government that tried to change the color of the civil
service would rapidly change its mood.

Determined white resistance seemed implausible in South
Africa, though minor disruption and a brain drain remained
worrying possibilities. As constitutional negotiations drew
nearer, the job facing the ANC's leaders looked more delicate
than ever. They would have to weigh black hopes and principles against the threat of white flight. White Zimbabweans
had been guaranteed twenty parliamentary seats under the
independence settlement. White Namibians retained some representation in their assembly via a multiracial party, the Democratic Turnhalle Alliance. Which kind of security would the
ANC offer whites in South Africa? Would any simple constitution suit such a diverse land?

4

THE QUEST FOR A
CONSTITUTION

A year after Nelson Mandela's release, a glossy pamphlet
appeared in the mailboxes of Johannesburg's white suburbs.
"The National Party is irrevocably committed to the creation of
a new, just South Africa," it declared. "You, as a voter, have
the right to ask: What will the new South Africa look like?" In
Afrikaans and in English, the pamphlet proceeded to lay down
the eight requirements that the new constitution should meet.[1]

1. The political dispensation must incorporate built-in guarantees and mechanisms which will make domination by a majority and/or a one-party state impossible.

The pamphlet did not say that the National Party, representing just over half the country's white minority, had itself
wielded absolute power without interruption since 1948. The
Nationalists never formally made South Africa a one-party
state, but that did not prevent them from banning parties that
commanded more support, such as the ANC. The parties that
did not get banned were those that the Nationalists did not
consider a threat.

2. A bill of human rights should be entrenched in such a way that it cannot be abolished or arbitrarily changed.

It was funny that the National Party had not got around to drawing up a bill of rights in all its four decades in government. As for abolishing or arbitrarily changing rights, the National Party could speak with authority on this matter. For much of the 1980s the state of emergency had empowered the white president to bypass both parliament and law courts, and rule instead by executive decree. Newspapers were censored, activists detained, organizations banned. In many such cases the victims had no right of appeal.

3. Any Government should have a limited term of office and elections must take place at regular intervals. Abuses such as the creation of "presidents-for-life," corruption, etc. must be made impossible.

The National Party, to be fair, always held regular elections, and never formally declared any of its leaders president-for-life. Informally, the Nationalists got fairly close to it. Daniel Malan, the first Nationalist prime minister, hung on in office until he was eighty; his successor, J. G. Strydom, died in the job; next came Hendrik Verwoerd, who ruled until he was assassinated. Verwoerd was succeeded by John Vorster, who held onto office for twelve years, then fell as a result of corruption, that other impermissible abuse mentioned in the pamphlet. Next came P. W. Botha, who ruled for eleven years until he succumbed to a stroke.

Skipping for the moment the pamphlet's fourth "requirement," consider requirement number five:

5. The free-market system and private initiative must be retained in the new South Africa. The right to own property, including land, must be respected, and there should not be arbitrary expropriation, or expropriation without proper compensation. Any taxation system should be a just one.

A free-market system? Private initiative? For years apartheid squashed both. There were rules about who could buy which house and who could perform which job. More rules made it all but impossible for blacks to set up businesses. A vast Afrikaner bureaucracy grew up to manage this red-tape nightmare; in 1990 it was reckoned that three out of ten whites worked for the state. Anglo American, the huge conglomerate which controlled more than 40 percent of the stock exchange, delighted in pointing out that it was dwarfed by the state; Gavin Relly, Anglo's chairman in the 1980s, called South Africa "one of the most socialist countries in the world." As to property ownership, land and fair compensation, the National Party taught black South Africans all about those. It evicted 3.5 million of them from their property in its crusade to rid "white areas" of blacks.

The sixth requirement, like the fourth, contained a gem to which we must return. The seventh demanded an "independent judiciary to pronounce judgements between individuals and also between citizens and the state." Under the Nationalists there were no black judges, and during the 1980s the state of emergency often prevented the judiciary from adjudicating between citizens and the state. Still, the Nationalists never quite broke the independence of South Africa's judges, who could be relied upon every so often to return a verdict that the government did not like. That leaves only requirement number eight:

8. The new South Africa's security forces must be properly managed and manned. Professional and well-trained defence and police forces, which are not subject to political pressure, are the best guarantees for the maintenance of a safe environment in which all can live and work.

A professional police force, unbiased politically! No doubt the victims of South Africa's white police force would say amen to that.

Requirements four and six contained no hypocrisy, which made them all the more alarming. "The reality of our national diversity dare not be ignored," declared the pamphlet's sixth paragraph. "Those people, therefore, who prefer to live, worship, work and play in specific communities must be able to do so in the new South Africa, but without laws compelling them to do so." The brave new order was apparently to include not only freedom of association but the freedom to dissociate as well. Once upon a time, whites' determination to dissociate from blacks was called apartheid.

The fourth requirement said:

4. The political system will have to make provision for leaders who uphold these values, even if they are supported by a minority group, to participate in the organs of government.

This was the most explosive clause of all. The Nationalists would insist that leaders of the white minority, notably themselves, should be guaranteed a role in government. They were set against winner-take-all parliamentary democracy, which they denounced as "simple majoritarianism." They made it clear to their supporters that South Africa's black majority would not be allowed unlimited power over whites. The Nationalists were quite right in saying that there is a role for checks and balances in any sound democracy. Pushed too far, however, this principle would leave the future government bound and gagged. It might prevent serious redistribution of wealth and opportunity. Without economic liberation, as the ANC never tired of saying, political liberation would be meaningless.

The pamphlet concluded: "Help us to build a new, just South Africa by supporting the National Party in word and deed." The Nationalists' requirements would have carried more authority if their words had been matched by their past deeds. As it was, their fine principles were stained with opportunism; and their less fine principles were likely to anger black South Africans still more. "Changing the constitution and scrapping obnoxious apartheid laws will not qualitatively, if at all, affect black life," went one typically wary black response to President De Klerk's reforms. "Neither will a vote put food in their pots, unless the said constitution is a reflection of the needs and aspirations of the underprivileged and exploited black majority." That was the view of Tsepo Sebusi, a member of the Azanian Youth League, as he explained it in an article titled "Don't Joke with Us, F. W."

The Nationalists' contortions were understandable, given the precedents in the rest of Africa. In the 1960s the departing colonists left straightforward democracies all over the continent; nearly all of them failed. The first elections after independence produced ethnically based governments, with minority tribes left out in the cold. The losers saw no hope of inclusion at future elections, so they lost interest in democracy. Minorities that were strong in the army organized coups d'état: that is what happened in Nigeria, the Congo, Sierra Leone and Togo.[2] Minorities that were strong in rich regions launched wars for secession: that is what happened in eastern Nigeria (Biafra) and northern Ethiopia (Eritrea). More often, minorities simply lost out. The big tribes tightened their hold on government and its profits. Sometimes they appeased others with token ministerships. Sometimes they did not.

In Zaire, Mobutu Sese Seko was known as president, field marshal and, in a self-effacing reference to the Bible, "the one who is and shall always be"; he plundered the mineral riches of southern Zaire to build a personal fortune and a palace in the village of his birth. In the Ivory Coast, President Félix Houphouët-Boigny was known more modestly as *le sage*; he too graced his home village, Yamoussoukro, with a vast basilica, by some measures the world's biggest. In Malawi, Hastings Kamuzu Banda is known as the "Lion" and "Saviour." In Zimbabwe, where democracy just about survived, President Robert Mugabe was nonetheless described as the "authentic, consistent and revolutionary leader"; one particularly ambitious politician said, "The Almighty has sent Zimbabwe his only other son."

The chiefs of precolonial Africa were replaced by a new generation of unelected leaders, their status displayed in personal fortunes, their supporters drawn from members of their tribes. Africa's traditional respect for elders discouraged opposition, except from friends who know a president well enough to differ with him, much as village elders would sometimes differ with a chief. In Zambia it was Simon Kapwepwe, President Kaunda's childhood friend, who in the 1970s ventured to start his own party (which Kaunda soon suppressed). In Zimbabwe it was Edgar Tekere, once among Mugabe's closest allies, who dared oppose him in the presidential election of 1990.

Between 1967 and 1990, when the wind of Eastern Europe's revolutions blew through Africa, power never passed from one elected government to another. Four of the continent's countries—Zimbabwe, Botswana, Senegal and Gambia—were nominally democratic. All were dominated by single parties, which allowed opponents to contest elections but did not expect to lose to them. Even in these rare democracies, minorities were deprived of the best jobs and privileges. It was hardly surprising that South Africa's white minority wanted to be different, and considered all sorts of minority protections in order to get its way.

Indeed other Africans had also tired of simple constitutions. Nigeria's first democracy, installed at independence in 1960, very quickly failed: in 1966 Ibo officers from eastern Nigeria staged a coup d'état, only to be booted out by a gang of northern officers later in the year. This experience, followed by the Ibos' war for the secession of Biafra, shocked the Nigerians into a range of constitutional ploys designed to contain the pressures of tribe. In the years that followed, they promoted ever greater devolution: the country's three regions were replaced by twelve states, then by nineteen, then by twenty-one. Nigeria's second democracy, which began life in 1979, laid down that the president must be elected not only by obtaining the greatest number of votes, but also by winning at least a quarter of the votes in two-thirds of Nigeria's states. This part of Nigeria's constitution worked well, though the corruption of the civilian politicians provoked another military coup in 1983.

Before long, however, the determined Nigerians resolved to try again. The military government of President Ibrahim Babangida promised a return to democracy, but of a type that would contain the tensions of religion and tribe. The newly legal civilian parties would not be allowed to mention either subject in their pamphlets and speeches. Moreover, only two parties would be allowed: this would force alliances between Nigeria's three main tribal groupings. At the start of the 1990s, as South Africans contemplated their own constitutional future, some Nigerians were complaining about President Babangida's blueprint, for a democracy that is hedged about with too many conditions ceases to be democratic. Somehow South Africa's constitution-writers had to balance the protection of minorities with the need for genuine pluralism.

Africa's constitutional failures had two main ingredients, and South Africa was free of one of them. On much of the continent, the president's word went unopposed partly for lack of powerful opponents. Despite the years of boycott, South Africa remained comparatively rich in independent institutions that could stand up to an autocrat. Its universities were full of outspoken lecturers; its business-leaders were not afraid to disagree with the state. Elsewhere in Africa it had been relatively easy to muzzle the few poorly printed newspapers; but South Africa had no fewer than a score of independent dailies, staffed by irreverent reporters of every race. Outside of Nigeria, no African country had so many sophisticated black professionals; and plenty of South Africa's black doctors and lawyers were ready to speak out against a future government, including one led by the ANC. Outside of Zambia, no African country had such powerful trade unions; and South Africa's union leaders declared that they had no intention of sacrificing their independence to become the labor wing of an ANC government. It was hard to imagine the ANC or any other future rulers keeping the lid on this caldron of opinion. After all, the white government had never managed it.

South Africans seemed irrepressible, but this rich variety of voices was hardly likely to promote democracy either. Like most of the continent's people, South Africans lacked a sense of common nationhood. Even the most tolerant democracies presume some basic unanimity; those who flout the constitution in Germany or the United States soon find that the tolerance stops. Without a minimum consensus, a country falls apart. With its communists and neo-Nazis, its Christians, Jews and Muslims, its Afrikaners and English, its Indians and coloreds, Xhosas and Zulus, Sothos and Vendas—with all its bubbling variety, how could South Africa build the basic consensus that democracy requires?

Anywhere in the world, it would be hard to write a constitution to fit such diversity. In South Africa diversity came on top of decades of deceit and conflict. It was not just President De Klerk's reborn National Party that sounded hypocritical. At every opportunity, Chief Mangosuthu Buthelezi chastised his black rivals for advocating violence. In fact his own party's role in Natal's violence had caused many more deaths than the ANC's desultory armed struggle ever had. Buthelezi projected himself as a democrat, a man of impeccable liberal credentials. In fact he practiced something very different from democracy in the homeland of KwaZulu. He had controlled it without interruption for nearly two decades. He doubled as chief minister and minister of police. The token legislative assembly never breathed a whiff of opposition. Anyone wanting a job as a KwaZulu civil servant, even a job as a teacher or nurse, was wise to join Inkatha. The party magazine was devoted to the cult of Buthelezi. It carried endless pictures of him: the chief minister in a dark suit shaking hands with various foreign heads of state; the chief minister in animal skins, addressing his Zulu people.

Besides the hypocrisy of Inkatha and De Klerk's National Party, apartheid had created a tradition of double-talk that was bound to bedevil constitutional discussion. Blacks had been excluded from white universities by the Extension of University Education Act. Pass laws were extended to women under the Abolition of Passes and Co-ordination of Documents Act. As a result of apartheid, Nationalist calls for federalism sounded to the ANC like a plot to maintain the homelands, and calls for protection of minorities smacked of suppressing the majority. Communists, liberals and white supremacists all declared for democracy; all meant different things. Rival gangs of Marxists traded obscure insults. When Joe Slovo, the Communist Party leader, accused impatient firebrands of "Pol-Potism" (after the murderous leader of Cambodia's Khmer Rouge government in the late 1970s), his enemies retorted that he was a mere "Luxemburgist" (after Rosa Luxemburg, an early democratic Marxist who died in Germany's failed communist revolution in 1919). In March 1990 Carter Seleke, a black-consciousness leader, said that the Communist Party was "shamelessly guilty of socialist betrayal of the toiling masses and their actions confirm our long-held belief that they were never socialist but petit-bourgeois liberal quacks who have mastered the art of abusing neo-Marxian phraseology."

South Africans did not even agree on who they were. "Black" could refer to people with black skin; or it could be a political term, describing all oppressed people, including Indians and coloreds; or it could even include a few whites who sided with the oppressed. Those who favored the inclusive meaning of "black" described people with black skin as "Africans," which caused whites, coloreds and Indians to protest that they also lived in Africa. The term "colored" provoked its own controversy. In the language of apartheid, it included people of mixed parentage, Bushmen, a few Chinese and the descendants of the Malays and Indonesians who were brought to the Cape by the Dutch East India Company. It was an ugly term, an attempt to make a racial category from a mix of very different people; but there was no easy replacement. Activists raised their arms to draw quotation marks in the air whenever this vile word was unavoidable. They referred pedantically to "so-called coloreds."

The biggest muddle concerned tribe. Black South Africans bristled at the mention of this subject. Whites had manipulated tribalism to suit their own ends; indeed, some modern radicals accused whites of inventing it. The anthropologists who first documented tribal differences in the early twentieth century had been imbued with contemporary Romanticism; and particularly with the view that the world divides into distinct communities of common blood and culture, whose natural expression is the nation state. Africa did not really fit this preconception. Politically, the continent divided into dozens of separate chiefdoms; but there were relatively few marked cultural differences to match. Often, neighboring tribes spoke similar languages, respected similar customs and tilled the soil with similar tools.

The anthropologists nonetheless sought out such differences as there were. It was not just that they were influenced by Romanticism. Any traveler who braves the uncertainties of far-off places likes to return with strange stories; anthropologists, who frequent remoter and less healthy places than most travelers, feel this need even more. To fend off doubts as to the difference between one tribe and its neighbors, anthropologists deployed a second fashionable preconception: social Darwinism, which involved the application of Darwin's evolutionary theory to social forms. If two tribes appeared culturally similar, this was merely because they were less "evolved" than European nations. Given time, slight tribal differences would flower; each politically distinct chiefdom would develop a distinct culture to match. The anthropologists' conclusions comforted the European audience they were aimed at, because they confirmed a familiar view of the world. In the words of Robert Thornton, an anthropologist at the University of Cape Town, "a vision of Europe was confirmed by a European vision of others."

However exaggerated it had been initially, the theory of tribal differences became self-fulfilling. Colonial rulers seized upon the idea of divisions among the Africans, because divided people are easier to rule. African chiefs began to present themselves as leaders of particular tribal groupings, because this was the best way to bid for grants and privileges from the new white boss. In the eyes of black nationalists all over Africa, therefore, tribal differences had been manufactured by whites and fawning elders, who kowtowed to colonial rule.

This was especially true in South Africa, where apartheid took the idea that tribes were undeveloped statelets to its logical extreme. Whites described blacks as a collection of "nations." Hendrik Verwoerd, who became prime minister in 1958, determined to make good this nationhood: he invented the homelands, each supposedly a reincarnation of an ancient tribal territory. The government pressed on with this program through the 1970s and 1980s. Black South Africa, said the official South African yearbook in 1976, consists of "separate ethnic groups, each with its own language, legal system, life-style and socio-political identity." The Afrikaners credited tribes with an exaggerated sense of identity, just as their Marxist archenemies exaggerated the sense of common purpose felt by members of the working class.

This caricature of anthropology bred its own reaction. By 1990 South African academics, distressed at the political consequence of past studies on tribalism, tended to the opposite extreme. Some refused to mention tribe at all. Others emphasized tribalism's artificial origins. Just as optimists blamed apartheid for race tension or economic difficulties, so anthropologists and political scientists suggested that, after apartheid, tribalism would fade. Black politicians, drawn from the educated people of the cities, found this entirely plausible. In the big townships around Johannesburg, different tribes merged into a South African whole. People spoke a patois which borrowed words from various African languages, as well as from English and Afrikaans.

In 1981 a survey in Soweto found that 85 percent of the township's better-off residents saw nothing wrong in marrying someone from another tribe;[3] on the best available estimates, between one-third and half of all Sowetans actually did so.[4] The divisions between the supposed black "nations" were so blurred that blacks frequently were assigned to the "wrong" homeland. Supposedly distinct African languages were actually fairly close: Zulu, Xhosa, siSwati and Ndebele were all Nguni languages; the differences between them were of dialect, not more. Tribal distinctions seemed all the more arbitrary as they neglected divisions within tribes. The Xhosa-speaking people divided into Xhosas, Pondos, Thembus and Mfengus; the Zulus were so divided that Natal had long been disfigured by feuds between clans.

Apartheid had exaggerated tribalism so grotesquely that black nationalists were inclined to dismiss it altogether. Besides, accepting the power of tribalism would have involved an admission of failure, for the ANC had tried to achieve supra-tribal unity since the day that it was founded. In 1912 the ANC's first manifesto declared: "We are one people: these divisions, these jealousies, are the cause of all our woes and of all our backwardness and ignorance today." The "National" in "African National Congress" referred precisely to the forging of one nation out of South Africa's disparate tribes.

Independence movements all over the world have united different factions in the struggle against whites. Their leaders believed that division had been conquered; but on the day of independence they were nearly always proved wrong. In the Indian subcontinent the campaign against the British gave way to a new fight between Hindus and Muslims. In the southern Caribbean the passing of white dominance opened a new conflict between blacks and Indians. In Zimbabwe the Shona and Ndebele people united briefly against white Rhodesia in the Patriotic Front; after independence the Shona-Ndebele bloodbath cost over one thousand lives.

As it approached its transition, South Africa seemed vulnerable to the same disappointment. Black nationalists continued to blame apartheid for all their country's conflicts. Yet the truth was that tribal tension was real in South Africa, however absurdly apartheid had exaggerated it. In 1990 Zulu hosteldwellers fought their neighbors in the townships; the ANC cited all manner of explanations but would not mention tribe. In the same year the movement's leaders appointed Patrick Lekota, an extremely able Sotho, to run the ANC office in southern Natal. When the ANC's local Zulu members were given a chance to confirm Lekota's appointment by ballot, they rejected him in favor of Jacob Zuma, the ANC's most prominent Zulu; Lekota left to work in the Orange Free State, home of his own tribe. The ANC's leaders persisted in denying tribe's importance; and yet their own identities betrayed their mistake. In mid-1989, ten of the twenty blacks on the ANC's National Executive Committee were Xhosa; Jacob Zuma was the only Zulu.[5] And after the ANC's party conference in July 1991, when the National Executive was enlarged to include eighty-two people, only two were Zulus.[6] There were perfectly good reasons for this. The Xhosas of the eastern Cape had enjoyed better education than blacks in other regions. They had formed the heart of the ANC's defiance campaign in the 1950s; in the following decade they had provided the breeding ground for Steve Biko's black-consciousness movement as well. Besides dominating the ANC, Xhosas outnumbered other leaders in the Pan-Africanist Congress and the Azanian People's Organization, two other theoretically non-tribal movements.[7] The ANC's leaders could not be blamed for the preponderance of Xhosas. The worry was their reluctance to admit it.

It was only natural that the Zulus, South Africa's biggest tribe, should resent their own exclusion and the Xhosas' preeminence. The few researchers who dared investigate the strength of tribal feeling found the Zulus relatively unmoved by the ANC's long campaign for tribal unity; Xhosas, by contrast, were all in favor of pan-tribalism, since their own people were its leading advocates. In 1986 a polling company called Markinor asked black women whether they thought of themselves primarily as South Africans, as blacks or as members of a tribe. In Soweto 20 percent stated that their first loyalty was tribal; in the townships around Pretoria, 30 percent did. The women from those areas came from a variety of tribes; but the pollsters also questioned women in the overwhelmingly Xhosa eastern Cape. There, only 19 percent said they put their tribal identity first. Zulus, by contrast, felt very Zulu: 55 percent of the women questioned around Durban declared that their tribe mattered more to them than being black or South African.[8]

Even more worrying, the Zulus' sense of tribal loyalty carried with it disdain for other peoples. A survey in the Durban township of KwaMashu found that Zulus regarded the Ndebeles as "backward"; Tsongas as "loose-living"; Xhosas as "clever" and probably dishonest. In fact, said the survey, "Zulus really get their ire up when they refer to the Xhosa," whom they regard as "too clever", "crooks," "scheming," "crafty" and "stiff-headed".[9] Likewise, in the townships around Johannesburg, Zulus were known for being proud, and especially proud of their language: if a black South African addressed a Zulu in English, he might be rebuked for speaking like a white. Zulus were also considered strong; they made good night watchmen and fearsome warriors. Even before the violence in the township hostels, the cry "The Zulus are coming!" had been enough to provoke panic in non-Zulu black communities. Many Zulus stated that they would never accept a Xhosa president.

Chief Mangosuthu Buthelezi played on the Zulus' sense of pride and exclusion. He liked to tell journalists that he had learned politics at his mother's knee, listening to the sagas of Zulu resistance against British settlers in the nineteenth century. His great-grandfather was King Cetshwayo, who routed the British army at the battle of Isandhlwana; the British later exiled his grandfather, King Dinzulu, to the island of St. Helena. The Zulus were proud of their martial forebears; they loved to be told by Buthelezi that those who would disband KwaZulu did "not understand the depth of the commitment that we have to each other as Zulu brothers born out of Zulu warrior stock." Their enemies should "know that there is an indomitable something in the Zulu character which is beginning to show now as Zulus draw together to say enough is enough."[10]

The ANC's leaders railed against Buthelezi for fomenting tribalism, declaring that without such unprincipled behavior this artificial nuisance would quickly go away. Yet tribal tension had existed long before Buthelezi stirred it; it even predated Verwoerd's mad scheme to turn blurred tribal divisions into independent nation states. In 1957 *Drum* magazine told the story of some Zulus who ganged up to punish muggers. They soon got carried away; they even beat up an old woman on the presumption that her son was a ruffian. "They smashed up houses without having done the most elementary research," *Drum* lamented. In the end the Zulus became so unpopular that another tribe, the Sotho, resolved to sort them out. One weekend the two sides went at each other with battle-axes, and some forty people died.[11] When *Drum* ran its first short story competition to encourage black writers, the winner was a tale of love across the tribal split. The sweethearts—one Sotho, one Xhosa—have to hide from angry relatives. They are seen and betrayed; the Xhosa Romeo ends up dead.

Nor was it true that tribal feelings were confined to Buthelezi's Zulus. A Tswana mother would tell her children to wash themselves regularly and be neat, lest they resemble the dirty Ndebele. Xhosas were said to make good artists and politicians; some Xhosa men therefore preferred to marry Sotho girls rather than their sharp-tongued cousins. Shangaan people were looked down upon as bumpkins; someone with garish clothes would be mocked for wearing "Shangaan colors." Vendas were renowned for sticking to themselves, even when they lived in Johannesburg's mixed townships. Sothos reputedly ate cats, though they were generally considered friendly. The Sotho greeting—"*Khotso*"—means "Peace"; the reply—"*A e ate*"—means "May it reign."

There should have been no shame in admitting to such simple prejudices, for they exist all over the world. The Irish are dim; the Scots are stingy; Yorkshiremen drink too much bitter. South Africa's stereotypes were no more mischievous and no more accurate. Diversity could be a source of fun as well as of friction, like the mix of foods and gods and tongues in any cosmopolitan city. Plenty of black South Africans prided themselves on their languages, switching from one to another in conversation like magicians riffling through a string of tricks. Tribal differences did not have to be dangerous, so long as South Africans recognized their importance and drafted their constitution accordingly. Unfortunately there was little sign of such recognition. The white right exaggerated the importance of tribes, regarding each one as a separate nation. Black nationalists tended to the opposite mistake, declaring that South Africans could live in harmony without acknowledging their divisions.

South Africa's established political parties were tainted with hypocrisy, while its previously illegal parties were handicapped by inexperience. Soon after its unbanning, the ANC's leaders set themselves a target of enlisting a million members by the end of the year; but by Christmas they had signed up barely two hundred thousand. The ANC was forced to postpone its party congress, planned for December, until the following July. This put off the time when the ANC's leaders would have a clear mandate to negotiate the new constitution; meanwhile both policies and leaders were weakened by impermanence. The ANC's young firebrands talked of shifting the struggle to the white areas; elder statesmen preached negotiation. From time to time Nelson Mandela announced a new initiative, then appeared to change his mind. In April 1991 he met Chief Buthelezi in the hope of calming the ANC-Inkatha fighting; afterward both declared that they were working together for peace; the next week Mandela denounced Inkatha for stoking the violence.

In the same month the ANC held a meeting with the Pan-Africanist Congress in Zimbabwe, after which the PAC announced that both parties wanted De Klerk's government replaced by an interim administration. Gerrit Viljoen, the government's chief negotiator, replied, "The confusion of leadership inside the African National Congress has apparently reached such a level that statements on ANC policy are now being issued by the secretary-general of the PAC." The following week Buthelezi said the ANC "is so floundering and so falling over each other in some kind of tumbled-up heap of people crying wolf that South Africa does not know whether the ANC's leadership is Arthur or Martha." Buthelezi's syntax revealed his own confusion.

The Pan-Africanists were even more bewildering. They had

launched their party in 1959, having split from the ANC in protest at the influence of whites and communists. The new party referred to whites as "settlers" in colonized "Azania." It adopted as its slogan "one settler, one bullet"; to those who doubted how literally this was meant, a letter to the *Sowetan* in 1990 explained that "waste of bullets is greatly discouraged." Like the ANC, the PAC was banned in the wake of the Sharpeville shootings, just a year after it was founded. The PAC's short legal life span perhaps excused its disorganization. Its policy was confused. It seldom held rallies. Even the funeral in November 1990 of Zephaniah Mothopeng, the PAC's old leader, drew a crowd of only three thousand. The Pan-Africanists denounced the ANC's decision to suspend the armed struggle and declared that their own military campaign would continue. The truth was that the PAC's armed wing was barely active. "We welcome the fact," said the ANC's Joe Slovo, "that the PAC has of today abandoned its thirty-year-old cease-fire." The thoughts of the PAC's exiled officials seemed a long way from insurgency. In November 1990 Zimbabwe's police arrested a resident Pan-Africanist for drug running.

The Azanian People's Organization was still less coherent. It had been founded in 1978 to embody the black-consciousness tradition, which had inspired the student uprising of 1976–77. Soon after that uprising, however, black consciousness had lost its most impressive leader when Steve Biko died in police detention. Black consciousness never quite recovered. AZAPO promised to free Azania, which it said belonged exclusively to "blacks": needless to say, the movement's leaders differed on who qualified for this description. They declared for "scientific socialism," but had difficulty explaining what this meant. They declared that AZAPO's armed wing was intent on seizing power, but even the seizure of a headline seemed beyond it. Like the PAC, AZAPO never showed its strength in rallies. Its leaders sat on broken chairs, denouncing the ANC as lackeys of the whites who paid for its plush premises. And yet AZAPO and the PAC did have a following. Intellectuals liked their stress on black self-sufficiency; in the townships, plenty of people sympathized with movements that wanted no contact with whites. Despite their incoherence, AZAPO and the PAC had a fair claim to a place at the coming constitutional negotiations.

A host of smaller parties clamored to take part. Seminars and conferences on the future constitution choked on a dozen different views; organizers even felt obliged to invite spokespeople from the discredited Indian and colored chambers of parliament. The ten homeland leaders occasionally demanded to join in too. Church leaders pronounced on national issues. Township committees were consulted. The Chamber of Commerce advanced a bill of rights. The black trade unions demanded labor courts with union representatives sitting in judgment, as well as the right to strike. They also declared that the economy should be "democratically planned"; that the unions should have a hand in the planning; and that there should be a free press. South Africa seemed hopelessly tangled in ideas and spokespeople; yet Mandela and De Klerk both insisted that all parties would have a chance to take part in negotiations. Both were nervous of hard-liners sniping from outside. Both were determined to include their allies.

Of all these splinters, the white right wing was the most awkward. Like AZAPO and the PAC, the right-wingers threatened to boycott the coming negotiations. Unlike some black hard-liners, they had at least a rough idea of what they wanted. Both the Conservative Party and the armed extremists to its right called for a white homeland. They clung to the idea that the survival of their culture depended upon political sovereignty. If the world would not let them subjugate blacks in all South Africa, the white right would settle for a more restricted sovereignty: they would hand part of the country over to blacks and rule the rest of it. They dressed their case up in grand historical language. "The second half of our century will go down in history as the time of restoration of national states," wrote Robert van Tonder, leader of the Boerestaat Party. And he continued:

In Africa no fewer than fifty-three new states emerged. . . .
In Europe . . . the Fresians, Flemish and Basques are on their
way to national sovereignty, while Lithuania, Latvia, Estonia,
Moldavia and others have more or less freed themselves from
the chains of Soviet empire. In the Soviet case, the entire
world applauds the disintegration process. Why then is it
different in the case of the only other archaic imperialist night-
mare-state left—South Africa?[12]

Van Tonder and his friends cheerfully admitted that their white
homeland would depend upon black labor. Economic interde-
pendence among neighboring states, they said, is what you
have in Europe.

The white right was divided on the character of this homeland and where precisely it should be. Van Tonder proposed a
Boer state, excluding not just English-speakers but also Cape
Afrikaners whose nineteenth-century ancestors had preferred
life under the British Empire to the rigors of the Great Trek.
The Conservative Party, by contrast, said the homeland should
be for all "Afrikaners," defined with an imprecision that
matched their opponents' definition of "black." The party was
proud of its support among English-speakers, so it declared
that anyone who embraced Afrikaner values would be welcome
in the new homeland. Did that include Colored South Africans,
whose first language was usually Afrikaans? Koos van der
Merwe, the official spokesman of the Conservative Party,
grunted at this question, then conceded that perhaps Coloreds
would qualify to join the Afrikaner homeland. And what of
blacks who claimed to identify with Afrikanerdom? No, they
could never be accepted, replied van der Merwe uncomfortably:
the cultural gulf between white and black was too wide.

Where should this homeland be? On another occasion van
der Merwe declared that it should occupy all South Africa except the bits where blacks and browns were living: thus the six
black homelands that had so far refused token independence
would have it thrust upon them; new "independent" homelands would be created for Indian and colored people; the black

townships would become independent city-states. Slightly more reasonably, van Tonder and Eugene Terre'Blanche's Afrikaner Resistance Movement demanded the revival of the nineteenth-century republics founded by those Boers who braved the Great Trek. These republics occupied much of the Transvaal, Orange Free State and northern Natal . . . in other words, a large chunk of the country.

A third faction was still more modest. The Afrikaner Volkswag claimed a piece of the Karoo desert in the northwestern Cape. The plan for this white homeland was drawn up by Professor Carel Boshoff, son-in-law of Hendrik Verwoerd, the prime minister who invented the idea of homelands for blacks. Boshoff called his dreamland Orandia. It covered a quarter of South Africa's surface, but it was poor and sparsely populated: it got only slightly more rain than the adjacent Kalahari desert. Much of the Karoo was utterly empty; it took at least six of its dry acres to graze a single sheep; the casual visitor might have easily supposed that humanity would be happy to give Orandia to the Afrikaners. The truth was that two hundred and fifty thousand colored people lived there; they outnumbered whites four to one. What was more, part of Orandia lay within the borders of Namibia, which had won its independence from South Africa in 1990, after nearly three decades of guerrilla war.

Some whites feared being overrun by blacks enough to leave their towns in the Transvaal for the wastes of Orandia. The occasional group bought up a village, and planned a new livelihood around cottage industries or vacation homes. The Volkswag started an investment organization to develop the land. Its most wild-eyed disciples talked of building a vast wall in the Atlantic to change the ocean currents and bring Orandia more rain. They declared that their colored neighbors would leave of their own accord if the white pioneers refused to give them jobs. But Orandia's people had no intention of pressing white self-sufficiency too far. They had grown used to armies of black helpers. Even the pioneer father seemed undecided. Carel Boshoff had formally founded Orandia in March 1990. A year later he had yet to go and live there.

* * *

White extremists had ideas that were unworkable; black extremists had no clear ideas at all. In the months after Nelson Mandela's release, both seemed undecided on whether they would take part in constitutional talks. Their reluctance was yet another obstacle to easy negotiations, although in the end the smaller parties could not derail South Africa's transition by refusing to take part. Their best hope was to seek the best price for their support from either the government or the ANC; for ultimately these two parties would decide South Africa's future. The National Party had the support of the armed forces, the civil service and just about everybody wielding power. The ANC had the support of numbers. If forced to, these two could impose the new constitution whether the smaller parties liked it or not.

During 1990 opinion polls put the ANC well ahead of all its rivals; one gave it an approval rating of 83 percent. It was quite simply the oldest liberation movement—on the continent as well as in South Africa—and its name had become synonymous with freedom to many blacks. Through the years of despair, black South Africans had looked forward to the day when the ANC would come home like a deus ex machina and deliver freedom and prosperity for all. To be sure, the high hopes on the day of Nelson Mandela's release were sinking by the end of the year; the crowds at ANC rallies were a tenth of their old size. Some supporters were disillusioned by the Congress's confused policies; some feared the preponderance of Xhosas in the leadership; more were disappointed by the township violence and the slow pace of reform. The unbanned ANC had proved incapable of calming the townships, let alone giving everyone a job. And yet it was hard to destroy the aura around the ANC's top leaders, who had spent years in prison or exile for the cause of liberation. It seemed almost certain that, in a free election, the ANC would win more votes than any of its rivals. It also seemed possible that it would win an overall majority.

Besides, disaffected ANC supporters appeared as willing to

defect to the National Party as to the antinegotiation hard-liners—reinforcing the impression that small parties would be unable to block constitutional talks. Black parties' confusion and the violence in the townships favored the Nationalists, who offered efficiency and order and were above tribal bias. "A black president sees a Xhosa or a Zulu," explained a black garage attendant in the northern Transvaal town of Messina; "a white president sees only a black." "Viva Comrade F. W. de Klerk," shouted children during the president's visit to Soweto in September 1990. That month a poll gave the National Party a 17 percent approval rating; De Klerk's personal approval rating was 24 percent, compared with 41 percent for Mandela.

The Nationalists sought to capitalize on this sympathy by opening their party to black members. Their smooth agents seemed likely to recruit hundreds of black conservatives: civil servants with jobs in the white-led bureaucracy, businesspeople whose shops had been looted by activists, parents shocked by children who preferred radical politics to schoolwork. The extent of black conservatism was evident from the strength of the evangelical churches. The Zion Christian Church, which by itself boasted 4 million members, had welcomed De Klerk's less enlightened predecessor at its Easter pilgrimage. Conservatism had been reinforced by the township violence after the ANC's unbanning, which seemed likely to push Indian and colored South Africans into the arms of the National Party. Returning from exile in 1990, an Indian communist was pounced upon by his rich aunt, who demanded to know whether he and the African National Congress planned to confiscate her house.

Between them, the Nationalists and the ANC were strong enough to force the talks ahead with or without the smaller parties. In the heady weeks after Nelson Mandela's release, the government's spokespeople predicted that talks would start by early 1991, and that a draft constitution could be put to a national referendum before the end of 1992. This soon proved too ambitious. South Africa needed time to live down its history of hypocrisy and bloodshed, repression and mistrust. In the months before the ANC's party congress in July 1991, the government and the ANC bickered over the shape of the negotiating table. The ANC demanded that the constitution be written by an elected assembly, so that each party's influence on the final document would be proportional to its national support. The Nationalists favored an unelected conference, with large and small parties taking part. At the same time, the ANC demanded an interim government; the Nationalists retorted that they had no intention of handing over power before the new constitution was in place. The two parties competed for the support of foreign opinion; both Mandela and De Klerk thought it worth stealing time from pressing domestic problems to travel lengthily abroad.

As the township violence continued, negotiations seemed to recede further. Blacks asked how they could negotiate with a government that did not control its policemen; whites asked how they could hand power to people seemingly unable to keep peace among themselves. In April 1991 the ANC lost patience with the government's failure to control the slaughter. It demanded the resignation of the ministers of defense and law and order by May 9 and said that if the government refused, the ANC would "suspend all exchanges with the government on the future constitution of our country." Journalists naturally reported this ultimatum, adding that the government would never comply with it. The ANC had been right to complain about the policing of the townships, but had spoiled its case by demanding too much of the government. (It took the Inkathagate scandal to bring about these two ministers' demotions.) Soon Mandela was climbing down, explaining that the ultimatum should not have been taken so literally. It was a fair way to cover up a gaffe; but the ANC went on to blame the incident on irresponsible reporting. This only worsened matters by raising questions about the future freedom of the press.

Throughout the ANC's ultimatums, President De Klerk refused to be put off. There would be no permanent block on negotiations, he promised, because South Africa had no alternative. If the ANC walked away from negotiation without good reason, it would lose its foreign support; already its old Eastern

European allies were more interested in making deals with South African businesses than in giving aid to the ANC. De Klerk, for his part, could not give up negotiation either, for he had no intention of risking another whites-only election, which would probably strengthen the right-wingers. In the end the arguments over the interim government and the constituent assembly would be resolved, and the two sides would devise a constitution. By late 1991, when this book went to press, events were justifying the president's optimism. The awkwardly named Convention for a Democratic South Africa, assembling over two hundred negotiators from a score of different parties, sat down for its first meeting in December.

To avoid another African failure, South Africa's new constitution would have to cater to the diversity of both race and tribe. The question was how to do it. The ANC's pan-tribalist, nonracial composition discouraged it from considering such things; besides, it was hardly organized enough to do so. The National Party, by contrast, had books full of proposals. Belgium's constitution sought to calm tensions between French and Flemish by devolving power to local government; the United States Senate reserves as many seats for Rhode Island as for California; Czechoslovakia has two national anthems, one Czech and one Slovak. National Party leaders devoured American books on "ethnic balance." They drew lessons from other countries' failures. Lebanon's constitution laid down that the president should be Christian, the prime minister Sunni, the speaker of parliament Shia. Those requirements were too rigid: Lebanon fell apart.

The government had a whole ministry devoted to "constitutional development." One morning in August 1990 I visited an earnest Afrikaner whose job was to research constitutional models. He sat in his office with his sleeves rolled up, flanked by a seventeen-volume encyclopedia on the world's constitutions and books from Oxford on freedom and the individual. Political discussion seemed painful to him. He frowned and fidgeted and looked at his shoes. He rubbed his huge forearms and looked out of the window. Yes, he conceded, South Africa's previous constitutions had been "undemocratic." And then: "The previous policy was a little bit forced. No, not a little bit. It was forced."

These thoughts had cost him so much introspection that I wondered what more I would get out of him; but when I asked about the future, he seemed to relax. "We must protect minorities, as John Stuart Mill said"—he seemed to derive comfort from this erudite citation. "Mill spoke of the 'tyranny of the majority.' " In the second chamber of parliament, for example, all "politically relevant groups should be represented as of right." How did he define relevance? Any group with the power to disrupt the country was relevant, he answered; in Spain, that would include the Basque separatists. Would these groups be defined by race? No!—and here he had the fluency of somebody reciting a familiar argument—groups could be defined by lots of different things. In fact, he had written a paper on this subject, and he rose to rummage in a large steel filing cabinet. He apologized that he had written it in Afrikaans, but he held it up for me to admire anyway. Groups could be defined by culture, religion or ethnicity, he continued. Who would define them? He sat down. Again the frown and the rubbing of the forearms. He began to answer, grew confused, then said, "We Afrikaners are good Calvinists, you see. We believe that God will look after us."

The constitutional planners had to do more than protect minorities, however they defined them. They had to do so in a way that was acceptable. At independence in Zimbabwe, whites had twenty seats reserved for them in a hundred-member parliament. Those seats brought whites no real power but plenty of resentment: after seven years, the black government scrapped them. That made whites fearful that more important safeguards, particularly the multiparty system, might be scrapped as well. A government that tampers with the constitution once is liable to do so again; Zimbabwe's unacceptable minority protection had left the minority more exposed than ever. South Africa therefore had to find constitutional mechanisms which protected racial and tribal minorities without mentioning them. The government had to encourage politicians to behave well, not lay down rules that politicians resented. They had to find ways of giving minorities influence, not just powerless parliamentary representation.

By late 1991, when the first constitutional talks were beginning, De Klerk's advisers had come up with various devices, all of which amounted to limiting state power. A bill of rights would protect many of the things that the party held dearest. It would guarantee the right of Afrikaners or Indians or Vendas to speak their languages and practice their religions. Schooling in Afrikaans, which would have the effect of limiting black enrollment, might still be permitted—as might schooling in Gujarati or Zulu. The bill of rights could be couched in the language of individual freedom; but it would have the effect of protecting the identities of minority groups.

The next principle for limiting state powers was to separate them. The judiciary would be made independent of the lawmakers in parliament. The executive would be separated from both. Each of the three elements of government could be made to police the others. The president's appointments, for example, might require ratification by the lawmakers; the president's policies could be challenged by citizens in independent courts. Whatever the details, President De Klerk was determined that his successors should have less power than he had had. The separation of the three arms of government would also restrict the power of the legislature. Parliament would have the right to pass laws; but the laws would be administered by bureaucrats who answered to the executive and would be interpreted by independent judges.

The Nationalists also considered means of discouraging the exclusion of minorities from each arm of government, as the interview with the earnest Afrikaner had showed. They talked of a rotating presidency and rules that would share executive powers among different parties. Thus any party with more than, say, 15 percent of the vote would have a right to a job in the cabinet. "The Swiss model," said President De Klerk to the

Financial Times of London, "provides a very interesting model, where the main role players are represented in the executive and where the executive operates on the basis of consensus." In September 1991 De Klerk had added detail to this proposition. At a special National Party congress he proposed that the presidency should be shared among the leaders of the three largest parties in the lower house of parliament. The chairmanship of this three person presidential committee would rotate. Decisions would be made by consensus. Each president would appoint followers to join a multiparty cabinet.

Even without such cumbersome arrangements, the future president could be encouraged to play to a broad constituency. Donald Horowitz, one of the American constitutional experts whom South Africans were fond of citing, suggested borrowing from Nigeria's experience: to be elected, the president could be required to gain votes from different regions. In South Africa this system would ensure that no president could be elected without a minimum of support from the Zulus of Natal or the Xhosas of the eastern Cape. This would encourage candidates to appeal to as many different groups as possible.

The electoral system could also be made to promote balance in the parliament. The Nationalists talked of a two-chamber parliament, with the lower house elected on proportional representation. This not only avoided the underrepresentation of smaller parties that came with the British first-past-the-post system, but also decreased the chances of a single party's having an overall majority, and therefore encouraged the formation of coalitions. This would give small parties influence as well as mere representation, avoiding the mistake made in Zimbabwe.

As to the upper house, the Nationalists tangled themselves in talk of representation for all "significant groupings." The problem of definition was inescapable. Racial grouping was clearly unacceptable to blacks; cultural and linguistic groupings, in a country where most people spoke several languages, seemed too vague to be useful. To placate those who objected to being grouped at all, the Nationalists had once proposed that they should join a "non-group group"; this was hopelessly

Byzantine. In the end, proportional representation seemed likely to win out: it was the only way of allowing groups to define themselves. If the Nationalists wanted to balance proportional representation in parliament's lower chamber with something different in the upper chamber, then regional representation, as in America's Senate, seemed the best option. President De Klerk had adopted this idea in his speech of September 1991, proposing that an equal number of seats be allocated to each of South Africa's nine development regions. More controversially, he suggested that, in each region, all parties obtaining more than 10 percent of the votes would share the seats equally among them. De Klerk said this would make the upper chamber "a house of minorities."

Next the Nationalists planned to devolve power to federal and even smaller regions. The smaller the states, the smaller the risk of excluding and thus alienating minorities. If, for example, the whole of Natal were to become a state, the ANC and Inkatha would both have a decent chance of winning it; either way, the loser would be unlikely to accept the result calmly. If Natal were divided into several smaller units, Inkatha and the ANC might win a few each, giving both good reason to respect the system.

In other parts of South Africa, devolution of power to small units might create more or less homogeneous groups of voters, which would relieve local elections of racial or tribal tension. In a mixed province, voters would side with their group. In a homogeneous province, they would be free to think of other issues. This principle had been applied with some success in India in the 1950s. The government created linguistically homogeneous states, which went some way toward changing elections from contests between rival language groups to contests of ideology.

The ANC's constitutional ideas were less clearly defined. The Congress firmly rejected the idea of an upper chamber of parliament representing groups, however defined; it described De Klerk's pro-minority regional representation as a means of retaining the "accumulated privileges of apartheid." But the ANC applauded talk of separation of powers, and had published a draft bill of rights, which found favor with the government's own law commission. The ANC's draft constitution, released in April 1991, had declared for proportional representation, rather than a first-past-the-post constituency system. It seemed to accept the idea of coalition government; in September 1990 Mandela had said that the first post-apartheid cabinet should represent a variety of parties, even if the ANC won an outright majority.

The ANC was suspicious of devolution, for in the past this had meant the infamous black homelands; and the Congress was determined that these should be reintegrated into South Africa. Yet it seemed likely that these suspicions could be overcome if it was shown that devolution would neither preserve the homelands nor allow mainly white suburbs to raise and spend taxes locally without sharing them around. The Nationalists insisted that these tricks were not intended. Moreover, it was clear that devolution was one way to placate the dangerous followers of Mangosuthu Buthelezi, who would surely fight ANC dominance at the center if they were denied some regional power.

Besides, devolution appealed to many of the ANC's own people, who had developed a taste for local government during the revolt of the mid-1980s. They had set up street committees to take charge of township issues, and declared for "people's democracy." The future constitution should not only give all South Africans a vote for the central government, they said. It should give them day-to-day control over local schooling, transport and streetlights. As a result of such pressure, the Congress's draft constitution called for "strong and effective" regional government—though it added that "the regions should not be devised so as to protect privilege."

On many constitutional issues, the ANC and the government did not seem far apart. The big exception was overt minority protection. At times the Nationalists had seemed drawn to various formulas for group rights; the ANC declared that all group protection was anathema. The closest the ANC had come to acknowledging the power of diversity was to talk of banning tribal or racial appeals from party manifestos, and of demanding that parties prove their nonsectarian support by publishing balanced lists of candidates. This seemed unlikely to be foolproof: the ANC, for example, would no doubt be able to supply evidence of its broad character despite its bias towards Xhosas.

In the end, these delicate constitutional questions would cause less excitement than a cruder trade-off. At independence in Malaysia, the rich Chinese minority got a guarantee of citizenship in exchange for a promise to share its wealth with the Malay majority. A dozen years later, the Malays were grumbling: the Chinese had got their citizenship immediately, whereas the Malays were feeling the benefit of affirmative action more gradually.[13] As South Africans approached their transition, however, this kind of bargain seemed attractive. In the future South Africa, whites were in danger of having their political rights curtailed, while blacks were in danger of being economically disadvantaged. It seemed reasonable to exchange political guarantees for whites with economic redistribution for blacks. The ANC's cry that political liberation without economic liberation would be worthless was perhaps an understatement: to many blacks in the townships, food and shelter mattered more than the details of the constitution.

As negotiations started, it seemed as though the grittiest arguments might be economic. For although the Nationalists accepted the need for redistribution, they demanded that guarantees on private property be enshrined in the bill of rights. They also wanted to guard against inflation by entrenching the independence of the central bank. Some even talked of fiscal promises that would bind the post-apartheid government: limits on the size of the budget, government borrowing and so on. The ANC, for its part, called for a workers' charter to be written into the constitution, and a role for its trade union allies in economic planning. The ANC's followers wanted a black president, to be sure; but they also wanted homes and jobs and health care. Perhaps most passionately, blacks wanted land.

5

THE LAND, THE SOIL, OUR WORLD

The big planes do not go to Nelspruit, so I flew from Johannesburg in a precarious nine-seater, crammed with huge Afrikaners returning to their farms. They looked uncomfortable in the suits and shining shoes that they had put on for Johannesburg. Their knees pushed up against the seats in front of them. There was no room to tip their chairs back. They swallowed the airline sandwiches in a single gulp. The white farms around Nelspruit, in the northeastern corner of South Africa, were big enough to make them rich. But I was on my way to the nearby homeland of KaNgwane, where black farmers practiced agriculture of a very different sort.

A smiling man in blue pinstripes met me at the airport. His name was Gija Nyambi and he seemed extremely eager to please. He carried my bag for me; he opened his car door for me; and on the drive from the airport he recited a long list of qualifications which whites are meant to like. He had a degree in agriculture; he had a diploma in journalism and another in photography; he had studied public relations on the side. When he had worked as an agricultural officer among KaNgwane's peasant farmers, he had been known for the wisdom of his advice. Now that it was his job to receive foreign visitors, he was known as the "Encyclopedia of KaNgwane." As well as being in charge of the homeland's protocol, Gija Nyambi wrote articles for the local newspaper; and occasionally he was called upon to act as driver for Enos Mabuza, KaNgwane's chief minister. "I am a multifaceted somebody," he laughed. He was not a radical somebody. He asked me what I expected of South Africa's future and then answered the question himself. White rule had its advantages, he assured his white passenger; you had only to look at independent Africa to see that. "So many what-d'you-call abortive coups. After independence, in the whole of Africa, there is what-d'you-call famine." He yanked the gearshift crossly. "Africa is always trouble!" We arrived at my hotel. Gija Nyambi jumped out, trotted around the front of the car to open my door and insisted on carrying my bag. Tomorrow morning we would set off for KaNgwane; he would fetch me at seven o'clock sharp.

South Africa's poorest people crowd into the homelands, set up by apartheid as dumping grounds for blacks. Until 1986, when the government abolished influx control, blacks without jobs in the rest of South Africa were legally confined to these poor patches of countryside and left to scratch a living from the land. For a time, the homelands and pass laws succeeded in their narrow aims. They saved the state the cost of paying out welfare benefits: the jobless and homeless could be dispatched to their huts. They saved industry the cost of decent wages: workers left their wives and children in the homelands, so employers paid only enough to support a single man.

But the homelands were too small to contain black misery for long. As populations grew, they became hopelessly crowded; by the 1980s desperate peasants were defying influx control, deserting their villages and building rings of shanties around whites' gleaming towns. The rush to the cities was hastened by the legalization of black trade unions, which drove up wages and increased the lure of urban jobs. For the sake of both the countryside and the overcrowded cities, South Africa's new government would have to find a way of relieving rural poverty. The answer would begin with a new policy on land.

Most land in the homelands was owned by homeland governments. Like land all over precolonial Africa, it was managed by chiefs. The chief was supposed to share it out among his people so that every household got a patch. The system was known as communal tenure: ownership was vested in the community, not in the individual who farmed each plot. The farmer paid nothing for the land when he acquired it, nor while he used it; if he left, it reverted to the chief without money changing hands. Communal tenure, which treated access to land as every peasant's birthright, worked fine in the precolonial era; land was plentiful, so there was no difficulty in giving people as much as they wanted. This state of abundance survived as long as Africans grew food only for their own families and so required only modest plots; and as long as there were vast tracts of virgin Africa to expand into.

Colonization destroyed both conditions. White settlers grabbed large chunks of farmland, blocking the constant migrations of Africa's tribes. At the same time, whites introduced the idea of producing for the market, which meant that farmers acquired a reason to want much more land. Africans' access to land was therefore restricted just when their demand for it increased; land had become scarce. In the next century that scarcity grew more serious, as medicine improved and population swelled.

The system of communal tenure had become anachronistic. It assumed that land was valueless and that people could have as much as they wanted. The truth was that land had become a fiercely contested resource. By excluding private ownership, communal tenure also dampened farmers' incentive to conserve the land. This did not particularly matter while land was plentiful, since the farmer who exhausted his fields could easily move on. As land ceased to be abundant, the bias against soil conservation mattered very much.

It was not just that communal tenure reduced the incentive to invest in conservation; it made it harder as well. From Thailand to Tanzania, peasants without land title have trouble getting loans, because bankers cannot reassure themselves that, in the last resort, the farmer will repay them by selling his plot. Besides, the absence of land title deprived bad farmers of the normal incentive to give up: under communal tenure, they would get paid nothing for ceding their fields to more ambitious neighbors. Africa's bad farmers therefore carried on half-heartedly, so Africa's scarce land was poorly used. Good farmers were frustrated because, however successful they were, they had no chance of buying out their neighbors. The result was that ambitious peasants left for the towns.

Before independence, African leaders denounced migrant labor for the toll it took on families; and by the 1990s they might have added that the separation of husbands from wives would ensure the spread of AIDS. They blamed the system on the colonists' low-wage policies, and while there were laws keeping wives and children in the villages, they were right. But they did not see that migrancy was also encouraged by the system of communal ownership, which many of them supported. So long as tenure depended on occupancy, miners and city workers would leave their families in the villages, to make sure that the chief did not give their farm to someone else. The overworked women, left to tend children as well as crops, usually farmed badly. But they coaxed enough corn from the soil to feed themselves, and they lived in huts built from mud and straw, which cost nothing. With life in the countryside so cheap, migrant laborers found it hard to justify the expense of bringing families to town. Communal tenure therefore preserved the separation of families long after the colonists' laws had been rescinded. In the popular imagination, Africa is the continent of the extended family. Many Africans find that even the support of the nuclear family is denied to them.

Gija Nyambi proved a most assiduous guide. For a whole day we crisscrossed KaNgwane, talking to farmers we found in the fields. Some appeared to justify the criticisms of communal farming. On a plot of land a mile from the road we found Anna

Sebiya, a tiny woman who was not sure how old she was, wielding a hoe a big as herself. She wore strings of beads around her wrists and ankles, the badge of a traditional healer. Under the most favorable circumstances, Anna Sebiya would not have been a model farmer; but communal tenure undoubtedly made her a worse one. If she had paid for the land, she would have had reason to work it energetically; or, if she found she had no time for it, she would have sold it to someone who did. As it was, Anna Sebiya had little time for farming and no opportunity to sell out. Her half-acre plot looked like a wasteland: a few wilting cornstalks stuck out of the powdery soil at random; here and there some peanuts had been planted, but not in anything resembling a row. She had no time for thorough weeding, she apologized; whenever she spent too long on her plot her patients complained. Besides, she had four children to look after. Could her husband help her with the farming? Her husband had four other wives and thirty children in all.

Slowly, farmers like Anna Sebiya were becoming more scarce. KaNgwane employed a team of white agronomists to turn subsistence farmers into prosperous producers, settled on bigger than average plots of land. Nyambi naturally introduced me to the most successful protégés. As young men they had deserted KaNgwane to find jobs elsewhere; now the prospect of making money from farming had brought them back home. James Nyambi (no relation to my guide) was doing well enough to have five laborers under him; Petros Sindane employed thirteen. Their land was irrigated. The white agronomists had arranged loans for them to buy the seeds and fertilizer they needed and had told them when and how to plant. They grew cotton, bananas and sugarcane. The cane paid best: on one plantation, the average farmer earned 35,000 rand a year.

This happy experiment seemed to defy the standard criticism of homeland farming; perhaps communal tenure did not stifle modern agriculture after all. KaNgwane's chiefs retained the power to allocate land; in theory, they could tell a farmer to pack up at any time. James and Petros both agreed that this was a worry; but the possibility of a future withdrawal of their land rights by an ANC government worried them much more. Indeed, the chiefs' power over their land had not stopped them from investing in it; one had even borrowed money to build his own dams.

Yet it seemed that success had come despite communal tenure rather than because of it. The whites had arranged the loan to build the dams, since bankers refused to lend to farmers without land title. The agronomists had had to ask the chiefs to choose motivated people to farm the new plantations, since motivation does not come automatically when land is given out free. They asked the chiefs to find people who were literate, who had some savings to invest in the new venture and who had gained experience of modern agriculture on a white man's farm. The chiefs seemed to have found the right people; the plantations were working well. But in time these carefully chosen people would grow tired. Since they could not sell their land, it was hard to see them passing it on to more determined successors. When land has no cash value, it makes sense to farm it badly rather than let it go.

Nyambi carried the biggest criticism of communal tenure hidden in himself. As the day wore on, he grew less obsequious. He spoke his mind on all manner of topics: the new people who had taken over his work among the subsistence farmers were lazy what-d'you-calls; London, which he had visited in the company of the chief minister, was what-d'you-call cold. We stopped at lunchtime at an agricultural station. The white boss was out, but his wife offered us some tea. A six-year-old hid behind her skirt. "Still shy," the mother said; "she's just started going to school." She beamed at her black visitor. "There are just five whites in her class. All the rest are little darkies, but she doesn't seem to mind." I looked at Nyambi. I wanted to apologize for being white. "What a racist," I said when we had got back to the car. Nyambi seemed to reconsider me. For the rest of the day, the driver with all his degrees and diplomas was not obsequious at all.

I asked him if he would like to farm. After all, he had studied agriculture at college, and had spent all those years advising

140

others on their land. It was a stupid question: of course he would like to, but there was no land for him in his chief's area. This seemed inconsistent with what I had been told about the new plantations, for which the chiefs had undertaken to find the best people; Nyambi was probably the best qualified agronomist of all the people in KaNgwane. I persisted: why did the chief not find him some land? Because, said Nyambi, he was not part of the chief's family. That ended the ambivalence about communal tenure that I had felt after meeting James and Petros. I now understood why they had felt happy to invest in dams and suchlike: if you were the chief's friend or relative, your land was secure. The system was not so good for Nyambi and others like him: however competent they were, they would not get land. Like all inequality of opportunity, communal tenure was inefficient; it prevented the best available people from farming the land. Given a chance, Nyambi would drop his protocol and driving. Showing people like me around was a frivolous occupation, he told me. "It's all a waste of time."

The talk of unfairness and missed opportunities led Nyambi to the much bigger injustice perpetrated by whites. Black South Africans rarely display personal anger to outsiders. They denounce oppression in the abstract, but they seldom talk about themselves. Perhaps personal tragedies become unremarkable; perhaps it is distasteful to discuss suffering with infinitely comfortable whites. It would be hard to get personal without being bitter; and bitterness is something which black South Africans nearly always suppress. Indeed blacks are so good at hiding their own suffering that whites could easily forget it ever happened. At the start of South Africa's transition, whites declared that after apartheid there should be a fresh start for everyone, glibly discounting the past.

This was truer about land than about any other issue, partly because the dispossession of black farmers was the biggest hardship inflicted by apartheid, and partly because healing it seemed impossibly difficult. In 1991, when the Nationalists published a white paper on land reform, they proposed merely to end the ban on blacks buying land in "white" areas; to begin with, at least, they offered no compensation to blacks who had lost their land. Yet more than a million farming families were dispossessed under apartheid (and more than 2 million lost their homes in the towns). When black leaders demanded compensation for these families, whites retorted that it would be impractical to excavate the past; if everyone tried to right the wrongs of history, Americans would have to leave their continent to the Indians and Australians would have to return theirs to the aborigines. But in South Africa the forced removal of blacks from their land was not the history of another century. It had happened to Nyambi when he was ten.

As we drove through one of KaNgwane's dusty hamlets, Nyambi ceased to contain himself. "Nineteen fifty-four!" I looked at him blankly. "Nineteen fifty-four: there was nothing here. We were taken here by force, all the people under the three Ngomane chiefs. The people were whipped with *sjamboks* [leather whips] and loaded into trucks; one of the chiefs who had resisted was taken away by helicopter and detained for three years. The people were dumped here, left to sleep under the trees. Thousands of sheep and cattle died, because there was not enough for them to eat in this new place. The people collected money to hire a white lawyer to take the government to court. The lawyer took the money and disappeared. We were here with nothing. It was twenty-three years before the first tarred road was built." His own house, the house of the homeland's chief officer of protocol, still had no electricity or running water.

Before the forced removal, the Nyambi family had been rich. It had owned a hundred hectares and four spans of oxen. The land had been in the family since the nineteenth century, when Gija Nyambi's ancestors fled to the Transvaal to escape Shaka, the Zulu king who impaled his enemies on sharpened sticks. Gija's father was a blacksmith and a good hunter. He shot zebra and wildebeest, so Gija's many brothers and sisters ate meat. The farm sold milk to whites in the area; the family stored surplus corn in secret granaries underground.

All this prosperity vanished when the land was declared

white. The new farmer offered to buy the dairy herd at an insultingly low price; Gija's father accepted because he had no choice. The new farmer erected new fences around his boundary; he built new buildings; he even bulldozed the family grave. Gija Nyambi laughed suddenly. The white should have known better than to disturb his dead grandfather. "The old man started making trouble. He blew the roofs off buildings and burned the crops. It was a terrible what-d'you-call!" After that Gija's family was given permission to visit the farm regularly, to pay its respects to the ancestral grave.

Of all the tests for the first post-apartheid government, none is harder than the land. South Africa's worst poverty occurs in the countryside, both in homelands like KaNgwane and among laborers on white farms. Half the population lives in the villages, where only one in twenty doctors practices; the average rural dweller earns less than half as much as the average city man. The legalization of trade unions in 1979 brought big gains for urban workers. But unions could not help subsistence farmers and had difficulty penetrating white farms. Private estates were particularly hard to unionize. Unlike big companies, which cared enough about their images not to ban trade unions, private farmers often kicked union organizers off their land. In 1989 a strike on Zebediela Citrus Estate in the northern Transvaal, reputedly the world's largest citrus farm, did win a wage raise and union recognition. It did so at a cost. The managers first tried to break the strike by sacking all the workers and calling in the police; fifteen people were hospitalized as a result of bites inflicted by the policemen's dogs. Other strikers suffered worse. On the Sapekoe Tea Estate in Natal, pickers were made to work ten hours a day, six days a week; and many suffered from ailments caused by dangerous agricultural chemicals. They went on strike. All 1,200 were dismissed. Police and soldiers assisted the management in booting them off the estate.[1]

Until 1986 apartheid trapped most black South Africans in the countryside, so rural labor was plentiful and cheap. South

Africa's Wage Act, which lays down minimum wages for selected industries, in 1987 set a floor for unskilled labor in some rural towns at forty-three rand a week. Yet even the official statistics, which relied on farmers' reporting of wage levels and therefore probably exaggerated them, suggested that farm wages were lower: in 1979, for example, the average per week for black workers was eleven rand—and that included an estimate for the value of payment in kind. On some farms, laborers got seven and a half rand for a week of ten-hour working days;[2] in 1978 the International Labor Organization estimated that sixty-five thousand South African children between the ages of eight and fourteen were among these exploited laborers. Some had been lured from the homelands under false pretenses, without the knowledge of their parents; others had parents too poor to object; still others had parents who worked on the same farm and who feared that protest would cost them their jobs.

True, farm laborers received some payment in kind, usually food rations, fuel or the use of some land. This seldom compensated for their pitiful wages, and could be worse than nothing. In 1990 Oxfam, a British aid agency, interviewed Willem Botha, a colored worker at a vineyard in the western Cape. He earned fifty rand a month. Each day his boss sustained him with seven tots of wine. Overtime pay consisted of wine too. "He is so dependent on alcohol," said the Oxfam interview, "that he regularly informs on fellow workers in order to get extra wine." This regime of alcoholic enslavement was called the dop system, and it was widespread in the vineyards of the Cape. A survey in 1984 found that thirteen out of eighteen farms examined plied their workers with more than one and a half pints (or just over a bottle) every day. Workers spent a fifth of their wages on binges in unlicensed taverns. Estate managers had learned to expect low turnouts on Mondays; wives and children had learned to expect beatings. Babies of drunken mothers were born with brain damage.

Most farm laborers were left to build their own houses, usually mud shelters with no running water or electricity. Overcrowding, bad diets and poor sanitation brought cholera, polio and tuberculosis. Ignorance brought other ailments. Workers injured themselves with machines and chemicals they did not understand; Chemwatch, a lobby group based in Durban, documented more than three hundred cases of deformed children born to parents who had been exposed to farm chemicals. Oxfam's study cited a 1988 report on farm schools near Port Elizabeth which found widespread malnutrition: "The teachers say the children are lethargic and cannot stand up when they have reading lessons. . . . Many of the children are losing their eyesight due to acute malnutrition."

It was up to farm owners to build schools for their dependents; the state provided only half the cost of construction. Left to farmers' consciences, education suffered. Eight out of ten farmworkers, according to Oxfam, could not read or write. In 1987 there was only one farm secondary school in the whole country.[3] One in three rural children attended school, and these lucky ones got only the most rudimentary teaching. When the rains came, they often came right through the roofs; when harvest time came, the children's help was demanded. In 1988 the government promised to stamp out this practice; the Education Act, after all, prohibited the removal of children from school. But far-flung farmers are not easily supervised. Many of the laws that protected South African workers did not apply to the countryside. The rest were seldom enforced.

The countryside required attention, yet it was not at all certain to get its fair share. The new government would be short of money; it would have to decide how much of its limited budget would go to the countryside and how much to the towns. Black politicians deplored rural poverty; but they lived in cities, and Marxism's emphasis on the proletariat had reinforced their urban bias. Besides, the liberation struggle had been waged primarily by people in the townships; when the spoils of victory were divided, they would expect a healthy share. Other African governments, confronted by the same dilemma, have almost invariably chosen to put the cities first: city people present their needs more articulately than peasants, and often back their arguments with riots.

The resulting discrimination against the countryside has taken several forms in Africa. Official marketing boards have bought the peasants' produce cheaply, sold it for more, and spent the profits on urban services. Exchange rates have been kept high, spoiling the peasants' chances of exporting their surplus and cheapening the imports that townspeople enjoy. It has been a costly mistake, since agriculture holds one of the continent's best hopes of generating new jobs and exports; and the neglect of the countryside has sent a flood of people to the slums that ring the towns. South Africa is the most urbanized country on the continent; the ability of its townspeople to complain and riot is unmatched. South Africa's politicians would be especially tempted to squeeze the peasants in order to keep the city people quiet.

Without sufficient money, it would be difficult to make a success of even the most enlightened rural policies; for land reform was bound to require new dams and silos and banana ripening rooms, not to mention more agricultural advisers and loans. The first black-led government would want to impose better employment practices on white farmers, and would aim to build more rural clinics and schools. All this would need money and administrative energy. But beyond the question of the resources necessary to make a success of enlightened agricultural reform, the bigger question was whether reform would actually be enlightened.

In 1991 President De Klerk's government repealed the Land Acts, which had reserved 86 percent of the land for whites. But it left open the questions of compensation for the victims of forced removals, the redistribution of land to blacks and the future of communal tenure. The ANC and its fellow black nationalists were set on compensation for dispossessed black farmers but were not sure how to organize it. If they tried to return some farms to their original occupants, they would set off a string of legal battles between past and present owners like those that followed the collapse of communism in East Germany. Yet blacks' sense of grievance would have to be satisfied somehow, and black politicians knew it. The ANC's Freedom Charter, drawn up in 1955 but still cited thirty-five years later, promised that the land would be "redivided among those who work it, to banish famine and land-hunger." The Pan-Africanist Congress demanded simply "the return of the land."

In October 1990 the ANC's Land Commission held a workshop on land reform. Afterward it reported that "the dominant understanding was that the government should nationalize the land and then give it back to the people." Wholesale nationalization without compensation seemed unlikely. It would infuriate not only white farmers, but also the banks that had lent money to them; it would disrupt agricultural exports and the local food supply, which the ANC promised to protect. Besides, a clause on property rights in the new constitution would probably rule out expropriation.

Still, some disruption of the land market seemed inevitable; "without state intervention, it will be economically impossible to carry out the land reform we need," said a spokesman for the Land Commission when it released a discussion document the following February. The new government would probably reserve the right of first refusal on any land that came onto the market; it might forcibly purchase some land and pay the owners partly with cash and partly with government bonds; it might even expropriate some unused land. To match its calls for one person, one vote, the ANC proposed one person, one farm: whites who owned more than one would be required to sell the extras.

It seemed entirely possible for the new administration to acquire large areas without provoking a white agrarian rebellion. In 1990 the government already held nearly 5 million acres of land in trust. These had been intended for transfer to the black homelands; since the homelands had become an embarrassment, President De Klerk planned to use the land to settle black farmers instead. Beyond these acres, the ANC would be able to define quite a bit of land as "unused"; a recent government survey had found that 9 percent of South Africa's farms were hardly ever visited.[4] Within the homelands, new land could be made fruitful by irrigation. Most importantly, plenty of white farmers would probably sell their land without being forced to.

Since the 1960s white small farmers had been selling out to bigger ones at a remarkable rate: judging from South Africa's confused statistics, the number of white farms halved to sixty thousand between 1960 and 1985, though it picked up a little in the late 1980s. There was every reason to suppose that whites would keep on selling. The efficient core of white agriculture was small: a quarter of the farms produced three-quarters of the country's total agricultural output. At the other end of the scale, two-thirds of South African farms were reckoned to be marginal and unproductive.

Some would fail because of their ecology—overgrazing and overcultivation had turned the soil to dust—so the new government's supporters would hardly thank it for settling them on these. But other farms would fail for financial reasons. During the decades of Nationalist rule, white farmers enjoyed subsidized credit, which encouraged them to borrow too much: between 1970 and 1990 white farm debt rose from 1.4 billion to 16 billion rand.[5] In the late 1980s, as the rural Afrikaner vote defected to the right-wing Conservative Party, the political argument for featherbedding white farmers disintegrated. Interest-rate subsidies were therefore cut; the government stopped paying the farmers artificially high prices for their produce. As a result, white farmers became incapable of servicing their huge debts; and many would sooner or later be obliged to sell. The new administration could easily encourage them to do so by introducing a land tax, which was rightly popular with the ANC. Besides increasing the pressure on indebted farmers, this tax would discourage rich Johannesburgers from buying land as a hedge against inflation and not bothering to farm it.

In 1991 the Development Bank of Southern Africa, which did most of the government's thinking on land reform, put the number of hopelessly indebted farmers at about three thousand (one thousand of those were hopelessly indebted to the state); together these whites probably farmed nearly 10 million acres. Add to that the nearly 5 million acres originally intended for the homelands, plus another 5 million that might be returned to recent victims of forced removals or found from land around townships, and the bank reckoned that black farmers could receive close to 20 million acres of land fairly quickly. If half that land were arable, blacks would find themselves farming 15 to 25 percent of South Africa's arable land. The bank admitted that its figures were only estimates, and had to defend itself against a storm of white protest when they were announced. Yet it seemed clear that the new government would be able to acquire plenty of land without resorting to expropriation.

Acquiring new land would be easier than deciding what to do with it. The ANC's Land Commission discussed a variety of possibilities. It compiled lists of pros and cons. It weighed state-run farms against cooperatives; it weighed both these options against private ownership; it found conclusions difficult. In all its deliberations, however, there was no sign that the ANC planned to move away from communal tenure. Indeed, the Land Commission declared that it should be encouraged. The report on its 1990 workshop stated that, in communal areas, "there should be no right to sell a farming plot"; and "there should be no right to rent out a farming plot, as it belongs to the community."[6]

As so often in South Africa, the origins of misguided policies were understandable, even admirable: they grew out of resistance to apartheid. In order to oppose the government's forced removals, blacks had to believe in their own idea of land rights, which meant communal tenure. Black resistance was heroic, so the faults of communal tenure went unobserved. "What I've seen in rural land struggles is that people fight for their notion of land rights, a notion which is much stronger than anything this present government has managed to impose," declared Aninka Claasens, a white who helped black communities to resist forced removals in the Transvaal. By 1990 Claasens was part of the ANC Land Commission, and her involvement in the resistance to forced removals had made her suspicious of the whole idea of private title. She wanted tenure to be decided according to who had been born on the land and who had worked it longest: in other words, the same kinds of criteria that chiefs were supposed to use in allocating communally owned land. Claasens worried that if communal tenure were replaced by private title in the homelands, white farmers and white companies would buy blacks' remaining land. Zola Skweyiya, another senior ANC figure, protested that capitalist land markets would "change the great divide between black and white in the rural areas to a deepening of contradictions between the rich and the poor in the countryside."[7] Communal tenure seemed the best way to ensure that as few people as possible were made landless.

The idea of land as birthright had a powerful allure; it attracted Pan-Africanists as well. In 1987 Essy Letsoalo, an academic with PAC sympathies, published a lament for the precolonial order, when every African had equal access to the soil.[8] Whites had destroyed this Eden to create landless laborers for their farms and mines; after apartheid, paradise should be restored. Letsoalo would have rejoiced in Petros Nkosi, a Transvaal peasant who told Oxfam's researchers:

> Our purpose is the land, that is what we must achieve. The land is our whole lives, we plough it for food, we build our homes from the soil, we live on it and we are buried in it. When the whites took our land away from us, we lost the dignity of our lives, we could no longer feed our children. . . . In everything we do we must remember that there is only one aim and one solution and that is the land, the soil, our world.

When land evoked such passion, it was hard to tell South Africans that the Eden of land as birthright could never be restored.

The romance with the soil, and with the simple life of the farmer, has possessed humankind since Virgil wrote his *Geor-*

gics. It was part of Afrikaner nationalism, especially in the 1930s, when Afrikaners were forced from the land into the hard world of the cities. It was hardly surprising that, as black South Africans arrived in the shanty towns by the thousands, the rural idyll should enchant them too. The capitalism of the cities was merciless: it failed to provide work for everyone; it meant orders from white men and homes in violent slums. Next to this, the precolonial peasant—self-reliant, at peace with his neighbors and with the elements—seemed an enviable figure. Since the 1960s reformers all over Africa had looked to the land to shelter their people from the cruelties of urban life.

The distaste for capitalism, and the romantic appeal of land as birthright, led some of these reformers to disaster. Like the ANC's idealists, Tanzania's President Julius Nyerere wanted to banish landlessness by breaking with capitalist patterns of land ownership. Soon after Tanzania gained its independence in 1961, *Mwalimu* ("the teacher," as Nyerere liked to be known) abolished private tenure; in 1967 he went much further. He announced his policy of *ujamaa,* or "African socialism"—"African" because the proposed collective farms were said to be consistent with Africa's tradition of communal tenure. Tanzania's people would live in consolidated villages, which would be easier to supply with seeds and fertilizer than huts scattered across the countryside. They would farm the surrounding land in cooperatives, which would achieve economies of scale not possible with small plots.

The hitch was that Nyerere's people disliked being made to embrace tradition. By 1973 only 15 percent of Tanzania's land had been collectivized; thereafter, the process proceeded partly by coercion. In the following three years more than 5 million Tanzanians were moved in the name of *ujamaa*—more even than were uprooted in South Africa by apartheid. Once they had arrived in these consolidated villages, the peasants were supposed to farm communally; but they resisted the idea so doggedly that eventually it was dropped. Nyerere's African peasantry seemed to doubt whether African socialism really sat naturally with Africans. By the 1980s Tanzania's government admitted that collectivization had brought food shortages. With much breast-beating, *Mwalimu* started to promote private tenure.

Ethiopia tried collective farming too. A year after the 1974 coup that overthrew Emperor Haile Selassie, the new Marxist junta nationalized all land. It set up peasant associations (which in fact were often led by students) to do the farming. It told the associations to create equal holdings for all members and to welcome in landless peasants whenever possible. This was intended to reduce landlessness; but accommodating newcomers meant redividing existing plots, destroying security of tenure and peasants' interest in conserving the soil. In time, the peasant associations were expected to eliminate private cultivation and go over to cooperative farming instead. In practice the associations refused; only 2 percent of cultivated land was ever farmed cooperatively. When the government's ideologues relented, the few cooperatives that had been established quickly folded; between March and June 1990 nine-tenths of them were dissolved. Fearing another change of policy, however, peasants still lacked the confidence to invest in their farms.

In the 1960s and 1970s Latin America's land reformers also experimented with cooperatives. They had equally little success, and by the end of the 1980s many cooperatives were being cut up by their members to make family farms. On the other side of the world, the Chinese came to the same conclusion. In 1978 they abandoned collective production in favor of small family holdings; by 1984 farm output had risen by three-fifths. Agricultural experts reckon that three-quarters of this increase came of the new enthusiasm bred by family control; the rest came from the extra incentive provided by higher food prices. The one example of successful cooperative farming comes from Israel, where the kibbutzim made the desert bloom. But the kibbutzniks began with special advantages. They had the determination characteristic of immigrants; they had financial help from foreign sympathizers; they had the bonding ideology of Zionism to overcome the squabbles and apathy that plague cooperatives elsewhere.

South Africa lacked these special conditions. The ANC's leaders yearned to give land to all their people, and to avoid the capitalist competition which would cause good farmers to prosper and weak ones to fail. Yet without private and secure tenure, South Africa's farmers were unlikely to conserve the land, or to produce enough food to feed the country. Without a land market, inefficient producers would continue to use land that could be better farmed by others, and migrant labor would persist. The idea of land as birthright played powerfully on the emotions, and wreaked havoc with the soil.

As in industry, so in agriculture: East Asia provided a model of how to reform land. After the second world war Japan, Taiwan and South Korea took farms from rich owners and gave them to their tenants. The land, in the words of the ANC's Freedom Charter, was "shared among those who work it." Now that they owned their farms, peasants became attractive to bank managers, since they could offer the land as security against loans. At the same time, the farmers acquired a good reason to borrow, since they and not their landlords would gain from new investment in their property. Land reform created more dedicated and sophisticated farmers: it served not only equality but productivity as well.

The second ingredient of Asia's land reform was the improvement of agricultural support services: farmers were provided with good seeds, enough fertilizer and advice from agronomists. In the decade after tenants became owners, the farms in these three countries stepped up their production. The newly prosperous peasants could buy more consumer products than before, stimulating industry. They soon accumulated deep pools of savings, which provided investment finance for the factories. Successful land reform set East Asia on its way to economic miracle.

Asia's success helped to make land reform fashionable in Latin America and Africa; but it was never quite repeated. Some Latin governments, notably Bolivia's in the 1950s, avoided the folly of cooperatives and tried to foster family farms. In most cases these failed because the government provided the land but not the support services. Even before land reform, Asia's big estates had been subdivided among poor tenants. In Latin America, by contrast, the big estates had been farmed as single units. Latin America's farm infrastructure—the barns, roads and tobacco sheds—had therefore been centralized; the new subdivided farms required new infrastructure to work. They seldom got it. Without new barns, the smallholders had nowhere to store their produce. Without new roads, they could not get their produce to the towns.

Africa's land reforms have been plagued by the same problems. With their bias toward the cities, African governments have spent their money on steel mills and stadiums, not on rural roads; besides, even excellent infrastructure could not have saved farmers from the food prices which governments kept low to please urban consumers. Yet the ANC's reformers could draw strength from one local precedent: peasants had prospered in neighboring Zimbabwe. There, one of the government's first actions after independence was to raise corn prices. Having given farmers a reason to produce more, the government set about enabling them to do so. It aimed to provide blacks with support services as good as those enjoyed by white farms. It did its best to provide transportation to take the farmers' food to market. It ensured that peasants could get credit. As a result, black farmers' food production rose fifteen-fold in the first five years of independence. In 1980 they had produced 7 percent of the country's marketed corn; in 1985 they produced two-thirds.[9] As in East Asia, redistribution and efficiency went hand in hand.

South Africa's 1.1 million peasant farmers were ripe for a similar revolution. Until the 1980s the National Party had lavished money and attention on white farmers, who enjoyed so many subsidies and tax exemptions that they paid just 30 percent of their nominal dues. The state's agricultural research and extension services were designed to serve white needs alone. Irrigation pipes delivered water to white farms rather than black ones. Black farms were off the main roads, so trucks did not collect their produce to deliver to the market. It was hardly surprising that the average laborer on a white farm produced six times what his peasant counterpart could manage. If the new government corrected the imbalance in subsidies and services, there was every reason to believe that South Africa's peasants would catch up as fast as had Zimbabwe's. With labor-intensive crops like corn and cotton, motivated workers counted for more than economies of scale: black family farms could outdo big white ones, provided they got the supplies and the services they needed.

The revolution had already started in small areas of South Africa, as my visit to KaNgwane showed. The banana and sugarcane farmers, who were lucky enough to find favor with their local chiefs, proved that smallholdings could prosper with the help of enlightened agronomists. Just as in the 1980s the white government had tried to appease township anger by building new houses and clinics, so it had tried to dent black rural poverty as well. By 1990 the Development Bank had committed itself to lending 60 million rand of mainly government money to projects like the ones in KaNgwane. Giving smallholders seeds, fertilizer and some simple advice had yielded wonderful results; the bank was good at telling journalists happy stories of peasants whose harvests multiplied by five in the first year of bank assistance. The challenge after apartheid would be to accelerate this process so that South Africa's black farms received as much support as white ones. It would mean building new roads, dams, rail links and electricity lines; persuading suppliers of fertilizer and seeds to deliver in smaller quantities; and reforming railroad tariffs so that small consignments were not prohibitively expensive. Banks and building societies would need to be persuaded that it was safe to lend to blacks.

In the first year after Nelson Mandela's release, the ANC did not rule out the possibility of cooperatives and state farms aimed at achieving supposed economies of scale. But Zimbabwe's example and the pilot schemes in the homelands seemed likely to prove persuasive. If the Development Bank's talk of nearly 20 million acres proved at all accurate, the new government would be able to settle a substantial number of farmers on small plots. In their first years of independence, Kenya and Zimbabwe had also created peasant smallholdings on formerly white estates: Kenya resettled 34,000 families on 3.7 million acres; Zimbabwe resettled 51,000 families on 6.4 million acres. In both cases, roughly 120 acres were required per family. If that ratio held for South Africa, the 20 million acres talked of by the Development Bank would be enough to resettle more than 160,000 families.

On top of this, black farmers might be able to acquire land as tenants. In the late nineteenth century white landowners reckoned black tenants were more productive than white ones[10] and were only too happy to take them on. In time the best tenants saved enough money to buy out their landlords; by 1900 blacks owned a quarter of a million acres of the Transvaal. The Land Acts stifled the growth of these black yeomen by outlawing black tenants as well as black ownership in 86 percent of the country: only labor tenancy, under which blacks paid for using white land by working half the year for the white owner, was still permitted. Given time and the scrapping of the Land Acts, that yeomanry could rise again.

Zimbabwe showed that half the Asian miracle could be repeated in Africa: properly supported, smallholders would thrive. In theory it would be easy to repeat the miracle's other ingredient: letting the smallholders own their land. In South Africa formal land title in the communal areas rested with homeland governments. The homelands would soon be disbanded; title would revert to the South African state. There would be nothing to stop the new government from subdividing this title and giving it to the homeland farmers. The only obvious obstacle to replacing communal tenure was the ANC's distaste for capitalism; and yet the precedents suggested that even determined African capitalists had difficulty entrenching private title on the land. Zimbabwe's government did not try to, which was one reason that migrant labor persisted. Most Zimbabwean peasants still farmed their communal plots. A minority farmed land which the government had bought from whites; but instead of giving the new black farmers private tenure, Asian-style, Zimbabwe's government gave out five-year leases. Similarly, Zambia's government distributed leases rather than title deeds to the new occupants of formerly white estates.

The one exception was Kenya. Not only did the Kenyan government distribute private title to the peasants it settled on formerly white plantations; it also introduced private ownership in areas where blacks had held land communally. From the outset, the program had its failings, particularly that it gave title deeds to men, not to the women who did most of the farming. The reform was resented for creating some landlessness, as the logic of the land market encouraged bad farmers to sell out. But the program's biggest shortcoming was that it did not last. To prevent subdivision of the land into uneconomical holdings, Kenya's government had tried to enforce a minimum plot size. The peasants disliked this, and the death of a farmer continued to be followed by the subdivision of land among his heirs. Where this entailed breaking the state's regulations, the state was simply not informed. The land registers, in which the new private titles had been inscribed after independence, fell rapidly out of date. As the new rules were ignored, their authority withered: in time, peasants reverted to taking their land disputes to tribal elders rather than to the courts.

Root and branch reform has no guarantee of working. The idea of private title offends rural people less than the idea of cooperatives, particularly when the establishment of cooperatives involves being moved into model villages. But no new idea, introduced suddenly by people from the alien city, is likely to be accepted happily by peasants. John Bruce, the director of the excellent Land Tenure Center at the University of Wisconsin, whose wisdom on Africa's land reform has contributed greatly to this chapter, suggests that it may be better to finetune communal tenure than to break with it. Thus in Botswana the chief's power over land was shifted to tribal land boards shortly after independence; some degree of continuity was preserved by inviting the chiefs to sit on the new land boards—though they tended to drop out in annoyance at their diminished status. More such compromises are possible: chiefs might, for example, be left to run communal grazing land, while cropland was given over to private tenure. Land markets could be introduced gradually; at first it would certainly be right to forbid rich whites from buying out black land.

In the end, however, private tenure is inevitable. Just as the enclosure movement of the seventeenth and eighteenth centuries spelled the end of the English commons, so enclosure by white settlers will ultimately kill off Africa's commons. In some homelands, communal tenure is already under pressure: in 1989 KwaZulu and QwaQwa passed laws permitting private tenure, not least because their people were neglecting land that they were not allowed to own. The question for South Africa is whether the transition from communal to private tenure will go smoothly, or whether it will be drawn out by government mistakes. The ANC does not seem likely to repeat the socialist errors of Tanzania and Ethiopia; nor does it seem likely to repeat Kenya's overimpatient reforms. In late 1991 the ANC's Land Commission appeared more vulnerable to the mistake of resisting modernization out of nostalgia for the precolonial age rather than encouraging modernization to proceed at a reasonable pace.

Whatever policy the ANC arrives at, its significance will extend more widely than the land. For the debate between ambitious and cautious modernizers represents Africa's greatest dilemma. Should the continent aspire immediately to European standards? Or should it protect the remnants of its precolonial past?

6

THE SHADOW OF TRADITION

Modernization is painful in any society. It creates a class of newly rich, resented by a class of newly poor. It sets the young against their elders. It breeds a powerful nostalgia for a mythical old order, under which life was simpler and happier and people were not so much the captives of efficiency and stress. During Britain's industrial revolution, for example, Luddites attacked the machinery of the modern factory; Dickens documented the misery of the new underclass; Marx proclaimed that the emerging industrial order was so unpleasant that workers would eventually revolt. Yet at least Britain effected its own industrial revolution. It suffered a lesser trauma than colonized countries, where foreigners imposed modernity fast from outside.

The colonists sought to justify themselves by breakneck modernization. It was for the supposed benefit of the colonized that Rhodes longed to bring "the whole uncivilised world under British rule." "Africa is still lying ready for us," he wrote as a young man; "it is our duty to take it."[1] Unsurprisingly, the colonized resented modernity even more bitterly than did the Luddites, for it was little more than a conquering creed. It was only natural that Marxism should collect its strongest following in the Third World, or that developing countries should be drawn to other forms of anticapitalism. In the Middle East traditionalists adopted Islam as their antimodern ideology: it embodied Arab history; it rejected women's rights, modern banking and other alien ideas. For Fidel Castro in Cuba and for the mullahs in Iran, anticapitalism was reinforced by anti-Westernism. The result was far more explosive than the pure revolt against capitalism that Marx predicted for the developed world.

The trauma of modernization is perhaps most acute in Africa, though the poverty of the traumatized has dampened organized revolt. Colonization was never briefer, nor imposed on people so many centuries behind their colonizers. In India and Arabia Europeans introduced modernity over a period of centuries; besides, both India and Arabia had developed proud civilizations long before the British or Turks arrived. They were literate; they produced fine architecture and painting; together they gave birth to the great religions of the world.

Africa was very different. Whites did not penetrate the interior of the continent until the 1880s, and in less than a century they were largely gone. Moreover, the first explorers found a people entering the Iron Age. Unlike the Indians and Arabs, the Africans were colonized before they had time to develop a grand heritage of their own. There were masks and textiles and some sculpture, though these were far less plentiful and splendid than Hindu temple carvings or Islamic rugs. There was an oral tradition of myths and stories, and a wealth of ceremony and ritual to match. But there was no precolonial literature, not much architecture, a history written down by white missionaries if at all.

This had a profound effect on the African leaders who took over at independence in the 1960s. Without a sophisticated African tradition to feel proud of, they accepted European attitudes and standards more than Indians ever did. This was most famously true of French Africa, where schoolchildren learned to read from textbooks which began, "Our ancestors, the Gauls . . ."; and where the colonized were treated as part of the French polity. In Paris the National Assembly included a handful of French Africans, elected by their people to represent their interests. As members of the assembly, two of the first generation of French African leaders (Senegal's Léopold Senghor and the Ivory Coast's Félix Houphouët-Boigny) participated in the drafting of the constitution of France's Fourth Republic; Senghor's French poetry earned him membership in the Académie Française. But even in British Africa the first generation of leaders was drawn from the minority schooled in British institutions, and they accepted these institutions' values more or less wholesale.

Hastings Kamuzu Banda studied politics in the United States and medicine in Scotland before returning home to rule Malawi. Zambia's President Kenneth Kaunda was guided in his search for the principles of national leadership by Arthur Mee's books for boys. Tanzania's first leader, Julius Nyerere, translated Shakespeare's *Julius Caesar* into kiSwahili. In Ghana at independence, a split soon developed in the ruling party between those who espoused the social democracy of the British Labor Party and those who had been involved with the Communist Party during their London days.

Some who could not go to London attended local imitations of the British public schools; in Uganda King's College defended British traditions so inflexibly that new teachers, freshly arrived from England, found the school's practices out of date. African clerks were taken into the lower ranks of the bureaucratic hierarchy, and were taught to prize the row of pens in their breast pockets.[2] The British also passed on their values through their colonial armies. The historian Ali Mazrui describes how, before becoming Uganda's dictator, Idi Amin prospered in the King's African Rifles because he showed "all the signs of colonial conditioning into dependency. . . . Within seven years he was promoted to lance corporal and was displaying the qualities which so endeared him to his British superiors—instant obedience, fierce regimental pride, reverence towards Britain and the British."[3]

South Africa's black leaders were not altogether different.

Sol Plaatje, an early ANC leader, translated Shakespeare into Tswana. Later Z. K. Matthews, prominent in the Congress of the 1950s, wrote: "I discovered that Shakespeare had things to say not only to his England . . . but also to me, a twentieth century African."[4] Since the late nineteenth century the sophisticated world around the diamond mines had produced a class of black Englishmen who held banquets to celebrate Queen Victoria's Diamond Jubilee in 1897, and who laid claim to Englishness by playing cricket. In the diamond town of Kimberley, Africans aspired to the Duke of Wellington Cricket Club and the Eccentrics Cricket Club, whose very names invoked the Empire.

People all over the world can read Shakespeare and play cricket without losing their identity, so long as they have a compelling home culture to balance the borrowed one. In South Africa the imported influence was hardly challenged. Even black nationalists who rebelled against white influence did not reject the values of the West: the black-consciousness movement, which led the 1976 protests, wanted above all education in English, not in Xhosa or Zulu. Black-consciousness intellectuals were inspired by ideas imported from America; the last thing they wanted was a return to African roots.

All over Africa, the rulers' identification with Europe has divorced them from the mass. It is easy to miss this, because precolonial Africa was so primitive that it left few visible marks. The cities of India and Arabia display their traditions in temples and mosques. Africa's towns are all office blocks and Woolworths; in the centers, at least, the precolonial huts are gone. Yet traditional Africa is still vibrant, even if it is not always visible to outsiders. The continent's people still worship their ancestors; they consult spirit mediums; they are loyal to tribal chiefs who still wield authority over communally owned land. Again, South Africa is not altogether different, even though it is richer than the rest of Africa, even though it was settled by the modernizing British more than half a century earlier than the rest of the continent.

The strength of traditional beliefs in South Africa is evident in a story from Nelspruit, the small Afrikaans town near KaNgwane where Gija Nyambi met my plane. In 1984 a cashier at Pick 'n' Pay, the local supermarket, was involved in a bus accident. Like the rest of the passengers, she was treated for minor injuries and discharged from the hospital. Unlike the other passengers, she became sick two days later and died. The following year another woman who worked at the supermarket complained of a headache; two days later she also died. A pattern was emerging. Each year, between April and June, one of Pick 'n' Pay's female employees would die: one scalded herself with boiling water; another was killed after a squabble with her neighbor; yet another complained of headaches, just as the second victim had. In all these cases, an apparently everyday misfortune turned fatal. The employee who scalded herself had been visited in the hospital by her colleagues soon after the accident, and had seemed in good health: her death was particularly mysterious. Pick 'n' Pay's employees began to suspect witchcraft. With each new tragedy, the suspicion grew.

In 1990 a woman who worked in the supermarket's meat department was hit by a truck as she got out of a bus. One of her colleagues claimed to have witnessed the accident from his car. He gave chase to the truck but it somehow disappeared. The same year another female employee slipped and broke her leg. It was set in the hospital, but the woman still insisted that she could not use it, even though X rays indicated that the break had healed. Meanwhile the workers found themselves beset by a host of smaller problems. The staff, especially the women, complained of burning and itching eyes, headaches and sleepiness. Some found their feet burned and itched as well. Others were said to menstruate continuously for as long as three months. Still others reported marital problems at home, which they blamed on the *thikoloshe*, a small hairy spirit with a single buttock and a penis so long that he carries it over his shoulder. Finally the workers were fed up. In January 1991 they appointed a committee to organize a visit to a traditional diviner, who would help them to undo the spell. Each worker

163

was asked to contribute 43 rand toward transportation and the healer's fee. The committee informed the managers and the police about the visit. A sign on the canteen wall announced that those who refused to be part of the expedition should consider themselves fired.

In the end 171 out of 184 black and mixed-race staff set off from Nelspruit in search of a diviner. Their buses took them to KaNgwane, where they sought villagers' advice on the local healers. They chose a witch doctor called Mayonyane Mpapane and arrived outside his hut as the sun was going down. The organizing committee presented Mpapane with the workers' money. Pockets were emptied of knives and guns. The healer's assistants divided the visitors into five groups and questioned each in turn. The interrogations went on until three o'clock the next morning, when finally the workers were permitted to sleep. They rose again after sunrise and were made to sit in rows to await Mpapane's verdict. The healer appeared before them. He ordered seven workers to be pulled out of the group. He told them to undress. He announced that they had conspired to bewitch their workmates, then ordered the culprits to smear themselves with dirty engine oil. Finally Mpapane declared that the accused should not be hurt or killed. On the way home the seven were quiet, which their fellows took for an admission of guilt.

When the workers returned to the supermarket on Monday, they demanded that the seven witches should be sacked. They also demanded the removal of four of the thirteen who, on the grounds that Christians could have no truck with witchcraft, had refused to join the expedition. The majority of the workers resented the Christians' indifference to the stream of fatal accidents; besides, the healer had said that one of these four was a witch. The white managers were bewildered. So were the region's trade union leaders, who stayed clear of the dispute. The managers were reluctant to punish apparently innocent people. They suspected that the healer had been instructed in advance to blame unpopular employees; besides, the firing of witches might be deemed an unfair labor practice by the courts.

The managers had little choice but to suspend the eleven on paid leave and to call in a team of social scientists to advise them what to do next.

The consultants found that the supposed witches probably had been unpopular even before the visit to Mpapane. Two were in charge of keys to different storerooms; they had refused to lend them out to colleagues who wanted to pinch groceries for their friends. A third "witch" held the job of supervisor. He was accused by the healer of using spells to make white managers "shiver and shake"; his colleagues agreed that this explained his exalted job. A fourth "witch" told the researchers that he had been unpopular since reporting some of his fellows for stealing meat. In fact six of the seven accused had privileged jobs; the exception was noted as a drunk.

The witchcraft was clearly a sham, but the consultants were at a loss to know how the supermarket managers should handle this unusual labor dispute. The workers would not agree to have the grievance taken to an industrial court, for the courts did not understand or respect black customs. They declared that if the managers refused to sack the witches, they would in effect be condemning the rest of the work force to death; and that the accused would be hounded out of the local townships whether they were sacked or not. The researchers asked the workers whether a very powerful diviner could cast a fresh spell to protect them. The workers replied that in the long run this would fail, since witches would respond with their own more powerful medicines: an escalation of spells would merely be expensive. The workers grew angry and called several brief strikes. Eventually they agreed to visit a second healer on the condition that if he confirmed the choice of witches, the accused would resign. This second consultation cleared three of the accused. The remaining four duly left the supermarket to seek work elsewhere.[5]

Black South Africans commonly invoke the supernatural to explain illness, a bad crop or a simple misfortune. Sometimes the spell has been cast by a disgruntled ancestor, as when Gija Nyambi's dead grandfather burned the white farmer's crops.

165

Sometimes it has been cast by living persons in contact with the spirits, as Pick 'n' Pay's workers thought. If benevolent, the person who casts the spell is a healer; if not, he or she is a witch. Witchcraft is often thought to explain the success of a rival, as with those who had achieved promotion at Pick 'n' Pay.

In the late 1980s Thomas Shabalala, a gangster who controlled an area of ten thousand shacks near Durban, was generally reckoned to have magic powers. Bullets fired at him would turn to water; legal charges would fail too. In 1989, when Shabalala was tried for the murder of four children, his protective spell was so strong that the magistrate fainted—or so local folklore claimed. Whenever the police looked for him, Shabalala hid by turning into a goat. This legend was so persistent that in the end a gang went to his house and burned the goat. The animal talked in its dying moments. People were dismayed to see Shabalala alive the next day.

Singers fear that jealous rivals may commission a witch doctor to steal their voices. Business owners hire witch doctors to jinx the competition and make their own enterprises thrive. Often the witch doctor requires not just a fee but human parts, which he uses as ingredients for his *muti*, or spell. One story has a successful Soweto businessman using an amputated white hand to guide him in his commerce; to prevent the hand from decomposing, he kept it in his refrigerator.[6] More commonly *muti* consists of internal organs. Rumors of murderers out to harvest human lungs and livers spread periodic panic in the townships, and sometimes in white suburbs as well. In June 1990 the *Sunday Times* reported that a witch doctor was offering a vast reward for a white child, whose organs he would use to end Natal's violence. A black nanny had apparently been offered 2,000 rand for the two-year-old she looked after; refused, the stranger upped the offer to 10,000 rand. The story worried one white resident enough to make a counteroffer, equal in value, as a reward to anyone who delivered the witch doctor to the police. In the remote homelands, black communities deal with witches more directly. A deputy minister in Venda was hanged for murdering someone for *muti*. More commonly, witches are burned.

The belief in witchcraft blurs into other traditions which are equally alive and well. The root cause of illness is thought to be supernatural, so the modern doctor who treats only physical causes is considered to have limited use; prudent patients consult both doctors and traditional diviners. Along with the diviners come herbalists, who treat the body rather than the spirit, but who claim to learn their potions from dead ancestors who appear to them in dreams. The diviners are also in contact with the ancestors and are the main custodians of the tribe's traditional laws. Their spiritual authority underpins the secular authority of the chieftaincy. When the chief contemplates a big journey or a difficult decision, he asks the diviner's advice. It is a way of ensuring that chiefs respect the wishes of the ancestors—and therefore the norms of their tribes.

Almost everywhere in Africa, the chiefs retain the loyalty of their people despite the efforts of modern rulers to promote the authority of the state. In 1985, when South Africa's white government still believed in depriving blacks of citizenship by putting them in homelands, it tried to impose independence on KwaNdebele. This was fiercely resisted, not because the Ndebele people understood the grand implications of losing South African citizenship, but because the man appointed to lead the new statelet did not come from either of the Ndebele's chiefly families. This affront to the traditional order provoked great violence. Shops owned by homeland politicians were burned down; dozens of buildings were destroyed. Only the minister of education escaped such treatment, even though he was resented for going about KwaNdebele's villages in a vast chauffeur-driven car. This minister was forgiven his ostentation because he was called Prince Cornelius and his father was none other than the supreme chief of the Ndebele tribe.[7]

In other homelands more sensitive leaders deliberately seek the cooperation of the chiefs. In KwaZulu Chief Mangosuthu Buthelezi appears before his people in tribal regalia and makes much of his relationship with Goodwill Zwelithini, who is Buthelezi's nephew and the Zulus' king. Enos Mabuza, KaNg-wane's chief minister until 1991, was careful to invite traditional leaders into his homeland cabinet. "Without chiefs," he told me, "rural people would lose interest in the political system, if they understood it at all."

Africa's first independent rulers embraced the ideas and attitudes of Europe; but their people were lodged in African tradition. The rulers took over the modern state from departing Europeans; but their people's first loyalty remained with the chiefs. The new governments built steel mills and stadiums; but most of their people still lived from the land. They published laws and policies in French or English; but many of their people could barely speak those languages and more could not read. African graduates became lawyers and judges; but peasants continued to settle disputes by tribal law. African graduates became doctors; but sick peasants continued to consult traditional healers. Modern ambitions and ancient loyalties rubbed shoulders, collided, but seldom combined in any useful way. Indeed a surprising number of the continent's problems result from the gulf between Africa's two worlds.

Soon after arriving in Zimbabwe I visited the market in Mbare, one of the capital's townships. A man introduced himself as International Unity and demanded my attention.

"This is for you," he insisted, holding out a stick.

"Thank you. What's it for?"

"For chewing. It will strengthen your backbone. Make you produce more sperm." When I said I didn't think I would buy any for the moment, thank you, International Unity looked deeply sympathetic. "So you do not have a woman?"

I gestured at my wife, who had been waylaid by another stall-keeper.

"But you do not have children?"

"We've only just got married."

"You see! Take this, she will have two babies at once!"

I had no idea whether the chewing stick harmed Zimbabweans' health, accelerated the already alarming birth rate, or was ineffectual on both counts, although I had been told that one popular aphrodisiac made from beetle wings sometimes caused stomach hemorrhages. In any case, the chewing stick worried me less than International Unity's views on AIDS: he advised his patients against using condoms and declared he could cure the disease with one of his potions ("Last price, ten dollars!"), so long as it had not yet reached the kidneys.

A whole row of the market was occupied by medicine men like this one. Nearly all black Zimbabweans visited traditional healers, who outnumbered modern doctors by around ten to one. So long as these influential people promised cures for AIDS, even the best government health campaign would not save the country. Large numbers of Zimbabweans would ignore the doctors' warnings because of the healers' advice. The ancient medicine undermined the new one.

Rival legal systems similarly conflicted. The colonists imported European legal systems; but, in the words of Rhodesia's rulers, they allowed traditional law to govern relations among Africans so long as it was not "repugnant to natural justice, morality and good conscience". This dual system was preserved by Zimbabwe's independence constitution, so ancient and modern law continued to clash. Modern law forbids reprisals against witches, but the chiefs' courts mete out punishment all the same. Modern law tries to protect women's rights; ancient law disdains them. In fact modernization has landed women with the worst of both worlds. Under the old order, a dead man's property is passed on to his brother, who therefore accepts responsibility to provide for the widows. In the towns, wives live too far from their brothers-in-law to be looked after by them if their husbands die; but this does not stop the in-laws from demanding the furniture the day the women become widows. Africa has upset the delicate balance of the traditional order, but has not yet achieved a modern balance to replace it.

The ancient-modern friction weakens government as well. The state sends its representatives to administer the villages, but the villagers prefer to answer to the chief. The two authorities compete and undermine each other; the main winner is confusion. A similar conflict prevails in the capital. Bureaucrats are paid to serve the state, but their traditional obligation is to look after their kinsmen. They therefore have difficulty choosing whether to be honest servants of the modern government or to steal from modernity to give to their tribe. Africa has failed to create uncorrupt civil services because its people do not identify with the modern state. Many do not even understand what the state is. In villages all across the continent, there are peasants who do not know their country's name.

Such conflicts and confusions help to explain why Africa fell apart after independence. The natural transition from tribal princedoms to supra-tribal nations had been interrupted by colonization, which squashed the first stirrings of the modern state—in Buganda (now Uganda), in Sokoto (northern Nigeria) and among the Zulus.[8] The colonists started to impose their own version of modernity, but they did not stay long enough to finish the job. Christianity challenged traditional worship. Modern government challenged chiefs. The cash economy impinged upon traditional agriculture. Migrant labor unraveled the close-knit family. Doctors threatened traditional healers. Schoolmasters questioned village lore. Yet none of these challenges were conclusive: Africa was caught halfway between the ancient and the new. The colonists bequeathed a confused society in transition, upon which it was hard to build. Perhaps it would have been better to be colonized properly, or not colonized at all.

Africa's rulers struggled with this legacy. On a whole string of questions, they faced the same dilemma that South Africa's black nationalists found in the land. Should they aspire immediately to European standards? Or should they protect the remnants of the precolonial past? A few of the continent's first leaders tried to strike a balance; they aspired to create a fusion of African tradition and modern ideas. Tanzania's Julius Nyerere proclaimed African socialism, though his view of what was African found little favor with African peasants. Zambia's Kenneth Kaunda founded African humanism, though the popular respect for Kaunda's grand sentiments declined as fast as Zambians' living standards. Kenya's first president, Jomo Kenyatta, who wrote a study of his Kikuyu people's traditions, was perhaps the most sensitive of all the early statesmen to African tradition. Most of the time, however, Africa's leaders were unapologetic modernizers. With their European schooling, they neglected primitive Africa, just as they favored the cities at the expense of the backward peasants on the land.

Africa's leaders have paid heavily for choosing to disdain tradition in favor of ambitious modernization. Their administrators in the villages tried to displace the chiefs rather than work with them; the result was that neither form of local government worked. Their doctors tried to displace the traditional healers rather than train them to hand out useful medicines; the result was that the doctors' sound prescriptions were drowned out by the healers' ignorant ones. A few governments tried to replace communal tenure with agricultural cooperatives or private holdings; the peasants resisted. Modernists did battle with traditionalists, rather than trying to reform them bit by bit. In the most extreme cases the battles developed, quite literally, into civil war.

In the last years of Northern Rhodesia, as Zambia was then called, a priestess named Alice Lenshina took on the transitional government (in which Kenneth Kaunda, the future president, was already a minister). Alice claimed to have died and been returned to earth by God; and her Church of the New Zion claimed sixty thousand worshippers. They were driven by the need to hunt down witches, a practice regarded as barbaric by both the government and the Roman Catholic Church. A traditional movement therefore collided with the modern state; and the traditionalists were so determined that they were prepared to fight the modern army. Alice promised that her spells would turn the soldiers' bullets into water. Actually seven hundred of her supporters died in the ensuing battles, and Alice herself was detained. A quarter of a century later, traditional rebellion remained very much alive. In 1987 another Alice emerged, this time in Uganda, promising that butter oil would protect her people against the army's bullets. Alice Lakwena's Holy Ghost movement marched under a standard of ritual fetishes; at its height it boasted some two thousand followers. The Holy Ghost fighters proved tougher opponents of President Yoweri Museveni's government than many of Uganda's other rebel bands.[9]

Africa's bigger post-independence bloodlettings are usually reported as ethnic feuds, stirred and manipulated by outsiders. The rebel armies in Angola and Mozambique got their soldiers from tribes that felt excluded by their governments; they got their weapons from South Africans and Americans, who disliked the governments' Marxism. This probably explains Southern Africa's civil wars as well as any single sentence; and yet at the same time the conflicts in Mozambique and Angola were about something else. Both were to some extent wars of modernization. After independence in 1975, Mozambique's government had declared that chiefs and spirit mediums had no place in the new socialist state. It rounded up hundreds of mediums and put them in reeducation camps; it transferred all local governmental powers to committees of the ruling party. The chiefs and spirit mediums therefore rallied to the rebels, taking a good number of their people with them; the insurgency grew more powerful and destructive than it might otherwise have been.

Angola's government was similarly dominated by modern-minded socialists, many of them born of unions between colonists and locals, which were common on Angola's coast. These mixed-race semi-Europeans had names to match their modern values: President dos Santos, Foreign Minister van Dunem, Education Minister Lopes Teixeira. By contrast, the rebel UNITA movement was made up of full-blooded Africans, led by a man named Savimbi. The government feared that UNITA was uncivilized because it burned witches and protected its men with charms. UNITA, for its part, called the government un-African. As in Mozambique, Angola's conflict was deepened by this clash with modernization.

African governments were certainly capable of learning from mistakes. By the early 1990s the wars in Mozambique and Angola were winding down, and Mozambique was trying to win back the support of traditional leaders. Next door the government in Zimbabwe also repented its earlier policy of sidelining the chiefs. It promised to reserve ten seats for chiefs in parliament; and it made some gestures in the direction of training traditional healers, rather than leaving them to misinform their patients. With a bit of instruction, after all, the healers could become useful; and since they paid for themselves by charging clients for their medicines, they would be cheaper than government nurses. The government therefore supported the Zimbabwe National Association of Traditional Healers, whose president, Gordon Chavunduka, bridged ancient and modern Africa neatly. When I visited him in 1990, he was also second-in-charge of Zimbabwe's nationalized industries; he was clever and elegant and believed witches should be dealt with sternly. Chavunduka ran workshops at which healers learned to prescribe sugar-salt solutions for diarrhea, and to avoid using the same razor blade to make incisions on different patients. This was more constructive than Mozambique's forced reeducation camps for mediums. The contrite Mozambicans sent a delegation to inspect Chavunduka's scheme in February 1990.

South Africans, too, could no doubt learn from their own mistakes; but it would be better to avoid them. Unfortunately the country's wealth and Western sophistication obscured traditional Africa; it made black leaders especially modern. Besides, apartheid had discredited the idea of deferring to tradition even more thoroughly than colonization had done elsewhere. Any suggestion that tribal practices should be allowed to adapt slowly smacked of the patronizing white attitudes of the past.

Although nineteenth-century imperialists justified their presence in Africa by modernization, they adopted a narrow view of whom modernity should serve. The British fostered an elite of African Englishmen, but they had neither the resources nor the philanthropic inclination to extend education to everyone. To justify the majority's exclusion, they talked of the dangers of giving blacks ideas above their station. In extreme cases, modernization was deliberately frustrated. To protect a fragile culture from the influence of Arab neighbors, Sudan's south was pronounced a "domain of social anthropology," and its subsistence economy was strictly defended against the cancer of economic progress. Plenty of Sudanese southerners still resent the British for treating their ancestors like museum exhibits rather than building them good schools.

White South Africans romanticized and promoted black backwardness still more, even while modernizing the economy. As blacks in the mines adopted Western habits, whites lamented the loss of their rural innocence. White writers, who had previously tended to ignore blacks, tried to capture the tragedy of modernization. In 1926 the novelist Sarah Gertrude Millin noted that "lately, the kaffir is being tentatively introduced" into white painting; around the same time Irma Stern was trying in her writing to reveal the "inner character" of Africans in their "natural environment."[10]

Fast economic development also spurred anthropologists to record African primitiveness before it was too late. They noted the impending change in black life-styles, but wrote up their research in a tense called the "ethnographic present," which encouraged some readers to believe that tribal people would behave forever the same way. The faster blacks flocked to the towns, the more writers such as Maurice Evans warned against the "breaking up of their present life, and with it of all standards of conduct and all the wholesome restraints to which they are accustomed". Ray Phillips, a Christian Welfare worker in the fast-industrializing area around the gold mines, wrote a book in 1930 entitled *The Bantu Are Coming*, in which he issued this dire warning:

All is ferment. In a generation the native people of this land are being compelled to bridge a gap which the white races have taken hundreds of years to cross. A native heathen father is sitting in his grass hut in the country, living his life and fearing his fears as did his ancestors before him. You ask him where his son is. "In Johannesburg." Today that son is in Johannesburg working as a motor-driver, piloting a high-powered motor-car through the thick of city traffic. Tonight this son will put on his correct evening clothes and spend the evening at one of the fashionable nightclubs. Tomorrow (Sunday) he may go to church, or he may listen attentively while the white agitator and his native assistants seek to arouse in him a spirit of revolt against the capitalist, the missionary, and the white labour leader.[12]

In the years between the two world wars South Africa's white rulers were at a loss to know what to do. They would have loved to halt the process of detribalization, but the officials who came into contact with blacks doubted it was possible. A certain Magistrate H. Britten, for example, told the Native Economic Commission that he naturally accepted the need to keep the tribal system going as long as possible. But he added, "Its breakdown is however inevitable and artificial attempts at retardation will be ineffective."[13] No such doubt disturbed the new National Party government that was elected in 1948. The Nationalists' determination to halt, in fact to reverse, black modernization far exceeded the British hostility to modernization in Sudan's south. The determination reached its high point in the 1960s with the scheme to send blacks to the homelands, those supposed reincarnations of their ancient tribal kingdoms: blacks were to give up their aspirations to be modern citizens of a modern state. Their education was designed (by the government's own admission) to prevent them from developing beyond menial roles. The Nationalists' propaganda stressed the futility of treating blacks like whites. "Traditional economics among the black peoples of South Africa is based on a subsistence rather than profit philosophy," said the government's official yearbook in 1985; Africans had no idea about doing things efficiently, because their subsistence philosophy excluded the ambition to produce more than they needed.

By exaggerating tribal differences, apartheid discredited all talk of tribalism. By exaggerating black backwardness, apartheid made it hard to recognize the power of traditional beliefs.

Apartheid made it particularly hard to accept that many rural blacks remained loyal to their chiefs, for the Nationalists had manipulated chiefs for their own ends. Here too they were following the British, who had done their best to bind Africa's chiefs into their own hierarchy of nobility. Lewanika of Barotseland, in what is now Zambia, attended the coronation of Edward VII in 1902: he was provided on his arrival with royal carriages; he attended tea parties with the Duchess of Abercorn. His hosts encouraged him to invest in an admiral's uniform for himself and scarlet coats for his servants, so that his court in Barotseland would acquire the right tone.[14]

The British were trying out in Africa the techniques of government that had worked well in India. In 1858 Lord Canning, the first viceroy of India, embarked on a journey through the northern states. It was the aftermath of the Indian mutiny against British rule, and Canning was intent on forestalling more of the same. At each settlement he called a "durbar," a term he had borrowed from the court rituals of the Mogul emperors. To these he summoned Indians who had refused to join the mutiny; he rewarded them with ancient Mogul titles (such as Raja, Nawab and Rai Sahib) and with special clothes and emblems, pensions and grants of land. Canning was trying to re-create the traditional system of leadership that had existed under the Moguls, with the difference that this time the chieflings would serve the British overlord instead.[15]

A century later Hendrik Verwoerd did very much the same. He became South Africa's minister of native affairs in October 1950, a position which under the law made him South Africa's most senior chief. "I am now actually the Great Induna," as he put it to his wife.[16] Verwoerd proceeded to visit African villages around the country, where he was received with traditional receptions fitting for a chief. The Great Induna and his underlings exchanged presents, and Verwoerd would then share a traditional meal of beer and porridge. The pageantry was both glorious and artificial, for the ceremonies had been revived on Verwoerd's orders after decades of disuse. In 1951 Verwoerd's Bantu Authorities Act replaced the European institutions that governed blacks with tribal authorities. The new administrators were chiefs, appointed and paid by the government. As in India, tradition and traditional leaders had been reinvented to serve white ends.

With salaries from the white state, chiefs ceased to answer to their people. The exceptions were deposed: Albert Luthuli, president of the ANC in the 1950s, was deprived of his chieftainship; Chief Edward Molotlegi, leader of the Bafokeng tribe, was forced into exile in 1988 after rebelling against Bophuthatswana's despotic homeland government. In the eyes of radicals, therefore, those who kept their chieftainships were collaborators; and many were flamboyantly corrupt. In the homeland of Gazankulu, the villages under Chief Joseph Manonsi were made to pay twenty rand per family toward the chief's new car; when the car crashed, they had to pay for the repairs.[17] In one district of what is now Lebowa, there were originally only five chiefs. By the 1980s there were more than fifty, each with his "appointment letter" from the white authorities. In black activist circles, "chief" became a synonym for "puppet."

All over Africa, the colonists manipulated chiefs; all over Africa, the chiefs' collaboration made them the first targets of black nationalists after independence. By the time of Nelson Mandela's release, South Africa's blacklash against chiefs had already started. ANC radicals railed against their hereditary privileges and called for a classless society. In imitation of attacks on black township councilors, the occasional group of homeland students would march on a chief's kraal. In 1990 the corrupt chiefs in the homeland of Ciskei were pushed aside by the Border Civics Congress, a pro-ANC group, which declared that henceforth it would exercise the chiefs' traditional functions. The people of Marapyane, a village in the homeland of Bophuthatswana, bought their chief a bus ticket and said, "OK! Now you can go and seek some other work."[18]

In the homeland of Venda, antiapartheid rallies featured the usual T-shirts—ANC slogans, trade union logos—but also some that demanded, "Stop Ritual Murders"; Venda's people were convinced that the chiefs had killed dozens of people for *muti* and had hired witches to turn others into zombies—mindless automatons who served them as slaves. A local branch of the antiapartheid United Democratic Front declared that Venda's young people were "totally convinced that by witch-hunting they are advancing the national democratic struggle." The *Weekly Mail* interviewed a resident of Thohoyandou, Venda's capital, who explained: "There is a feeling that once Mandela and the ANC is there, the witches will be snuffed out. . . . I say we should round up all the witches in Venda and take them to the stadium in Thohoyandou where they can all be shot."[19] Here was the backlash against traditional figures at its crudest. The coming of black rule would bring the triumph of modernity. Africa's backwardness would be vanquished by force.

The biggest backlash against chiefs had started in Natal. Like the civil wars in Mozambique and Angola, the ANC-Inkatha feud was in part a war of modernization. Chief Mangosuthu Buthelezi's Inkatha Freedom Party described itself during the 1980s as a Zulu "cultural movement," a guardian of tribal tradition. Buthelezi's enemies in the ANC hated to hear tribe mentioned. Naturally older Zulus, particularly the tribal chiefs, tended to support Inkatha; younger, urban Zulus tended to favor the ANC's modernism. Buthelezi and his ally, King Goodwill Zwelithini, played on the chiefs' fear that a future ANC government would turn on them. On holidays called to honor the memory of Shaka, the greatest of the Zulu warrior-kings, Buthelezi and Goodwill would appear before the chiefs in leopard skins. Their speeches would be introduced by *izimbongi*, praise poets who sing the martial achievements of the Zulu royal line, kindling the pride and blood-lust of the audience. Then King Goodwill would challenge his chiefs to prove their authority. What had happened to the traditional respect of young men for their elders? "Everything Zulu is being ridiculed. Our cultures are now being torn apart." The implication was that, to prove themselves worthy of their status, the chiefs should punish young ANC supporters for their uppity modernism.

When in 1990 the ANC-Inkatha battle spread to the townships around Johannesburg, people still seemed to divide on the issue of modernity. Well-educated township Zulus looked down upon Inkatha, with its appeal to chief and tribe. According to one such sophisticate, the Zulu journalist Nomavenda Mathiane, Inkatha was for poorer Zulus, such as those who lived in single-sex hostels and slept on concrete bunks. The hostel-dwellers proved Mathiane right by rallying to Inkatha, whereas the rest of the townships (which included a large number of Zulus) tended to remain loyal to the ANC. In the middle of the modern townships, Inkatha gangs killed their enemies with traditional Zulu spears.

South Africa had all the conditions for a destructive clash between tradition and modernity. Its black elite had embraced European ideas and standards. Its black majority was still drawn to African tradition. Apartheid had made it hard for the elite to treat tradition moderately. In some areas, the consequent battle had already started.

And yet there seemed a reasonable chance that here, at least, South Africa would defy the continent's sad precedents. In some of their statements, the ANC's radicals would denounce chiefs wholeheartedly; but a note of qualification usually crept in. In 1990 the ANC's workshop on land drew attention to "the need to denounce and scrap all the corrupt practices pertaining to chieftainship that have arisen in the course of our colonial history," as well as "the need to refrain from making any new laws which reserve a privileged position for chiefs and headmen." It declared that communities should in future elect their leaders, which sounded like a demand for a repeat of the mistakes made in Zimbabwe and Mozambique. But the report on the workshop also noted that some dissenting voices had spoken in the chiefs' defense. The following January, the day after unknown gunmen killed thirty-eight people in Sebokeng town-

179

ship, an ANC speaker delighted his audience by denouncing witch doctors and Inkatha in one breath: both, he said, should be exterminated. But the same rally displayed the ANC's respect for traditional symbolism: Oliver Tambo, the Congress's ailing president, was presented with a spear and shield, symbols of the ANC's guerrilla wing.

Dr. Ntatho Motlana is a thoroughly modern South African. He works in an airy clinic; his telephones bristle with special buttons; his body bristles with energy. He was detained with Winnie Mandela in 1969; he is the Mandela family physician. Every five minutes or so as I interview him, one of the telephones rings—"The bishop is sick? Ask him to come here! I can't come, I'm busy!"—and then he goes back to my questions. What, I wonder, does Dr. Motlana think about chiefs?

> I'll tell you. Throughout this continent, when the Nyereres, the Kaundas, the Mugabes were in the bush, they all knew that the clever British had used the chiefs in their policy of indirect rule. The chiefs were hated. . . . During the wars of liberation these people said they would abolish the chieftaincy. But they have continued to use chiefs in the same way as whites did. And that is absolutely shameful! If you ask my opinion, I would certainly say that we need to abolish the chief with his corruption and nepotism. He has no place in modern-day Africa. We need elected village committees. Chiefs are known among activists for what they are: lackeys of the system.

Motlana seemed true to his telephones and airy clinic: the first question about chiefs produced the stock condemnation. But the next questions produced something more complicated. Yes, there had been good chiefs: the ANC's Albert Luthuli had been the best of them. (Nelson Mandela also had chief's blood; but he had renounced his traditional rank as a young man, when he joined the modern struggle.) True, some chiefs were still respected: at college Motlana had shared rooms with Francis Matlala, a chief from the Bafokeng tribe. "Nobody in town regarded him as anything but a bloody student who drank too much. But people from the rural areas would come and pay tribute to him. *Kgosi*, they would call him, which means king." And yes, sometimes the respect was actually deserved, for the chiefs could be faithful servants of their people:

> Among my Tswana-speaking people the system has served us well. Chiefs are not despots. If there's an issue to decide, a *kgotla* is called, which a chief does not attend. The men of the village sit under the morula trees. Morula trees? Don't you know them? Those are the ones that produce fruits that drop to the ground and ferment and when the elephants eat them they get drunk. So the men sit under these trees and sit there until the agreement has been reached. The women bring them drink, but no beer—beer comes at the end of the whole thing. Then the chief is called in to announce the decision of the tribe. He is only a chairman.

The first instinct was to denounce chiefs; but many of the more thoughtful black leaders were willing to concede that chiefs could be constructive. Some ANC spokesmen carefully distinguished their attacks on Inkatha's use of tradition from their respect for tradition itself; thus the ANC journal, *Sechaba*, censured Buthelezi in 1984 with an article entitled "The Tradition Betrayed." The ANC's Constitutional Guidelines, published in 1988, included just four clauses on the shape of the future state. One was devoted to the need to democratize chiefs; this might presumably involve returning to the time remembered by Motlana, when chiefs deferred to the views of their counselors. After the Congress's unbanning, its officials went out of their way to address groups of local chiefs in remote villages. And since 1987 chiefs had started to join Contralesa, a pro-ANC organization that balanced the traditionalist appeal of Buthelezi's Inkatha. Buthelezi took unkindly to this rival; "a spear in the heart of the Zulu nation," he called it. But by 1991 Contralesa had won fifteen hundred chiefs over to the ANC camp. Among the converts was Prince Mcwayizeni Zulu, whose rank in the Zulu royal family was second only to the king.

Sampson Ndou, an ANC activist who helped to organize Contralesa, was wide awake to the dangers of a future black government ignoring the chiefs. "The traditional leaders is not something that you can wish it away by writing a clause in a constitution or a government gazette. The traditional leaders are there. They are a reality." Sampson Ndou weighed his words carefully, speaking slowly and watching as I wrote them down. "And I do not agree that they are all traitors. You cannot have a sector where all the people become traitors. It has not happened in the history of man." And he added, "If we do not organize them, somebody else will. And we will have in future our Renamos [the rebel army of Mozambique] and UNITAs. We won't have peace in South Africa with these people left out." Like Dr. Motlana, Sampson Ndou remembered a time before white manipulation, when chiefs were not the despots they subsequently became. *"Khosi ndi khosi ngavhathu,"* went the proverb of his Venda people: a chief cannot be a chief without his people; he owes his power to them.

If the ANC opted for the tactful modernization of the chieftaincy, there seemed every chance that the chiefs would cooperate. On my visit to KaNgwane I met an elderly chief called Eric Ngomane, who as a young man had done all he could to escape the responsibility of his high birth. He left his kraal to work in Johannesburg, and when his father died he ignored the messages to return to his village. His uncle was dispatched to fetch him. Ngomane escaped by moving to another township. The uncle searched for months until he found the young chief; then he dragged him away from the lights of the city, back to the duties to which he had been born. KaNgwane's more junior chiefs seemed even more attracted to the modern world. All had finished secondary school, and some had been to college. My guide introduced me to a younger Chief Ngomane—"He has grown only with his bones"—who had a big white sedan and natty trousers that changed color with the light. The younger Ngomane proudly showed me his offices, which comprised a study and a large auditorium which he used as his court. The study was equipped with a ceremonial spear, a smart Olivetti typewriter and a novel by Wilbur Smith.

Tactfully treated, both generations of Ngomane would welcome modernity. But my trip to KaNgwane also suggested the damage that might follow if the chiefs were provoked. Everyone I met seemed ready to support their traditional leaders in a confrontation with the modern state. The homeland's chief minister, Enos Mabuza, assured me over breakfast that KaNgwane's people identified much more closely with the chiefs than with the state. James and Petros, the two wealthy farmers, feared that a future ANC government would interfere with their farms. My guide, Gija Nyambi, to whom the chiefs had failed to grant any land, directed his anger at the coups and famines that had come with black governments elsewhere in Africa; and he railed against the disdain of South Africa's black politicians for the truly poor people who lived on the land. There were two kinds of apartheid, he told me. One divided black and white, the other divided countryside and town: "They get better services than we do, but we are all South Africans." As for Anna Sebiya, the healer and subsistence farmer, she had not heard of South Africa or F. W. de Klerk or Nelson Mandela; but she did know the name of her chief. If South Africa's future government mistreated them, KaNgwane's chiefs would start a new war of modernization with their people's support.

Contralesa's campaign to recruit chiefs to the ANC camp held out the hope of healing the division between traditional and modern leaders, between countryside and town. The campaign was supported by some of the ANC's most senior figures. The older Congress leaders remembered Chief Albert Luthuli. They recalled that the ANC's founders had seen nothing wrong in chiefs' privilege; "Chiefs of royal blood," began Pixley Seme, the ANC's founder, in his speech to the movement's inaugural meeting in 1912. But by no means did all ANC people set store by these memories. Most young activists saw chiefs as puppets. As with so many other issues, ANC opinion seemed to divide by generations. And in the first eighteen months after Nelson Mandela's release, the old guard seemed uncertain of its control over the young.

The clash between ancient and modern Africa turned on more than chiefs. South Africa's new government would have to contend with parallel legal and medical systems, not to mention the dilemma over communally owned land. The country's modern law courts were dominated by white lawyers and judges, who understood little about customary law. Yet customary law was widely practiced in the countryside, in courts like the large auditorium I was shown by the young chief I met in KaNgwane. Just as in the rest of Africa, disputes could arise between customary and modern law. Customary law regarded a dead man's brothers as heirs to his estate; Roman-Dutch law recognized the widow's claim. The ANC's legal spokespeople seemed uncertain which side they would favor. They professed respect for customary law; but they also cast themselves as champions of women's rights.

The ANC's policy toward traditional healers was equally vague. Like Zimbabwe, South Africa was full of medicine men who claimed to have a cure for AIDS. Professor Ruben Sher, South Africa's leading AIDS expert, received regular visits from such people. Some came with herbs; one swore he could overcome the virus with a rusty nail. Ignored, the healers would undermine the future government's efforts to control AIDS. Constructively harnessed, the healers constituted a ready-made army of primary health care workers. Unfortunately, traditional healers seemed to attract as much animosity as chiefs. Ntatho Motlana, that thoroughly modern doctor, had delivered lectures on "the tyranny of superstition." He denounced whites who romanticized herbalists. "All races of mankind," he told me, "have gone through the phase where they believed that disease was caused by ill will and that kind of bloody nonsense." Motlana ignored his telephone. Africa was passing through that stage as well, he continued, and it was not being helped by outsiders with the "racist attitude of locking my people into the tenth century, telling them to throw magic bones or dream. That kind of crap. Pseudo-psychological mumbo-jumbo. Makes me absolutely livid. Medicine is happening on computers now!"

Even the well-to-do Sowetans who came to Motlana's private clinic visited traditional healers too, and their advice undermined Motlana's. "A patient comes to me with cervical cancer. And I tell her that all she can do is have the mouth of her womb cut out. It is completely curable. And she says, no no no, I don't want to lose my womb. So she goes away and sees a traditional healer, who gives her herbs or something. And then months later she comes to me again. And by that time it is too late. That patient is going to die." I could understand why this made Motlana furious. But the question was what to do about the healers' damaging prescriptions. What did the modern doctor think about Mozambique's policy, as pursued by the country's first president, Samora Machel? "Samora Machel locked up all the charlatans . . . that's why I love Samora Machel! He just locked them up!" And what did Dr. Motlana think of Gordon Chavunduka, president of the Zimbabwean healers' association? "That man! He is absolutely dangerous!"

With luck, the ANC's old guard might prevail over the young radicals, forestalling further wars of modernization between the old order and the new. Judging by Motlana's outburst, a black-led government would be less likely to apply the same moderation to traditional courts and healers, or to forestall the confusion of dual systems that had troubled other African states. Beyond these questions, however, lay the hardest challenge of all. South Africa's new leaders would have to accept that economic progress is slow. Ancient Africa could not hope to share the living standards of modern Africa immediately. If the future government tried to bridge the economic gap between ancient and modern too quickly, it would hurt the very people whom it wanted to help.

At independence all over Africa, idealistic leaders aspired to European standards for their people. All over Africa, this ambition backfired. The new governments said thatched huts offended decent standards, so they built concrete tenements too expensive to maintain. They said companies should pay their people decently, so they made workers too expensive to employ. They paid out grand sums for grand industrial projects; they paid again for the white expatriates needed to make the factories run. In almost every area of policy, Africa's first independent rulers tried to make their countries look like Europe in the space of a single five-year plan. The first trouble with Africa's modernization was that it provoked traditionalists. The second trouble was that it was pursued too ambitiously, so that it almost always failed.

South Africa is especially vulnerable to this trap, because whites' conspicuous affluence has encouraged the idea that the country can afford European standards for everyone. Blacks want the gleaming schools, houses and hospitals that whites have had; they want the same job security; they want the same pay. Surely this could be achieved by abolishing apartheid? During the 1980s the white government lavished five times as much on the welfare of each white citizen as it did on each black (Indians and mixed-race people came in between). White old-age pensions were twice those for blacks. White state schools got four times as much per pupil as did black ones outside the homelands, and nine times as much as in the homeland of KwaZulu. Each white had four times as much spent on his or her health as non-homeland blacks did, and ten times as much as those in the homelands. The result of this lopsidedness was that, during the 1980s, some two hundred white schools were closed for want of pupils, while black classrooms overflowed. Until hospitals were desegregated in May 1990, Johannesburg's whites-only hospital had a thousand empty beds.[20]

Correcting this madness would appease blacks' sense of injustice, but it would hardly dent black needs. If the seventy-four hundred white classrooms empty in 1987 had been opened to blacks, just a fifth of the shortage in black schools would have disappeared. Besides, it takes more than buildings to educate people; many teachers in black schools were underqualified, especially in important subjects like mathematics. Equally, a few thousand extra hospital beds would not make blacks healthy. Various surveys suggested that a third of black children under fourteen were underweight and that half the rural black population suffered from chronic malnutrition.

Providing decent homes for blacks would be even harder. In 1990 the black housing shortage was said to come to 1.8 million units. Another 2.9 million housing units would be needed to accommodate the population growth expected by the turn of the century. Yet in 1988 the government managed to build just 1,300 new homes. Servicing the new houses would be as hard as building them. Two-thirds of Soweto's people had no running water; countrywide, more than four in five black households had no electricity.

The demands on the treasury would be bottomless. The future government could save some money by axing apartheid's parallel bureaucracies (different legislatures and ministries for each race group, not to mention the mini-ministries in each of the ten homelands). It might also save money by trimming the defense budget. Beyond that it would have to raise taxes, which might threaten the economic growth on which better living standards ultimately depend. In 1990 one South African academic suggested that it would cost 55 billion rand to bring black housing, health, education and pensions up to standards enjoyed by whites, meaning that taxes would have to rise from 27 percent to around half of South Africa's gross domestic product. The truth was that the new government would not be able to afford European standards for everyone. Like it or not, it was also true that if South Africa destroyed the comfort of the skilled minority, some of those skills would leave. The first post-apartheid government would have to accept that it could not bridge the gap between rich and poor immediately. It would have to accept that overambitious modernization backfires.

South Africa's white government already understood this. In the 1980s it had tried to improve black living standards, conscious that an angry underclass had nothing to lose from revolt. It had looked at the backlogs in housing and education, and had admitted that they could not be made good. Indeed, with the black population growing at 2.5 percent a year, it would be hard to prevent the backlogs from getting worse. The government therefore settled for unambitious modernization, aiming not at European standards for everyone but at tackling basic needs. Rather than building houses, the government installed running water and latrines. Rather than aim at proper jobs for everyone, it cut back the regulations which made it hard for jobless people to employ themselves. Backyard welders were no longer required to fill out endless safety forms; hawkers were no longer chased off the streets. Blacks were allowed to run minibuses in competition with the government bus company; by 1990 the Southern African Black Taxi Association comprised forty-nine thousand members, owned eighteen service stations and had even made a bid to take over its state-owned rival. The government made a great show of fostering black entrepreneurship. In 1988 President Botha ceremoniously presented three black hawkers in central Pretoria with hot-dog stands, and accepted a meal of *pap-en-vleis* (potato and meat) from another.

South Africa's black leaders found it altogether harder to adopt such pragmatism. They had fought for so long to get rid of apartheid; it was difficult to accept that political liberation would not necessarily bring economic liberation in its wake. Trained in Europe, the ANC's leaders cited with approval Sweden's welfare state. But Sweden's per capita gross domestic product was eight times South Africa's; and by 1990 even Sweden had decided that its welfare programs were more generous than its economy could sustain. Black trade unionists and politicians demanded a minimum wage. Unfortunately companies usually cope with higher wages by hiring fewer people; and already one in three black South Africans had no formal job. Likewise, most black leaders opposed the loosening of health and safety regulations that governed township businesses. Deregulation threatened trade unionists, who worked for big companies competing against township craftspeople; besides, black leaders resented the notion that township businesses need not stick to the same health and safety standards demanded by whites. Yet many hard-up black consumers were glad of cheaper goods and services, even if they were less safe or healthy; and many unemployed people in the townships would be glad of a backyard job. Black leaders favored regulation in the name of European standards. The truth was that European standards were unattainable. Many South Africans would get African jobs and African services or they would get nothing at all.

If South Africa's black leaders could accept this, they would be closer to avoiding the other traps of modernization that had plagued the rest of the continent. Recognizing that Africa would grow out of poverty slowly was akin to recognizing that there would be a gradual shift of loyalties from healer to doctor, from chief to government, from communal tenure to private ownership, from tribal to modern law. None of these shifts could be made to happen quickly. South Africa's first black-led government would have to continue installing running water and latrines in the townships, rather than building everyone a house. It would have to train village health workers rather than doctors; and the best candidates for basic health training would be the traditional healers. South Africa would have to accept different standards of legal qualification: in a country where the supply of education was limited, it made no sense to demand that routine legal problems be dealt with by university graduates. Modernization would have to be coaxed along with tact and sensitivity. It could not be made to happen in one great bound.

7

ACROSS THE BORDER

Suppose that South Africa had reached the point of political transition ten years earlier. It is the early 1980s. Angola and Mozambique, which won their independence from Portugal in 1975, are still in the grip of pro-Soviet rulers, as yet unhumbled by economic failure and ruinous civil war. Zimbabwe, independent since 1980, has elected a Marxist government too. Further afield, the Russians have recently invaded Afghanistan; and in Central America the pro-Soviet Sandinistas have consolidated their hold on Nicaragua since their revolution in 1979. The West's geopoliticians are worried. Communism has advanced steadily since its victory in Vietnam. American power has retreated, pushed back not just by communists but by Islamic fundamentalists as well. Iran's bearded mullahs have chased the pro-American shah out of the country; they have held the staff of the American embassy hostage; they are supporting and encouraging anti-American fundamentalists throughout the Middle East. Libya has become trainer and sponsor of guerrillas from the Palestine Liberation Organization, the Irish Republican Army, even the Moro National Liberation Front, an army of Muslim extremists from the south Philippines island of Mindanao.

To overcome their sense of weakness, the Americans have

elected Ronald Reagan, a president who promises to look communists and fundamentalists straight in the eye. Reagan is beefing up the United States' armed forces; he is deploying new missiles in Western Europe; he talks dreamily of his Strategic Defense Initiative ("Star Wars," his detractors call it), a scheme to make Americans safe forever by building an antinuclear shield over their heads. In the developing world, the United States does not shrink from sending the marines to control Lebanon's mayhem or from bombing Libya to punish it for terrorism. And, in the name of something called the "Reagan doctrine," America has started to supply weapons to far-flung rebels fighting communist regimes: the mujahedin in Afghanistan, the UNITA rebels in Angola and the "contras" in Nicaragua.

Now, imagine that South Africa is about to acquire a government dominated by the ANC, which is in turn led at least partly by communists. The strongest power in Africa is in danger of tipping to the Soviet Union, thus consolidating communism's hold in Angola, Zimbabwe and Mozambique. Those who believe in the domino theory of geopolitics fear that, if South Africa falls to communism, other countries in the region—Botswana, Zambia—will soon follow. This prospect is unsettling. An alliance of the Soviet Union and Southern Africa would control an alarming proportion of the world's minerals. It would account for 22 percent of its diamond production and 40 percent of its gold production;[1] and it would dominate world markets in several "strategic" minerals (particularly chromium, platinum, palladium and rhodium),[2] on which the world depends to make environmentally friendly attachments for car exhausts and a variety of special steels. A minerals cartel involving the Soviet Union and South Africa could threaten the health of Western industry as acutely as does OPEC, the oil cartel led by Saudi Arabia.

The hard men in the Reagan administration, who have successfully argued for the support of anticommunist fighters in Afghanistan and Nicaragua, declare that an ANC takeover in South Africa is unthinkable: it must be blocked by force. Liber-

191

als plead that an ANC government would include democrats as well as communists; but their entreaties have already been ignored in the case of Nicaragua, where the early Sandinista cabinets included moderates as well. Besides, South Africa has an excellent candidate for support under the Reagan doctrine, a man cleverer and more presentable than most of Nicaragua's contra leaders, and infinitely more so than the Islamic fundamentalists of Afghanistan's mujahedin. That man is Chief Mangosuthu Buthelezi, who has visited Ronald Reagan at the White House, and who denounces communism and revolution whenever the opportunity arises.

It is not difficult to imagine that, if South Africa's transition had occurred a decade earlier, the ANC-Inkatha fighting might have turned into an outpost of the Cold War, with Russians and Americans backing their local friends. Instead, South Africa's white government survived into the 1990s, by which time geopoliticians scarcely worried about whether the new rulers would be pro-Soviet or not. The disintegrating Soviet Union seemed pitiful, not threatening; Africa's onetime Marxists were promising elections and bidding hard for Western aid. In 1991 Angola's pro-Soviet government made peace with Jonas Savimbi, the rebel commander whom President Reagan had backed. Zimbabwe's self-proclaimed Marxist leader, Robert Mugabe, quietly shelved his plans for a one-party state. In Ethiopia President Mengistu Haile Mariam, who had long been propped up by the Soviet Union and its allies, gave up the unequal struggle against three separate rebel armies and fled. There was no longer the remotest danger that the Soviets might grab control of the continent. If the ANC's communist wing did come to command South Africa's future government, plenty of people would fear for South Africa's economy. But not even a full-scale communist takeover in South Africa would provoke intervention from the outside world.

Yet South Africa would always be a worthwhile ally. The rich world has no interest in alienating a country which, besides its strategic minerals, is the key to a subcontinent. South Africa's ports and arms and industry dominate the southern half of Africa. In 1987 its gross domestic product was fifteen times as big as Zimbabwe's, fifty times as big as Mozambique's; in all black Africa, only Nigeria came near to it. Eskom, South Africa's electricity company, generated 60 percent of the power on the continent. Countries as far to the north as Zaire and Malawi were forced to trade through South Africa's ports, not least because South African-backed rebels had sabotaged rival routes to the ports of Angola and Mozambique. Economics and logistics made South Africa the natural base for multinational companies in the region; the rich world's business leaders would expect their governments to cultivate good relations with South Africa, so that their commercial interests could be protected and furthered. Besides, if the rich world wanted to save Africa from hopelessness, it would have to do its best to keep the continent's most dynamic economy afloat. A prosperous South Africa might pull its neighbors up with it. A stagnant South Africa would leave Africa's well-wishers without a single success story to sustain their morale. For the sake of its interests and its conscience, the rich world would give South Africa aid.

Besides, the end of the Cold War did not mean the end of conflict, as was proved by the war over Kuwait. Iraq's dictator, Saddam Hussein, showed by invading that country that regional powers could create nasty problems for developed countries, particularly if they presided over bits of the world blessed with strategic minerals. It took the most sophisticated bombing campaign in military history to free Kuwait. South Africa's army hardly matched Iraq's war machine; but it was strong enough to overshadow Southern Africa. Its 250 tanks compared with Zimbabwe's 43 and Zambia's 60;[3] the South Africans had repeatedly demonstrated the reach of their army with raids on the neighboring states. South Africa's future rulers were likely to cut the defense budget; but the army's regional dominance seemed certain to continue. The West had no interest in provoking the government that commanded the strongest army in this region full of minerals, not to mention Western companies and aid.

South Africa's ability to harm the West's interests extended beyond the size of its army. In a world increasingly threatened by terrorism, let alone the prospect of more Saddam Husseins, the West sought to control the behavior of arms-making countries, lest they equip extremists with ever more lethal devices. Since 1977, when the United Nations prohibited them from importing weapons, the South Africans had doggedly built up a weapons industry of their own. Indeed, in 1987 South Africa's defense minister called the arms embargo "a blessing in disguise": it had caused the development of Armscor, South Africa's state-owned weapons manufacturer, which employed twenty-three thousand people and exported 1.8 billion rand worth of weapons a year.[4] Armscor made everything from rifles to armored personnel carriers; in 1991 it unveiled its first helicopter gunship.

Armscor's ability to damage Western interests was demonstrated by the case of the G-5, one of the world's best long-range guns. Gerald Bull, the G-5's Canadian inventor, had designed the gun for the American army in the mid-1970s. The Americans never used his blueprint, partly because of budget cuts and partly because they believed that a new generation of missiles made long-range artillery unnecessary. Bull therefore sold his design to the South Africans, who soon produced the G-5 for their war in Angola (it was not only the Americans who supported Angola's rebels against the Marxist government). South Africa exported the gun as well; a noted customer was none other than Saddam Hussein. Saddam so approved of the weapon (or so the intelligence gossips had it) that he commissioned Bull to build an even bigger version. In March 1990 Bull was mysteriously assassinated. Two weeks later the British authorities seized some suspicious pipes: they appeared to be parts of a vast gun barrel, and they were en route to Iraq. Iraq claimed the material was to be used in its oil fields. After the Gulf War, in August 1991, inspectors from the United Nations visited the country. Hidden in the mountains of northern Iraq, they found a gun with a barrel some 160 feet long.

Then there was the small matter of South Africa's nuclear

program. In July 1991 South Africa formally renounced nuclear weapons by signing the Nuclear Non-Proliferation Treaty, opening its nuclear facilities to inspection by foreign teams. The precise state of the country's nuclear research until then had been secret; the South Africans were happy to let others believe that they might possess the bomb. Such evidence as did exist suggested that South Africa's nuclear program had made considerable progress. A Central Intelligence Agency document, written in 1979 and obtained through the United States' Freedom of Information Act, estimated that South Africa "has by this time acquired sufficient fissile material for the fabrication of several nuclear devices."

According to the Natural Resources Defense Council, the lobbying group which obtained this document, South Africa's nuclear preparedness made a mockery of its new willingness to sign the Non-Proliferation Treaty: South Africa's signature would not take away its ability to construct a nuclear weapon at short notice. As the CIA put it in another document in 1980: "Once a ready weapons capability is assured, Pretoria may well be willing to sign the NPT or at least accept international safeguards." And: "Even if Pretoria placed all nuclear production facilities under international safeguards, for example, foreign specialists would reason that a previously amassed secret stockpile of weapons-grade uranium probably was being maintained."[5]

A near-nuclear power, sitting on one of the world's richest stocks of minerals, dominating a subcontinent: South Africa would never be entirely forgotten by the world. Black politicians in the U.S. Congress would ensure that post-apartheid South Africa received reasonably generous American aid. Some of Japan's growing aid budget would no doubt find its way to South Africa too. The European Community, for its part, increased its aid to South Africa from 80 million to 200 million rand in 1991. Among Western nations, however, Britain was perhaps South Africa's most natural friend. Britain had been the colonial power; and after apartheid South Africa was expected to rejoin the Commonwealth, from which it had been ejected in 1961.

English was the nearest thing South Africans had to a national language; as many as a million white South Africans held British passports. With 170 companies in South Africa at the end of 1990,[6] the British were by far the biggest investors too (though Germany, Japan and the United States were more important trading partners). Besides, the British government was less preoccupied elsewhere than those of most other powerful countries. It was less engrossed in the opening up of Eastern Europe than other European powers, especially Germany. It did not share America's preoccupation with the newly prosperous countries of East Asia. As a result, Southern Africa was still relatively untouched by the general ebb of British power.

At times it seemed as though ANC radicals might rebuff British friendship. Some older members of the Congress still remembered Britain as the opponent of Hitler's racism, but the fresher memories were of Britain under Margaret Thatcher, who had done her best to alienate the ANC. In the mid-1980s, as South Africa's police crackdown swelled the indignation of Western television audiences, Mrs. Thatcher enjoyed being different. She scorned the Congress's arguments for sanctions, saying that they would merely lower black living standards and resisting their imposition both by the Commonwealth and by the European Community. She denounced the ANC's armed struggle as terrorism, even though the Congress normally avoided harming South African civilians. She praised President P. W. Botha's limited reforms. Mrs. Thatcher seemed to see the Afrikaner government rather as she saw herself: an obstinate people who championed order against communism, defying self-righteous liberal protest. The ANC hated her for it.

When I first visited South Africa, in 1987, black politicians almost invariably interrupted my questions to deliver a diatribe against Thatcher and Reagan, anticommunists who had sided with white rule. But America's image among black South Africans had improved slightly in 1986, when the U.S. Congress defied President Reagan and imposed the tough package of sanctions laid down in the Comprehensive Anti-apartheid Act. Britain underwent no such redeeming revolt against its premier; it consistently resisted other countries' calls for stiffer sanctions. After Mandela's release, Britain led the movement within the European Community to lift restrictions on trade and new investment, ignoring the ANC's pleas that they should be retained until after the coming constitutional negotiations.

In May 1991 Mrs. Thatcher, by then no longer prime minister, visited South Africa as a guest of President De Klerk. Whites received her as a heroine. They granted her the freedom of the city of Johannesburg; a farmers' association named a fruit after her; Pik Botha, the foreign minister, greeted her at the airport with a rose. The ANC snarled that Margaret Thatcher's visit "reminds us of those dark apartheid days when the regime could continue violating human rights knowing fully well that it had the support of such people internationally." Mrs. Thatcher was nothing less than "the accomplice of the enemy of humanity."

Yet the promised demonstrations against Mrs. Thatcher's visit turned out to be restrained; and Nelson Mandela thought it worth spending forty minutes on the telephone with her. Despite their resentment of Britain's stance on sanctions, black South Africans' respect for the country appeared considerable. The paradox was illustrated in the person of Sir Robin Renwick, Britain's ambassador to Pretoria since 1987. Renwick denounced sanctions and extremist black leaders bluntly. He was on remarkably good terms with the National Party, even when it was led by the autocratic P. W. Botha: "Renwick is almost a member of the cabinet," as one South African journalist put it. Yet none of this prevented Renwick from maintaining contact with the ANC after its unbanning, or from inviting its leaders to dinner to meet members of the far-right Conservative Party. His farewell party, in 1991, featured Nelson and Winnie Mandela, among others.

In the end, the ANC leaders would forget their distaste for Mrs. Thatcher and would welcome British investment and aid. The same would surely be true of relations with other rich countries. When Nelson Mandela visited Japan in 1990, he condemned the country's "absolutely insignificant" contribution to his people's struggle. Equally, America's CIA was said to have supplied the white police with the tip-off that led to Mandela's arrest in 1962; and President Ronald Reagan had joined Margaret Thatcher in opposing economic sanctions. Yet there was little doubt that, if Japanese aid began to flow, the past would soon be forgiven. And in 1990 New York City feted Nelson and Winnie Mandela with a ticker-tape parade, the highest and messiest honor known to the city; Mrs. Mandela spoke emotionally of how much she had adored it.

Although it was clear that the West would not forget South Africa, and that South Africa's new government would not rebuff the West, few South Africans were content to see their future foreign policy purely in terms of the world's rich nations. Even if South Africa could look forward to some aid, it was also true that the rich world would devote more money and attention to Eastern Europe. Now that there was no danger of losing the Cold War to the Soviets, one of the arguments for aid to Africa had disappeared. The Europeans and North Americans were building free-trade areas within their continents; they showed little inclination to open their markets to exports from developing nations.

South Africans therefore felt the need for foreign friends outside the rich world. One promising area was Eastern Europe, whose people might prove good customers for South African products, which were less sophisticated but cheaper than the equivalents from the West. Most frequently, however, South Africans talked of developing their links with the rest of their own continent. "South Africa's destiny is inextricably linked to that of its neighbours," said Neil van Heerden, South Africa's chief diplomat.[7] "In our part of Africa, South Africa has an important role to play," said President De Klerk, after a meeting with King Hassan II of Morocco in 1990. "We must move nearer to each other. There must now be closer economic links. We must become a fully fledged economic region."[8] It was a theme De Klerk returned to on all his trips abroad.

Optimistic South Africans set great store by this vision. Neil van Heerden painted a picture of a reborn region, with South Africa free of the stigma of apartheid, with peace in Angola and Mozambique: "If we can stop these wars, our part of the continent can take off."[9] That takeoff would involve growing trade within the region, now that apartheid and the barriers of sanctions were falling away. South Africans made much of the fact that their products were designed for Africa's climate and conditions, as well as for its poverty; South African industry still churned out things that Europeans had forgotten—coal-fired stoves, stove-heated irons, battery-operated televisions. South Africans boasted that their salespeople knew how to do business on the continent; and that they could serve their customers more easily than Europeans, whose headquarters and warehouses were farther away. Perhaps South Africa's big companies might even invest across the border, and succeed where European businesses had failed. The optimists had a point. It was true that foreign investors did not always under-stand the continent; and that South Africa enjoyed the advan-tage of shorter lines of communication and supply. But it was also true that business is tough in Africa, however experienced you are.

The story of Lonrho, the most celebrated British company to have stuck it out in Africa, shows how important it is to understand the rules of the continent, and how hard it is to make money even so. Lonrho was originally short for the Lon-don and Rhodesian Mining and Land Company; its managers were African specialists from the start. In 1962 "Tiny" Rowland took over its leadership, at a time when many British investors were retreating from Africa along with British colonial rule. Rowland was not a typical British businessman. He had been born in India of German parents; throughout his successful life he bore an outsider's grudge against the British establishment, blaming it, among other things, for frustrating his ambition to control Harrods, London's grandest store. As other companies left Africa, Rowland chose instead to diversify Lonrho's interests northward from its base in Rhodesia (and, more discreetly, into South Africa as well).

Lonrho flourished, but only by employing some unusual tactics. Other foreign companies feared nationalization. Rowland insured himself against this calamity by becoming the nationalizers' personal friend. Wherever he did business in Africa, Tiny Rowland made a point of getting to know the president. Rowland flattered the leader and won his confidence; he gave him courtesy rides in the Lonrho jet. In various countries Lonrho owned a local newspaper, which made the flattery especially effective. Presidents Kaunda of Zambia, Banda of Malawi and Moi of Kenya came to know and trust Rowland, who would fly from one palace to another, bringing news to each leader of what the last had said. The Rowland charm also worked well on leaders whom misfortune had befallen, or who had not yet made it to the top. Thus Rowland befriended Nigeria's federal government in the late 1960s, when it was fighting its war against the Biafran secessionists, whom several governments and corporations had chosen to back. Likewise, Rowland befriended Uganda's future president, Yoweri Museveni, when he was still a guerrilla leader in the bush. Both the Nigerians and Museveni later repaid Rowland for his support in hard times.

Other foreign investors despaired at Africa's instability. Rowland saw it as an opportunity and a challenge. He disliked Rhodesia's war of independence, for it disrupted Lonrho's mines and farms. He also disliked white rule in Rhodesia, for white rule meant economic sanctions, which blocked off the oil pipeline that connects Rhodesia with the Mozambican coastline—and Lonrho owned the pipeline. Rowland therefore promoted the replacement of white rule in Rhodesia with black rule and peace. He supported Joshua Nkomo, one of the two guerrilla leaders, who later said in his autobiography that he trusted Rowland like "a son-in-law." Rowland also flew Rhodesia's white prime minister, Ian Smith, to peace talks in Zambia in 1977 and 1978.

In 1971, in the same spirit of business and history-making, Rowland had helped to restore General Jaafar Numeiri, a friend of his, to power in Sudan: when a group of communist officers took advantage of the defense minister's absence in Yugoslavia to stage a coup against Numeiri, the Lonrho executive jet was rolled out to fly the minister home.[10] This timely help naturally increased Rowland's standing in Sudan, which he hoped to use as a bridge between his investments in Africa and his ambitions in the Middle East. Unfortunately Lonrho's main project in Sudan, a vastly overambitious sugar plantation, was located in the country's south, where civil war made agriculture difficult. In 1984 Rowland therefore tried to do Numeiri another favor by organizing peace talks with the rebels. That effort failed; Numeiri fell from power again, but Rowland remained friends with the rebels nonetheless.

Mozambique, torn by civil war and famine, was full of the adversity on which Rowland thrived. When I went there in March 1990, the country seemed incapable of sinking lower. The fighting between the government and Renamo, as the rebel army was called, had spread to every corner of the country. Half Mozambique's 15 million people were short of food; 1 million had fled abroad. The rebels specialized in gratuitous brutality: they forced children to execute their parents; they sliced off ears and noses. With an annual income per capita of $100, Mozambique's people were the poorest in the world. The government had bravely embarked on an economic reform program in the midst of this mayhem. With the help of the World Bank, it was doing its best to persuade businesses to invest in the country, to create local wealth and jobs. Not surprisingly, few foreigners were anxious to invest in a war zone. Lonrho was undeterred.

There was a power cut the day I visited Lonrho's office in Maputo, capital of Mozambique. In fact there were power cuts most days, because Renamo had taken to blowing up the power lines that fed the city. I walked up several flights of stairs in the dark (the elevator ran on electricity), sweating in the humidity. When I got to the top I found an atmosphere of perfect composure: Lonrho's office took power cuts in its stride. The company had installed a small standby generator; the lights were on; so was the air-conditioning. John Hewlett, the local manager, was giving instructions for two people to visit one of Lonrho's nearby farms; they would go in a company aircraft, since the threat of a Renamo ambush made the roads too risky. Hewlett wore a pink button-down shirt, a loud tie and checked trousers. He had the roguish good looks of Michael Caine in one of his roles as a master criminal. He seemed to revel in his job.

Hewlett summoned me into his office, where we sat on either side of his considerable desk. That farm, he said, was damned profitable; but it took some defending. I looked at him inquiringly. "Last weekend our new irrigation equipment was attacked. Friday night and Saturday night. Renamo wasn't looking for food. It wanted to blow up the irrigation equipment." He picked up a pack of photographs and started dealing them at me across the desk. "See those guys," he said, pointing at two dead security guards; "they were ours, but they went down fighting." Other photographs showed some senior Mozambican politicians visiting the cotton fields; it went without saying that Lonrho dealt with the top people in the government. On President Chissano's recent visit to London, I was told, he had of course called upon Tiny Rowland; Hewlett gave the impression that Chissano's meeting with Margaret Thatcher had been almost incidental. Yes, it was possible to make money in Mozambique, but it took guts and a special kind of character. "I came out here five years ago," said Hewlett, "with nothing but a briefcase and a pat on the back from Tiny." Now Lonrho's Mozambican farms were earning 1 billion meticais ($1.3 million) a year, even though the company had to pay for a private army to defend them. And Hewlett was moving into new areas, refurbishing a hotel, securing an automobile distributorship. He had even started prospecting for gold.

* * *

Not all South African companies would relish this style of doing business, however well placed they apparently were to sell to the African market. South Africans who talked optimistically about their future trade with black Africa usually pinned their hopes on the example of one company. The Premier Group's products made it a natural exporter to Africa. It sold staple foods like bread and cornmeal, as well as cheap cosmetics; "Ninety percent of our products go into black tummies or onto black faces," said Peter Wrighton, the company's chairman. Premier was known to be trading on the continent despite its wars and poverty, and despite African leaders' public calls for sanctions against apartheid. Nobody was quite sure how much African business Premier was doing, for the company kept a low profile: it had no wish to embarrass its pro-sanctions African clients by publicizing their double standards. Since Mandela's release, however, the atmosphere had changed. When I met Wrighton in late 1990, he seemed happy to talk about his African operation. He even offered to show it to me. So in April 1991 I boarded Premier's company jet in Johannesburg and set off to see how rewarding African trade could be.

I was taken to Mozambique, Malawi, Zambia and Zaire. At each stop the plane delivered a few South African comforts to Premier's local managers: Johannesburg newspapers, frozen milk, cans of insect spray. At each place I learned a little more about business in African conditions. Zaire and Mozambique presented the most extreme challenges. In Lubumbashi, capital of Shaba province in southern Zaire, the local Premier manager never ventured out without "*quelques millions*" of the devalued currency. These might be needed to pay off marauding policemen or officials; Zaire was the only country, he joked, where the gangsters have a uniform. The Zaire operation had also to contend with telephones that were bad even by African standards; the Premier man sometimes went for weeks without being able to contact the Johannesburg headquarters. This made it all but impossible to run a trading operation: Premier's shop in Lubumbashi was supposed to stock everything from flour to beer to secondhand clothes, which came in huge, multi-colored bundles all the way from New York. Without decent telephones, Premier could not order new supplies when stock ran low. Premier's frustrations had driven its executives to consider investing in a private satellite link between Lubumbashi and Johannesburg. In the view of the hard-pressed Lubumbashi manager, it would be money well spent.

With Zaire's currency losing value by the day, it was important to convert Premier's local earnings into dollars quickly. The trouble was that the best exchange rate was to be had in the capital, Kinshasa, some thousand miles to the northwest. Twice a week, therefore, Premier's shop in Lubumbashi loaded trolleys full of banknotes onto an aircraft bound for Kinshasa, where they were collected by an agent with the right sort of contacts. Premier also had to contend with the tricky question of smuggling. As part of its policy of winning the trust of local governments, Premier did pay import duty. This put it at a disadvantage against Lubumbashi's Greek and Lebanese merchants, who were evidently less scrupulous. The city's shops were stacked high with gleaming televisions, stereos and cameras, all at knock-down prices; one offered half a dozen different types of video recorder; Laura Ashley fabric went for about $3 a yard. Lubumbashi's senior customs officials received only meager civil-service salaries. Somehow or other they lived remarkably well.

In Mozambique the main problem was the war. The trucks that delivered Premier's food to Maputo were frequently ambushed. At the time of my visit, one driver was killed in the same place where his brother had been killed two years previously; witchcraft was suspected. Besides importing food into Mozambique, Premier had a contract to manage the state-owned chicken farms. War had destroyed most of Mozambique's agriculture, so it was hard to find local corn from which to make the chicken feed. When I visited Premier's feed factory in Maputo, I found that it was using sacks of Texan food aid, which might otherwise have relieved the hunger of Mozambique's peasants. Hunger drove the peasants to steal Premier's chickens, so Premier's farms were guarded by armed men; in fact security guards made up one in ten of the chicken farm's employees. The machinery at the slaughterhouse was decades old and broke down constantly. The manager complained particularly about his ice-maker: whenever it gave out he lost his entire stock of carcasses to the African sun. In 1980 a complete set of new machines—from scalder to plucker to freezer—had been delivered by the Danish government. A decade later the equipment rotted in crates in the slaughterhouse yard, unopened because of some obscure argument between the Danish and the Mozambican governments.

Malawi was uncomplicated. It was a poor country with not much to spend on Premier's products; but it was pretty well free of corruption. Like Mozambique and Zaire, Malawi was unembarrassed at trading with South Africa. In Zambia, by contrast, the sanctions campaign had until recently obliged Premier to pose as a British company. Its people had London addresses on their business cards; faxes from Johannesburg came via an office in London to protect the Zambians' sensibilities. Somehow these sensibilities had not prevented Premier from managing Zambia's state-owned mills for a period, or from running a warehouse in the northern town of Kitwe, or indeed from exporting to Zambia raw materials for the country's chicken industry.

Premier's ability to do business in Zambia owed much to the nerve of Albert Nelissen, the Belgian chairman of Premier's international division. Nelissen first went to Zambia in the early 1980s, when the Zambian government officially disapproved of contact with South Africa. Whites from South Africa were not allowed in. But Nelissen knew a black South African who knew some powerful Zambians, and he set off without a visa. When he arrived in Lusaka, Zambian officials were there to meet him. The next day he met President Kenneth Kaunda. The meeting went off famously: like Tiny Rowland, Nelissen had a way of charming presidents. Kaunda invited Nelissen back; on his second visit he was accompanied by Tony Bloom, then the

Premier Group's chairman. From then on Nelissen was welcome in Zambia. He would fly to Lusaka regularly in the Premier jet, often bringing with him a crate of champagne. He would hire a suite in the Intercontinental Hotel and stack his champagne in the refrigerator. As visitors started to arrive, the bottles would start to emerge. Albert Nelissen would stay up into the small hours in his suite in the Intercon, doing deals with his African friends.

Like Lonrho, Premier went to great lengths to win the loyalty of senior politicians. On one of his visits to Zambia, Tony Bloom was asked by a cabinet minister if he could help with a little problem. Christmas was coming, and Zambia was short of wine. Bloom phoned his deputy in Johannesburg and told him to arrange things. The wine was duly flown to Lusaka airport, and the minister in question was informed. Unfortunately the minister did not have the ear of the customs officials. Worse, his political rivals did have their ear, and were determined to use the wine to humiliate him. The scandal was leaked to the local papers. There were unpleasant banner headlines. For days on end the wine stayed on the tarmac, festering in the sun and the tropical rain.

In the late 1980s Albert Nelissen got a call from Zaire: President Mobutu Sese Seko wanted urgently to see him. Nelissen got into the Premier jet and flew halfway up Africa. Mobutu explained his problem. His new palace in Gbadolite, the village of his birth, was nearly complete. It had marble façades, crystal chandeliers and a runway long enough to accommodate the presidential Concorde. But it did not yet have a garden: please could Premier see to it? Mobutu stipulated that his garden should be in flower at Christmas, which was just a month or so away. Nelissen returned to Johannesburg. He bought 2 million rand worth of flowers. He hired several aircraft. A ready-made garden was dispatched into the middle of Africa, complete with gardeners to replace the Zairean bush with flower beds. Everything was to President Mobutu's satisfaction; but then he was taken by another fancy. He wanted a chicken farm. Nelissen had little choice. After all, Premier knew considerably more about poultry than about landscape gardening.

Another convoy of aircraft, this time carrying hens and coops, flew across the continent. Everything went according to plan: the bush was cleared away; the coops were set up; Premier even installed a smart new slaughterhouse, replete with machinery that would have made the Mozambicans jealous. When everything had been put in place there emerged one irritating problem. The hens were not laying. Different Premier managers gave me different versions of this story: some claimed that the hens had been traumatized by the experience of air travel; some said they were given the wrong feed. Whatever the truth, something had to be done. Christmas was coming. The president was expecting some distinguished guests; he must have a poultry farm to show them. So Premier sent one more plane north into Africa. It was loaded with eggs, one to be tucked under each chicken. "A European company," said Peter Wrighton, "would never have done that."

As my trip with Premier proceeded, the character of Albert Nelissen became its main fascination. The legends that surrounded him suggested an uncanny gift for inspiring trust and confidence: President Kaunda made him welcome in Zambia, President Mobutu confided in him the most sensitive of business. Even before he led Premier into Africa, Nelissen had had a special way with customers. People who remembered his days as manager of Premier's marketing in Natal claimed that he outwitted rival sales people in valley after valley. He was said to be a master of the road show, a technique which worked on the principle that every cluster of villages had a choir, a football team and a troupe of traditional dancers. Premier would arrive in a remote area and announce that it would set up a stage and a sound system. It would be the first time that the choir's singing had been amplified, or that the dance troupe could perform on a proper stage. On the appointed date, thousands of people would come from all over the countryside. They would sit on the ground and watch their cousins performing—on a stage decorated with Premier brand names. The festival would last until sundown and sometimes the next day.

Another Nelissen technique began with a visit to a school. The Premier salesman would ask to see the headmaster. He would promise him a set of new blackboards, a soccer field or whatever he most needed—in exchange for a large number of empty Premier corn bags. The headmaster would go to his children and tell them to make sure that their families bought only Premier corn. The scheme worked miraculously. Whole valleys were cleared of the opposition's brand name. Nelissen's marketing assaults also included parties. There would be a big bonfire, a couple of sheep on spits and a generous supply of alcohol. Nelissen would drink with the best of them, with the chiefs and the elders and the owners of the local shops. At the end of the evening, when the mood of drunken fellowship was at it warmest, Nelissen would rise to speak. He was a friend of this community. Premier was a friend of this community. He and Premier would look after them, supplying all the corn that they could possibly need. All he wanted in return was a bit of loyalty. Sure enough, Premier's food would displace its rivals in that valley's shops.

These, at least, were the stories told of Nelissen. (Later, in Johannesburg, I asked him about them. He grinned rather naughtily and admitted to "some funny tactics.") The subsequent African adventures were clearly in character. But the African exploits had the extra fascination of moral ambiguity. Nelissen was hobnobbing energetically with the likes of President Mobutu, whose personal fortune was reputedly as big as Zaire's $8 billion national debt. And Nelissen was selling food to Africa in order to make money; the bigger his profit margin, the less his impoverished customers would eat.

Yet Africa was better off with profit-seeking suppliers than with no suppliers. Africa was better off with business leaders who humored its autocrats than with business leaders who shunned it. It was hard to condemn a company prepared to risk its cash in Africa, which was crying out for all the trade and investment it could get. Indeed, in the mid-1980s Premier's managers were seen by enlightened Mozambicans as heroes: they delivered millions of rand worth of stock to Maputo, at a time when South Africa's armed forces were blowing up ships in the city's port. The Mozambican government could have seized Premier's assets in retaliation; Premier's warehouses could have been attacked by armed gangs. Premier took the risk anyway. It was this kind of gesture that won Albert Nelissen his friends in Africa.

I eventually met Nelissen in Lubumbashi. He arrived at the airport in the Premier jet, which had delivered me to the city earlier that day. A Premier jeep and a Premier minibus drove up to the plane as it waited on the tarmac; the token customs and immigration officials did not even try to make these vehicles wait in the parking lot outside. Half a dozen Premier employees got out and prepared to meet their boss. I got out too, and stood in the warmth of an African evening, watching a big bear of a man squeeze through the jet door and steady himself on its steps. Nelissen shook hands with his reception committee, grinning and grunting at each one. Then he handed his passport to a Zairean, a man retained by Premier for his expert knowledge of airport officials and how much each must be paid. Nelissen boarded the jeep. The convoy drove into Lubumbashi, leaving the passport expert to transact his delicate work.

The party reassembled over supper. Even by African standards, the luxury of Lubumbashi's restaurants contrasts impressively with the poverty all around. The mussels and frogs' legs are flown in from Europe; so are the cheeses and the ample choice of wine. Nelissen sat at the head of the table, grinning and grunting at his band of followers, tucking his food into his heavy cheeks. He spoke only occasionally, with a thick Belgian accent and a watery lisp. I sat next to him and tried to get him to talk about his African exploits. He was easily drawn into defending the morality of his position in Africa, which he did mainly by attacking all the other white intruders who had done the continent down. He railed against rapacious colonists, against ineffectual Western aid donors and especially against "briefcase salesmen," a breed of slippery traders who swarmed across the continent, defrauding the poor Africans of their meager wealth. Nelissen denounced the Greek and Lebanese merchants, who wanted only to get rich quickly and take their money home. He denounced multinational companies who paid their staffs in foreign currency, so that the wealth generated by their businesses never went near their African hosts.

It was easy to see how Nelissen's denunciations won him friends in African governments; but was Premier really any different? Nelissen grunted. White Africans, he replied, were committed to the continent; they alone treated its people with any decency at all. "Us establish in Africa. Paying tax, employing locals, training locals. Us give them a complete package." That was why Premier was so respected in the continent. Now that apartheid was going, Nelissen's good name in Africa was earning him more invitations than he had time to accept. The presidents of Mauritania and Ghana, he assured me, wanted urgently to see him. So did the vice-president of Kenya. Nelissen's reputation was impeccable. "Us never dropped anyone. Us never—how do you say it in good English?—us never screw anybody."

Premier did indeed prove that South African companies could do business on the continent. At the start of the 1980s its international division consisted of ten people and an annual turnover of 1.2 million rand; by the time of my visit it boasted more than a thousand employees and a turnover of 200 million rand. Premier International showed every sign of further expansion. The waning of apartheid was bringing Nelissen new invitations; the waning of statist economics was bringing new opportunities. As African governments started to privatize state companies, Nelissen's political contacts gave Premier an excellent chance of buying those it liked. In Mozambique, for example, it might buy the chicken farms it managed; and if the civil war stopped and the economy brightened, the demand for chickens would grow fast. Zambia's mills, which Premier had also managed for a time, might prove equally attractive. Indeed it seemed a fair bet that, by the turn of the century, Premier would be running flour mills and chicken farms all over the continent. It would be a fitting reward for the long and difficult years of getting established in black Africa. "We've paid enormous green fees," said Peter Wrighton, the Premier Group's chairman. "Now we're hoping to play the golf course."

Africans as well as South Africans talked brightly of this kind of expansion. They hoped that Premier's example would inspire other big South African companies to take the place of Western businesses, which, battered by world recession, were drawing back from risky places and satisfying their diminished appetite for adventure in Eastern Europe. Without South Africa, Africa risked falling victim to an unkind irony: just when the continent's governments were coming around to the virtues of private investment, the world's investors were moving away. Africans talked nervously of the northern hemisphere's emerging trade blocks, fearing that these would not favor exporters from the developing world. The fears rekindled some enthusiasm for the Preferential Trade Area for East and Southern Africa, an organization which tried ineffectually to develop regional trade. In 1990 the PTA invited South African business groups to sit in on one of its meetings, where rhetoric tended to get the better of simple measures like lifting tariffs. In imitation of the European Community, the conference proclaimed a program for monetary harmonization; this scheme was to incorporate South Africa, as soon as apartheid was gone. After all, the British Empire had given most of the region a common language, legal system and administrative tradition; why not a common currency too?

Such hopes were clearly too ambitious; but the waning of apartheid was already delivering some practical benefits. In the 1970s and 1980s South Africa had fueled the civil wars in Angola and Mozambique, which had ruined those countries' economies, disrupted the transport routes used by their landlocked neighbors and contributed to famines that claimed millions of lives. The United Nations, piling estimate upon unsteady estimate, put the cost of South Africa's military aggression at $60 billion for 1980–88. That dwarfed the $5.3 billion of aid attracted

from antiapartheid sympathizers by the Southern African Development Co-ordination Conference (SADCC), set up in 1980
by the region's black-ruled states. By the UN's estimates,
SADCC's economic output might have been more than 40
percent higher than it was at the end of the 1980s had it not
been for South African destabilization. Angola suffered most of
all in terms of lost production; Mozambique lost most lives.
Zimbabwe, whose access to Mozambique's nearby coastline
was cut off by the Renamo rebels, was forced to trade through
South Africa instead. According to the UN, the extra transport
costs came to more than $700 million between 1980 and 1988.
Longer transport routes cost Malawi $500 million. On top of
that, Malawi had to play host to nearly a million Mozambican
refugees.[11]

By 1990 President De Klerk's domestic reforms were reflected
in a different kind of foreign policy: South Africa had changed
from bully to benefactor. It withdrew its support from the Mozambican and Angolan rebels; both movements proceeded to
meet their respective governments to talk peace. The South
Africans also started to send aid to Mozambique, sometimes
to repair the very infrastructure which South African–backed
rebels had helped to destroy. At Mozambique's independence
in 1975, the port of Maputo had handled more than 6 million
metric tons of South African cargo a year. Attacks by the Renamo rebels had reduced that to 250,000 metric tons; now the
new South Africa was helping to pay for the port's repair. In
1988 the South Africans signed a deal with the Mozambican
government to rehabilitate the hydroelectric plant on the huge
Cahora Bassa dam; among other things they donated 10 million
rand in nonlethal military aid to the soldiers guarding the power
lines from Renamo. This project would eventually produce
more power than Mozambique needed; the surplus would be
exported to South Africa and other neighboring states.

South Africa's interest in its neighbors' infrastructure had
given birth to other projects too. The South Africans were helping to finance a vast water project in the tiny mountain kingdom
of Lesotho. The scheme aimed to divert Lesotho's rivers so

that their water could be exported to the industries around Johannesburg; among other feats of engineering, this would involve a thirty-four-mile tunnel. The project would eventually cost $2 to $3 billion (if the consultants' estimates were accurate) and would include the building of a new hydroelectric plant. Eskom, the South African electricity company, talked grandly of linking this to Cahora Bassa in a single regional grid; indeed, the company's visionaries foresaw a whole series of new dams along the Zambezi River, which runs between Zambia and Zimbabwe and into Mozambique. There was an appealing logic to all these projects. South Africa had the skills and money to develop the region's resources. The resources would feed South African industry. The neighbors would gain export revenues and jobs.

Mining seemed to hold out the hope of more such regional cooperation. De Beers, the South African company that dominates the world's diamond market, was involved in big mines in Namibia and Botswana, as well as smaller ones in other neighboring states. In February 1991 De Beers announced an agreement with Tanzania's government to prospect for new mines in the north of the country. South African mining expertise was also at work in Namibian gold, Botswanan soda ash (an ingredient of glass), Zimbabwean nickel and Mozambican coal.

If they felt confident of political stability, South Africa's mining companies would no doubt be interested in increasing their involvement. They might buy stakes in the run-down copper mines of Zambia and Zaire. They might follow Lonrho's lead in Mozambique and start looking for gold. The biggest prizes would come in Angola. The country's mines, notably its diamond mines, had been disrupted by the civil war; peace promised lucrative contracts. Angola's agriculture and hydroelectricity were also alluring. The prospect of foreign investment in Angola made the country seem interesting to foreign salespeople as well; for investment would boost the country's exports and hence its ability to pay for imports. Besides, Angola's oil wells were already earning some $2 billion a year in foreign exchange; once that money was no longer devoted to the civil war, it could be spent on civilian imports. Amid all the hopes for renewal in Southern Africa, the prospect of a turnaround in Angola was perhaps the most exciting.

Elsewhere in the region, the potential seemed more modest. Already 85 percent of South Africa's trade with SADCC's member countries consisted of exports from South Africa; until the neighbors started to sell more, there was a limit to how much they could buy. Some optimists declared that the figures showed how much the Africans were buying already: in 1990 a tenth of South Africa's exports, and a third of its manufacturing exports, went to sub-Saharan Africa. The passing of apartheid would no doubt cause that trade to grow. But the effect would not be dramatic: most countries had continued to trade quietly with South Africa throughout the sanctions years. For most African countries, the main block to trade with South Africa had nothing to do with politics; it was a simple question of poverty.

SADCC's combined gross domestic product of $25 billion was half of Portugal's, a quarter of South Africa's. Its people were dispersed and inaccessible, and might soon be decimated by AIDS. Poverty was why Western businesses, unencumbered by sanctions, were leaving the continent; poverty was why even Africa's most dedicated traders were looking elsewhere. Lonrho had expanded out of Africa; the continent was contributing only a small proportion of its profits; soon after I visited him in Maputo, John Hewlett set off to investigate Eastern Europe. And despite all those pressing invitations from African presidents, Albert Nelissen took the time to visit Moscow in 1990. He befriended Russians as easily as Africans; he came home with contracts to sell South African beer and brick-making machinery.

Brisker regional trade would depend on new investment; but there would be no flood of South Africans (or anybody else) anxious to invest. The prospect of power cuts, bad telephones and bribery made most investors shudder. For the foreseeable future, a plantation in many parts of the region would require an army of security guards; a new mine might require hundreds of miles of new roads. Besides, South Africa's wealth was limited. Its companies were not investing enough at home to employ more than a fraction of the thousand youths who joined the work force every day. Thanks to white emigration and poor black education, South Africa was short of skills; it could ill afford to send hundreds of consultants and technicians off on African projects. In their optimistic moments, Zimbabweans and Mozambicans talked of enrolling their people in South African universities and training institutes, which were considerably more sophisticated than others in the region. But South Africans fretted that their colleges could not accommodate enough of their own people. Measured against its neighbors, South Africa looked like a rich country with plenty to offer. Measured against domestic expectations, South Africa could not spare a penny. "The expectation of Africa towards South Africa is enormous," said Albert Nelissen. "Us can't supply. Us can't give what Africa expects."

As South Africa began its process of transition, the ANC's leaders clung to the ideal of regional cooperation. They declared they would not tolerate the gap between South Africa's prosperity and the region's misery. "Greater regional economic cooperation," said one ANC document, should be constructed "along new lines which will not be exploitative and which will correct imbalances in current relationships." This kind of talk matched the rhetoric of other African leaders, who were forever proclaiming African solidarity. Their rhetoric had included frequent condemnation of apartheid, which made the ANC's leaders all the more inclined to talk in the same vein. Black Africa, through the Organization of African Unity, had backed the ANC's campaign for sanctions. It seemed that soon an ANC-led government would be in a position to repay the continent with investment and aid.

Yet the truth was that Africa's support for the ANC had very often been no more than rhetorical. Of SADCC's ten member countries, only two—Angola and Tanzania—had refused to admit a South African trade mission. None of South Africa's immediate neighbors had permitted the ANC to set up military bases on its territory, for this would have invited trouble. South African commandos periodically blew up supposed ANC hideouts in the region's capitals; and in 1985–86 the South Africans blockaded Lesotho's pro-ANC government until it collapsed. Officially, the ANC sympathized with the region's black governments, accepting that South Africa's military preeminence gave its neighbors little choice. Unofficially, some ANC leaders were resentful. In 1990 Chris Hani, the head of the ANC's military wing, complained that in the past ANC "exiles would be photographed and fingerprinted in the neighbouring countries, especially in Botswana, Lesotho and Swaziland, and we were convinced that these reports were made available to the South African police".[12]

It seemed unlikely that an ANC-led government would bring a rush of generosity toward the neighbors. In some respects, the opposite seemed more probable. During its years of international isolation, South Africa's white government had been prepared to pay handsomely for African friends. It had given aid to Botswana, Swaziland and Lesotho via the Southern African Customs Union, a regional common market which collected tariffs jointly, distributing a sizeable slice of these revenues to the smaller states. The white government had also accepted thousands of migrant workers from Mozambique, Swaziland and Lesotho, despite the alarming unemployment among black South Africans. It had even given aid to Mozambique, despite the huge backlog in housing, schools and hospitals at home. It was hard to imagine an ANC-led government spending money on its neighbors while it was besieged by demands from its own people. The neighbors realized this, and worried. Half Lesotho's gross national product was earned by the one hundred and sixty thousand Basotho employed in South Africa; the cover caption of a local magazine read: "Would Lesotho sink without apartheid?" Pariah South Africa had been prepared to pay for friends. Black-ruled South Africa would not need to.

For all the talk of regional unity, plenty of entrepreneurs in

Zimbabwe and Zambia were terrified by the prospect. A unified currency and a free-trade zone were the last things they wanted; the end of barriers to trade with South Africa would mean the end of their businesses. With few exceptions, they could not hope to compete against South African producers. The South Africans had newer machinery, better-educated workers, lower transport costs, less red tape, reliable telephones, a convertible currency, efficient banks and a stock market. Even in Zimbabwe, the most sophisticated of the neighboring economies, the visa lines outside the South African trade mission extended for yards along the street: Zimbabweans longed to shop and work in the region's ritziest economy. The lure of the local superpower was such that consumers would pay higher prices for its products. In 1990, when Zambia began to import South African beer, the local Mosi brew was soon pushed to the back of the shelves. The South African beer was twice the price; but it was smartly packaged and more alcoholic. Stylish Zambians adored it.

In one big way, however, the end of apartheid would serve the region well. Evil South Africa had masked the neighbors' failings. It was used to excuse economic failures, Zimbabwe's state of emergency, the unwillingness of the Angolan and Mozambican governments to recognize their rebels' legitimate complaints. For more than thirty years, said a document released by SADCC in 1990, the region's leaders strove for black liberation. The ejection of colonial white governments had absorbed the region's energies in the 1950s, leading up to the British departure from Tanzania in 1961 and from Malawi and Zambia in 1964. It took years of armed rebellion to rid Angola and Mozambique of the Portuguese, who finally left in 1975, after Portugal's own revolution against Salazar's dictatorship. In 1979 another guerrilla war ended, and white-ruled Rhodesia gave way to Zimbabwe. Now, in South Africa, the last domino was falling. The fight against white rule was over. The region's governments could put black welfare first.

This had already started. By the time of Nelson Mandela's release, all the SADCC countries were grappling with the real

217

problems that crippled their economies: not apartheid, but overblown exchange rates, fat bureaucracies and useless controls. In 1988 the region's economy grew faster than its population for the first time in a decade. Angola and Mozambique, the two onetime Soviet clients, applied to join the International Monetary Fund. Tanzania's leadership, which had founded African socialism, talked less about cooperatives and more about market incentives. In 1990 food riots failed to scare Zambia's President Kaunda into abandoning his economic reforms. Zimbabwe started to liberalize its economy the same year.

Zimbabwe also lifted its state of emergency, which had been in place for twenty-five years. During the course of 1990, Mozambique declared for democracy; Angola accepted it in principle; Tanzania promised to consider it; Zambians won the right to a referendum on it; Namibia's new constitution enshrined it; and Lesotho planned on it. Since Botswana always had it, only Malawi and the mini-kingdom of Swaziland were still wedded to the continent's autocratic traditions. In October 1991, these Southern African stirrings achieved their first big breakthrough. Zambia's President Kenneth Kaunda was voted out of office in a clean election, after twenty-seven years of uninterrupted power.

The high hopes for regional cooperation were understandable. Humiliated by sanctions, white South Africans naturally longed for their isolation to end. Battered by white South Africa's army, neighboring states naturally longed for the regional superpower to acquire a sympathetic government. In fact the end of apartheid would bring some benefits, but of a limited kind. By reining in the rebels it had once supported, South Africa could help to end the civil wars in Mozambique and Angola. Companies like Premier would expand their presence on the continent, bringing badly needed investment and technical skills.

Both these developments promised to help the region's economies, which was essential if the new democratic experiments were to succeed. People with little or no tradition of democracy do not usually deem it a good in itself. They demand the vote in the hope that it will bring prosperity; if they find that instead they get poorer, they often lose interest in democracy. Such disillusion, exacerbated by left-wing violence, opened the way to a string of military coups in Latin America during the 1960s and 1970s. In October 1991, just a month after Togo shook off twenty-four years of dictatorship, three unsuccessful army mutinies seeking to restore the ancien régime showed that disillusion could undermine African pluralism too.

Besides economic help for its neighbors, South Africa could improve the prospects for the region's new democracies by setting an example of tolerance and fair voting, free association and free speech. In the end, this might prove the greatest service South Africa could offer to the region. One robust democracy would encourage wavering democrats throughout Southern Africa. It would provide working proof of the benefits of pluralism and would dispel the suspicions of some Africans that democracy is a white invention not suitable for them. Yet, as rival parties killed each other in the townships, post-apartheid South Africa seemed far from certain to meet high standards of democracy itself.

8

THE TAMING OF UNGOVERNABILITY

Africa's poverty, and the limits that it sets to cross-border investment, remind South Africans how far they can fall. The continent's weak economies and weaker records for democracy reinforce one another. Poor citizens do not understand democracy, so are manipulated by autocrats who give them only token votes. Poor workers do not work productively, so Africa's economies have failed. Poor civil servants are easily seduced by bribes, so Africa's bureaucracies are rotten. Millions of the continent's people lack the basic conditions—education, health, shelter—that they need to fulfill their own potential, and therefore the potential of their countries.

In South Africa's newspaper columns and weekend seminars—business executives debating the future at dozens of provincial gatherings, black activists arguing with white tycoons—there lurked the fear that failure in one area of policy would trigger failure in the rest. Without industrial growth, there would not be enough jobs to relieve pressure on the land. Without wise land reform, the demand for city jobs would grow beyond control. A large army of jobless youngsters would mean restless townships; without calm townships, economic development would be hard. A weak economy would cause skilled whites to emigrate, which would weaken the economy still more. If South Africa could not solve its domestic problems, it could not help its poorer neighbors; impoverished neighbors would in turn compound South Africa's difficulties by reducing opportunities for trade.

It was impossible to disentangle South Africa's troubles; and yet one challenge did stick out. South Africa simply had to conquer the culture of ungovernability and the violence that it bred. Ungovernability poisoned the country's efforts to rebuild itself more than any of the other interlocking problems. Ungovernability deterred foreign investment, for it is hard to produce much with workers who live in violent townships and fear for their lives. The violence also delayed the start of constitutional negotiations, because it created bitter suspicions between rival black movements, as well as between black and white.

Most fundamentally, the culture of ungovernability undermined South Africans' commitment to regeneration. The struggle against apartheid had made a virtue out of boycotts and demonstrations; many township teenagers thought disruption virtuous even after the struggle had been won. They continued to believe in strikes and boycotts, not seeing the need to improve productivity in the factories. They continued to call for international sanctions, rather than encouraging foreign companies to invest. The great reconstructions of the twentieth century—those of Japan and West Germany after the Second World War—depended more than anything on thrift and hard work. In South Africa Nelson Mandela called for discipline in the townships, but his appeals were often ignored.

Taming South Africa's underclass would depend, in part, on the health of the economy. About one in two black South Africans are illiterate. Something like one in three workers do not have jobs. Twenty million live in houses without electricity. Such people have no good reason to be disciplined; hard work and thrift are meaningless without jobs to do or money to save. To give the underclass a stake in the new order, South Africa needs an economy that can generate hundreds of training pro-

grams and thousands of jobs. And yet the taming of ungovernability depends on more than money. Countries with similar
economies, and with similar mixtures of middle class and underclass, can develop very different political cultures, ranging
from violent social conflict to relative peace. There could hardly
be a better demonstration of this than the contrasting experiences of Brazil and Colombia.

Like South Africa, Brazil and Colombia are both classed as
"middle-income" countries in the World Bank's league tables;
like South Africa, both have violent slums. In many ways,
South Africa resembles these Latin countries. They share pol-
ished white leaders with sentimental ties to Europe, and companies that export worldwide. They share impoverished nonwhite
peoples, living in shanties or squatting on patches of fast de-
grading land. In Brazil nearly half the farmland is owned by 1
percent of farmers, a distribution roughly comparable to South
Africa, where apartheid awarded the white minority 86 percent
of the land. Other forms of wealth in Brazil are distributed as
unfairly; the top tenth of the population hogs 51 percent of it,
compared with 50 percent in South Africa.[1] Colombia's disparities of wealth are less appalling; but it still has an elite that
discusses Don Quixote in the capital, while two in five Colombians never get beyond primary school.[2]

Yet Brazil and Colombia, despite their similarities, have developed very different political forms. The black and brown
people who live in Brazil's slums are poor and prone to violence;
at times the crime rate has caused government officials to talk
darkly of a "civil war." But the underclass has never seriously
disrupted Brazil's public life. Brazil's generals returned power
to the civilians in 1985, making way for national elections in
1986 and 1989. Both were won by conservatives who enjoyed
the backing of Brazil's business establishment. Neither victor
felt the need to play to the anger of the underclass, to encourage
it to think that violence against the rich was justified or that a
radical redistribution of wealth was its right. Even Brazil's left-
wingers were relatively restrained. The Workers' Party demanded land reform and fairer wealth distribution. But by the

last leg of the 1989 election it had dropped its talk of socializing the means of production; and in any case, it lost. The culture of revolt, so remarkably strong in South Africa's townships, was remarkably weak in Brazil's.

Colombia's underclass seethed with revolt. From the 1960s to the 1980s its bitterness was expressed in a bewildering array of guerrilla groups, inspiring their impoverished brown followers with the promise of revolution against rich whites. They blew up oil pipelines and attacked government offices; they even laid siege to the Palace of Justice in 1985. The ungovernability of the left was matched by violence from the right: hit squads with links to the official security forces routinely killed trade unionists and other spokesmen of the dispossessed. Then there were the cocaine barons, with their own lists of enemies—critical journalists, determined judges—whom they murdered as well. In 1988 Colombia's murder count was put at eighteen thousand; at least a fifth of these were attributed to politics or drugs. Not surprisingly, democracy suffered under these conditions. Some left-wingers refused to take part in the elections of the 1980s, and went on bombing and killing right through the campaigns. Others did abandon their guns for a shot at the ballot box. Right-wing hit squads murdered more than four hundred of them, including both the leading left-wing candidates in the 1990 campaigns.

Brazil's mix of skyscrapers and shantytowns breeds crime, but in general life goes on. Colombia's inequalities have given rise to so much violence that both democracy and justice have been undermined. Brazilians can reasonably hope that if they sort out their economy, wealth will spread gradually from the white suburbs to the slums. Colombians know that their surprisingly steady economy is being sapped by violence all the time. Guerrilla sabotage of oil pipelines and electricity pylons has cost Colombia millions of dollars in lost production. In 1985 the average Brazilian was just 24 percent richer than the average Colombian. By the end of the decade, however, that gap had grown to 112 percent.[3]

Colombia and Brazil suggest a lesson for South Africa. The

damage wrought by an underclass depends on more than the health of an economy. It depends as well on the mindset of the poor. Unlike Brazil, Colombia has a history strewn with political violence; indeed the decade of the 1950s is known as "La Violencia," a time when two hundred and eighty thousand Colombians were killed. This tradition of violence has taught Colombians to fight in order to change things, and to do so in organized gangs. The act of organization is a big step on the ladder to instability: coordinated violence is many times more dangerous than disjointed crime. Anywhere in the world—from South America to Sicily—a mugger becomes really destructive when he joins a mafia; a bitter slum-dweller or right-winger becomes deadly when he joins an armed guerrilla band. Organized violence stifled Colombian democracy during the 1980s. Mostly unorganized crime merely inconveniences Brazil. The biggest danger to South Africa's post-apartheid prospects is not the anarchy of teenagers. It is that the teenagers may be led.

Who might provide such leadership? South Africa's long years of struggle have created a tradition of extremist rhetoric, and in the early 1990s extremism sometimes seemed to get the better of the moderates like Nelson Mandela. The South African Communist Party, with a secret membership that was thought to include many top ANC officials, had supported the Soviet Union throughout the Cold War; and it was unclear whether communism's collapse had genuinely persuaded the party that democracy was good. The black trade unions, founded in the 1970s with the help of white communists, led a series of violent strikes in the ensuing decade; non-striking workers were sometimes killed. Both communists and trade unions had at times reveled in the language of ungovernability; and both were influential groups within the African National Congress. As President De Klerk began the unraveling of apartheid, however, one spectacle of ANC extremism eclipsed all the rest.

The story of Winnie Mandela captures both the heroism of black resistance to apartheid and the dark side of the culture that resistance bred. Her courage survived years of separation from her imprisoned husband, 491 days in solitary confinement and constant bullying from the state. Journalists prized her comments; foreign dignitaries lined up to see her; the University of Glasgow could think of nobody more suitable to elect as its rector. She was acclaimed the "mother of the nation"; yet in the late 1980s Winnie Mandela led a gang of torturers, whose behavior far exceeded anything that could be justified by the antiapartheid cause. She seemed to revel in extremes of violence that other black leaders refused to condone: "Together, hand in hand, with our boxes of matches and necklaces we shall liberate this country," she declared in the midst of the mid-1980s anarchy, as though the murder of suspected collaborators with burning tires drenched in gasoline were cause for great pride. Here was an organizer of the underclass who might ensure that South Africa remained ungovernable for years.

Nelson Mandela met Winnie in 1957 and quickly arranged a divorce from his first wife. Many of his friends disapproved of this second marriage: he was a Xhosa nobleman of nearly forty, she a pretty upstart barely half his age. Besides her looks, however, Winnie did have the distinction of being the first black South African to qualify as a medical social worker; and in the decades to come the strength of her character was proved beyond doubt. In 1963, the year after Nelson's capture and imprisonment, the government "banned" her: she was confined to her home from dusk to dawn; she was forbidden to meet more than one person at a time; she was not allowed to attend public meetings. In 1969 she was arrested, and she spent the next seventeen months in prison. Then, in 1977, she was banished to Brandfort, a small Afrikaner town in the middle of nowhere. Winnie and her two daughters lived there without water, stove or electricity; but she was soon setting up community projects, establishing a clinic and generally refusing to be cowed. Her example inspired new dignity among the people of Brandfort, upsetting the quiet subservience that had been the rule before.

In 1985 Winnie returned to Soweto in triumph, a celebrity

among her own people and abroad. She declared herself a member of the ANC, at a time when nobody else in the country dared to do so. She wore ANC colors, though the courts had been known to jail a man for five years for drinking coffee out of an ANC mug. But her brave obstinacy was soon channeled into less worthy causes than the clinic at Brandfort. Within a year she founded the Mandela United Football Club, aiming, she said, to "remove the boys from the streets as part of a program to cut down on petty crime." Stories began to circulate of the club's misdeeds. It was blamed for hacking to death Masabatha Loate, one of the leaders of the student uprising of 1976. It was said to have punished two teenage boys who had unwisely insulted a club member by dragging them off to Winnie's house, carving "VIVA ANC" and "M" into their flesh, and applying battery acid to the wounds. Then, on December 29, 1988, the team kidnapped four boys from a Methodist mission house in Soweto. The events that followed were to spread the disenchantment with Mrs. Mandela throughout Soweto and beyond.

The most famous of the four boys kidnapped that day was Mokhetsi Seipei, or "Stompie" for short. Stompie was barely ten years old when he started his career in politics. He was swept up by the mid-1980s rebellion; he rose to lead an army of young comrades; at the age of eleven he was arrested. While in prison, Stompie is said to have been tortured and to have betrayed some of his fellow activists to the police. True or not, this rumor made Stompie a target of the comrades' wrath. After his release, he sought shelter in the Methodist mission. The shelter was imperfect. The thugs from the Mandela United Football Club came and removed Stompie and three young men who happened to be playing cards with him. Nine days later the body of a boy was found in a ditch with its throat slit. The police eventually identified the body as Stompie's. He was fourteen years old.

Stompie's three friends survived to tell the tale: first in various public statements,[4] then, in more detail, during the trials of football club offenders, as well as that of Mrs. Mandela herself. In interviews with journalists before the trial, the victims claimed that they had been taken from the Methodist mission to a room in Mrs. Mandela's backyard, where they were informed that "Mummy" wanted to see them. Mrs. Mandela (again, according to the victims) arrived and hit one of them in the face. Then the football team joined in. Mummy reportedly took up a *sjambok*, the leather whip much loved by South Africa's policemen, and beat the captives before leaving the field to the footballers again. One of the victims, Thabiso Mono, later told the court that he was lifted into the air and dropped on the floor, then trampled and beaten with a shoe. Another, Kenneth Kgase, described how Mrs. Mandela and her bodyguards repeatedly punched and whipped him, switching occasionally to karate kicks. While this was going on, "Mrs. Mandela was humming a tune and then dancing to the rhythm," said Kgase to the court; she also told the four victims that they were "not fit to be alive." This session lasted perhaps ten or fifteen minutes, and by the end there was blood on the walls. Two days later Stompie was taken away by Jerry Richardson, the "coach" of the Mandela football team. When Richardson returned to the Mandela household, he had blood on his shoes.

At her trial, Mrs. Mandela denied this version of events, and the verdict went some way to vindicating her. She was found guilty of kidnapping, but not of assault. Yet the verdict was hardly comfort to Mrs. Mandela, whom the judge described as "a calm, composed, deliberate and unblushing liar." Lies had indeed surrounded the case for quite some time. When the police first claimed to have found Stompie's mutilated body, Mrs. Mandela told John Ellison of the London *Daily Express*, "Stompie is not dead. He was taken away from here in good health." The court that tried Jerry Richardson decided otherwise: in August 1990 he was convicted of Stompie's murder and sentenced to death. In another interview Mrs. Mandela declared, "The youths in my premises did not abduct any children. This is the room where they claimed to have found these blood-splattered walls. This is the lie that has been going on and on and on." The prosecution later submitted forensic evidence of blood traces on all four walls and on the curtains of a shed in Mrs. Mandela's backyard. They also found blood on the ceiling. A police expert testified that there was a strong possibility that the blood was that of Pelo Mekgwe, one of Stompie's three friends. Mrs. Mandela's defense did not contest this evidence.

The trial was marred by intimidation as well as lies. Soon after it began in February 1991, Pelo Mekgwe disappeared. A local newspaper reported that he had been led away from the Methodist mission, where he was still staying, in the company of people from the ANC; the ANC rather feebly denied that it had been "organizationally involved" in the abduction. That left two of Stompie's fellows as witnesses for the prosecution; and they appeared too terrified to talk. One, Kenneth Kgase, explained that he did feel a strong duty to testify against Mrs. Mandela. But he felt an even stronger urge not to die. "I've got to make a choice between my obligation and my life," he said. "I really want my life, I like my life." The judge threatened the two recalcitrant witnesses with five-year jail sentences, which might have been renewed for the rest of their lives. They nonetheless refused to testify, and the court was forced to adjourn.

When it reconvened three weeks later, the witnesses had recovered their nerves. The trial proceeded over the ensuing three months, and ever more gruesome details emerged. Kgase stated that, after his own punishment, he was made to join the torturers. His victim was Andrew Ikaneng, a former footballer who had incurred his teammates' displeasure by resigning. Kgase held this man down while Jerry Richardson slashed his throat with a pair of garden shears. Kgase also claimed that Stompie had been made to "confess" to betraying four activists when he was beaten and questioned by the police. The murder of Stompie therefore resembled so many of the 1980s, when hundreds of black South Africans were killed for collaborating with the state. But the beating of the three other victims had been different. During their ordeal, Mrs. Mandela had allegedly tried to get Kgase and his friends to admit to having had homosexual relations with Paul Verryn, the Methodist minister who ran the house where they stayed. These beatings had nothing to do with the struggle. They were a punishment for supposed homosexuality, and for practicing it with a white.

At the close of her trial, the judge accepted Mrs. Mandela's alibi: that she had been in Brandfort at the time of the kidnapping and the subsequent assault. But he declared that Mrs. Mandela had authorized the kidnapping; to imagine that it had taken place without her knowing was like imagining "Hamlet without the Prince." The judge also found Mrs. Mandela guilty of covering up the assault after it had happened. For these crimes, Mrs. Mandela was sentenced to six years' imprisonment. She announced immediately that she would appeal; and in 1991 nobody could predict whether she would eventually be locked up. But Mrs. Mandela's personal fate was less important than what she meant for her movement. Was she an aberration? Or did she represent a powerful faction within the ANC?

At times Winnie Mandela did seem formidably powerful. The photographs of Nelson Mandela emerging from prison show a smiling Winnie by his side, and she stuck there with the same determination that she had shown in Brandfort. She became interim head of the ANC Women's League; a member of the ANC's executive in the Johannesburg region; chair of her ANC branch in Johannesburg; and (with an irony not lost on her detractors) head of the ANC's welfare department. She achieved all this despite the charges of kidnap and assault that hung over her, and despite a string of provocative remarks. In August 1990 the ANC suspended its armed struggle as part of its negotiations with President De Klerk. The Congress's armed wing was barely active anyway; but the suspension of violence was a useful way to placate the white hard-liners who were making life difficult for the government. Three days later this gesture was rudely undermined. Winnie Mandela told a crowd that the suspension of the armed struggle was "a strategy. It does not mean the cessation of violence." To reinforce her militancy, she took to wearing designer military outfits and promising her audiences that if the white government did not

deliver more reform quickly, the ANC would resume its guerrilla campaign.

Mrs. Mandela was still speaking in the slogans of the struggle; the legacy of ungovernability, which her football team had
come to symbolize, was far from being tamed. With Nelson at
her side, Mrs. Mandela's pronouncements were bound to catch
the headlines, and to alarm South Africans who valued democratic ideas. But Nelson Mandela was already seventy-one
when he came out of prison; Winnie could not count on him to
guarantee her prominence forever. To survive in politics, she
needed other supporters. She would require the backing of a
hard-line coalition within the ANC.

In early 1991 a prominent Soweto leader told me that if Nelson Mandela died suddenly, he would not be surprised to see
Winnie take over the leadership of the Congress. This was an
extreme opinion; but few doubted that Mrs. Mandela enjoyed
a power base independent of her husband. Some of her supporters, like the elderly Alfred Nzo, were drawn to her out of
expediency: Nzo knew he was unpopular with ANC members,
but hoped to hang onto his job as the Congress's secretary-
general by enlisting her support. (In Nzo's case, this strategy
failed; he fell from high office at the ANC's party congress in
July 1991.)

But other voices, unprompted by opportunism, also echoed
Winnie Mandela's militancy. Indeed Radio Freedom, the ANC
station which broadcast from exile, made Mrs. Mandela's pronouncements sound tame. In December 1990 a bulletin from
Addis Ababa declared, "We must mount the biggest offensive
yet," which should consist "not only in words but in mass
militant actions on the ground." The radio's verdict on a year
of President De Klerk's reforms was that "nothing much has
changed." When De Klerk made another reformist speech the
following February, promising to scrap the remains of statutory
apartheid, the ANC organized a demonstration outside parliament. The protest amounted to a declaration that this remarkable reformer was not remarkable enough—and it showed that

Mrs. Mandela was by no means alone in her attachment to the militant reflexes of the past.

The militants apparently included some extremely powerful figures. Next to Mrs. Mandela, white South Africans most feared Chris Hani, a leading contender to take over the ANC's leadership once Mandela's generation left. Still in his forties, Hani was chief of staff of Umkhonto we Sizwe, the ANC's army, which guaranteed his popularity among the militant youth. He had a politician's way of putting opportunism before principle. He played to the indiscipline of the comrades, letting it be widely known that he had opposed the suspension of armed struggle, and echoing Mrs. Mandela's talk of a return to the bush. "I think we need to have a lot of what I call revolutionary patience," said Hani. "But of course there is a limit to patience." If the government failed to rein in its white policemen, "it is going to be very difficult for the ANC to maintain the suspension of the armed struggle."

Hani seemed perfectly willing to play on tribalism too. After his return to South Africa in 1990, he spent much of his time away from the capital, drumming up support among his Xhosa kinsmen. He held court in Umtata, capital of the Xhosa homeland of Transkei, in a manner that recalled the Xhosa chiefs of the past. His protégés filled the ANC's regional committee. This tribal power base, and his association with the armed struggle, made Hani a formidable figure. What was more, he was a member of the South African Communist Party, which gave him the backing of many of the most influential figures at the top of the ANC.

Next to Winnie Mandela and her football club, the prospect of a communist president alarmed moderate South Africans more than anything else. Winnie Mandela raised the specter that ungovernability would be entrenched and organized, stifling democracy in the post-apartheid state. Many South Africans feared that communism would stifle free speech and fair elections just as surely. The white government had played up the evils of communism during the Cold War, emphasizing the economic chaos wrought by pro-Soviet black governments in other African states. Anticommunism blurred with white supremacism and became an important part of the government's justification for excluding blacks from power. A black government would mean communism and chaos, went the crude rhetoric of the 1970s and 1980s: just look at Angola and Mozambique. It was every liberal's nightmare that the rhetoric might be proved right.

The South African Communist Party was unbanned in February 1990, at the same time as the ANC. It was hard at that stage to estimate its power with any confidence, because its membership was secret. In July, however, the party announced the names of twenty-two of its leaders. The list at once confirmed the communists' influence. Nine of the twenty-two leaders were also on the ANC's policy-making National Executive Committee. Together, those nine made up a quarter of the National Executive's thirty-seven members; and it was quite possible that other communists, whose identities were still secret, were on the executive as well. Besides Chris Hani, the open communists included Joe Slovo, the Communist Party's white general secretary. Though his health was failing, Slovo was among Mandela's closest advisers; he was chosen to represent the ANC in its first talks with the government in 1990.

The communists' influence at the top of the ANC was matched by their standing among the rank and file. Hani and Slovo were both popular speakers at township rallies, not least because both were identified with the armed struggle (Slovo had preceded Hani as Umkhonto's chief of staff). Communism was guaranteed popularity among the radical youth because the white government had preached so much against it. Besides, the communists had a long pedigree of opposition to apartheid, having quickly made up for a period of whites-only membership in the early 1920s, when they rejoiced in the slogan, "Workers of the world unite for a white South Africa." By the end of that decade, the communists were encouraging black trade unions and winning over black converts at meetings and night schools. In 1950 the party achieved the distinction of becoming the first opposition group to be banned.

Even Nelson Mandela, who in the 1940s tried to get the communists expelled from the ANC, had to admit that they were dedicated allies. "Theoretical differences amongst those fighting against oppression is a luxury we cannot afford at this stage," Mandela told the judge during his trial in 1964. "For many decades communists were the only political group in South Africa who were prepared to treat Africans as human beings and their equals; who were prepared to eat with us, talk with us, live with us and work with us. . . ." In the years that followed, the alliance between the Congress and communists was reinforced by support from the Soviet Union and its allies, who supplied military training, weapons and scholarships to the ANC.

With their long pedigree of opposition to apartheid, and with a membership that included so many senior leaders of the ANC, the communists' standing and influence were undoubted. The question in the 1990s was what communism meant. At times the communists themselves seemed unsure. At a conference in 1990 Essop Pahad, the party's chief spokesman, was asked how he could support the socialist economic policies that had failed so badly elsewhere. Pahad replied that his party had noted the collapse of communism in Eastern Europe, but would never abandon its "dreams"; he was later confronted in the lunch line by a liberal, who told him that he would be better off devising his political program while he was awake. On other occasions South Africa's communists declared Eastern Europe proof that socialism would fail without democracy; they therefore committed themselves to "political pluralism now, for the post-apartheid phase and in the period of socialist construction."

Whatever their vision for the future, the communists' language did not suggest that they expected to arrive at it fast. Indeed Slovo denounced those who thought socialism could be established quickly in South Africa. He declared them guilty of "Pol-Potism," which was a grand way of saying that impatience would backfire. In the meantime the role of the party would be to represent the working class: "We need a powerful mass ANC within which the working class remains the leading social force," said a leading communist quoted in *Mayibuye*, the ANC journal. "But we also need an independent party of this working class." Being a communist seemed to involve hazy utopianism plus left-wing economics and a commitment to speak for workers. It did not seem to be about supporting a one-party state, nor about stirring up the ungovernable youth.

Or did it? In 1990 Pallo Jordan, the ANC's clever director of information, accused the communists of "intolerance, petty intellectual thuggery and political dissembling." It was true that communists figured disproportionately in the top ranks of the ANC's army, and that they were notably fond of radical talk. In 1990 some fifty communists were locked up when the police uncovered Operation Vula, a plot to smuggle arms into the country. Ronnie Kasrils, a prominent white communist who had once been in charge of the ANC's military intelligence, escaped arrest for his involvement and went underground. He would appear at press conferences and meetings periodically, and his writings would pop up in the local press. In one left-wing journal he gave warning of the supposed danger that negotiations might "come to eclipse other forms of struggle." The ANC's official policy was that demonstrations and rallies served negotiation by keeping up the pressure on President De Klerk. In the mouths of some militants, however, it sounded as though the opposite were true—as though negotiation were merely an outgrowth of the more important business of disruption. And in December 1991 a congress of the Communist Party revealed the limits to moderation once more. Joe Slovo, who retired as general secretary, to be succeeded by Chris Hani, proposed to the congress that the word "democratic" precede "socialism" in the party constitution, and that the long-standing commitment to Leninism be dropped. His followers rejected both suggestions, though the communists' commitment to regular multiparty elections was confirmed.

South Africans could not be sure that the Communist Party had genuinely abandoned the communism of the Cold War, even if the party's leaders issued reassuring statements from time to time. Equally, many of the ANC's seemingly moderate statements could be interpreted pessimistically. Radio Freedom, in that same broadcast at the end of 1990, declared, "The ANC belongs to the people. It is the people's movement. Whatever the mood of the people, the ANC has to reflect that in its own strategy." It sounded democratic; but what room for opposition did it leave? It seemed that opponents of the ANC were also the opponents of "the people": that they were traitors, no less. Likewise, the Congress believed, officially, in freedom of the press. But it added that the press must behave "responsibly": intrinsically evil doctrines like racism and fascism should on no account be aired. Responsibility had been a favorite word with the white censors of the past.

The ANC seemed just as capable as the National Party of using this term selectively. When white policemen stirred up township violence, the ANC praised journalists who reported it. When Winnie Mandela came in for criticism, her followers railed that "trial by media" was unfair. Even the *Weekly Mail*, a staunchly antiapartheid newspaper which had in 1988 been banned for a month by the National Party, was resented by the Mandelas for its coverage of Winnie's trial. Kaizer Nyatsumba, a black columnist from the *Sunday Star*, complained in 1990 that "journalists—especially black journalists—are expected to sing praise-songs. Either that, or suffer abuse—verbal, physical, and character assassination." "Some," he continued, "have been manhandled for asking 'tough' questions at press conferences."

When Mrs. Mandela was sentenced, her radical supporters threatened riots. Throughout the trial she had come to the courtroom in a style to which few black South Africans are accustomed, flanked by guards recruited from the township youth. On March 21, the anniversary of the Sharpeville killings, she arrived in a suitable black dress, set off smartly by a scarf in the green, yellow and black of the ANC. The court adjourned early that day, and Mrs. Mandela proceeded out of the grand building and into Johannesburg's crowded streets. The usual retinue of guards accompanied her, with green, yellow and black tassels tied around their foreheads or looped over their shoulders in the manner of military brocade. One guard seemed particularly proud of his red sunhat and very dark sunglasses; another was distinguished by his money belt, which was Day-Glo yellow and pink. Winnie crossed the street in front of the court building and marched into an office block to talk to her lawyer. The guards waited outside. From a nearby car they produced a large and rather tattered ANC flag, which they unfurled self-importantly among the pedestrians and shoppers who compete for room on Johannesburg's pavements. They also produced a giant wooden model of an AK-47 assault rifle, argued a bit among themselves, then left the comrade with the bright belt to hold it. He stood in front of the lawyer's office, this teenager with torn gym shoes, balancing a toy gun nearly as tall as himself. To anyone who knew the stories of the football club, this public procession was not a reassuring sight. And yet it was hard to believe that these children with their makeshift uniforms could really threaten South Africa's future peace.

Winnie Mandela and her militant allies could not be dismissed. The youths in the townships were a powerful constituency, and plenty of black leaders seemed more inclined to play to their taste for militancy than to preach discipline and restraint. Winnie Mandela's talk of resuming the armed struggle was echoed by other powerful voices, some with the authority of the Communist Party. Yet the ANC also included people who realized that irresponsible leaders could entrench ungovernability and lock South Africa into violence of the Colombian sort. In the months after the ANC's unbanning, it became the obsession of political pundits to discern the balance between the two sides.

The ANC's power struggles were often obscure. Its members were reluctant to identify themselves clearly with hard-liners or moderates, partly for fear of exposing the ANC's divisions in public and partly for fear that forthright positions might cost political support. ANC members were especially reluctant to criticize Mrs. Mandela openly, lest Nelson take offense. As the months unfolded, however, positions did emerge. Several ANC branches protested Mrs. Mandela's appointment as head of the welfare department. Others pointed out that her election to the executive of the Johannesburg region, held by open ballot in the presence of both her and her husband, had hardly been fair. In May 1991 Mrs. Mandela's position as interim head of the ANC Women's League was due to be confirmed by ballot. For two days the conference delegates debated whether to hold the vote in public or in secret, knowing that many would shrink from opposing Mrs. Mandela openly. In the end the conference opted for a secret ballot. The women voted for Mrs. Mandela's rival by a majority of two to one.

The biggest test of the ANC's mood came in July, at the party's conference. More than two thousand delegates met for five days—and for much of the nights—at Durban University sports hall. It was the first time in three decades that the ANC had held such a vast gathering inside the country to elect its leadership; it was the first chance ordinary members had had to show whether their loyalties lay with the moderates or the hard-liners.

The result demonstrated the hard-liners' strength. The new National Executive Committee, enlarged to eighty-two members, included some twenty-five suspected communists. Of all the candidates standing for committee membership (as opposed to one of the top five ANC offices), Chris Hani came first. Although Thabo Mbeki, the moderate foreign affairs spokesman, came second, the prominence of hard-liners was marked. Third place went to Joe Slovo, the Communist Party secretary-general. Ronnie Kasrils, the communist who had been on the run from the police during much of the previous year, came seventh; during the conference his comment on the township violence was, "There is a role for rudimentary weaponry. Nicaragua and Salvador have shown this." Winnie Mandela came twenty-sixth, with the votes of nearly half the delegates.

At the same time, however, the radicals failed to secure any of the ANC's top five jobs. Harry Gwala, generally reckoned among the Communist Party's more dogmatic leaders, ran for the post of ANC deputy president. He was soundly defeated by Walter Sisulu, an elderly prison graduate who had spent much of the period since his release appealing for discipline in the townships. The moderate old guard took two other top positions: Nelson Mandela was elected unopposed as president; Oliver Tambo, the ailing hero who had led the ANC through its three decades of exile, became national chairman.

The choice of the younger men, who filled the jobs of secretary-general and deputy secretary-general, was even more revealing. The junior of these two jobs went to Jacob Zuma. He had the distinction of being the ANC's most senior Zulu—and the ANC was aware of the need to counter accusations that it was an anti-Zulu party. But Zuma was also distinguished by his reputation as a negotiator. He had mediated successfully in the ANC-Inkatha fighting in Natal. He was not thought to be a communist. He had no record of preaching ungovernability to the township youth.

The job of secretary-general went to Cyril Ramaphosa. He repeatedly declared that he was not a member of the Communist Party, and was known and respected for his work as head of the National Union of Mineworkers. Since 1982 he had built the union up from almost nothing; by 1991 it boasted more than three hundred thousand members. Ramaphosa's proven organizational ability was likely to prove useful to the muddled ANC; within a month of his election he was reorganizing party headquarters and exerting an influence that suggested Chris Hani was no longer the leading candidate to succeed Nelson Mandela. But the new secretary-general's administrative skills were possibly less significant than his record as a negotiator. Ramaphosa's instincts were a world away from the blanket calls for no compromise that came from some quarters of the ANC. He had learned through his experience of wage bargaining that real gains in black living standards come through compromise. This had won him the respect of white executives: he was "without the shadow of a doubt the most competent negotiator I have come across anywhere," said Bobby Godsell, head of labor relations at Anglo American Corporation.[5] Ramaphosa had demonstrated his attitude toward ungovernability by denouncing Mrs. Mandela in 1989, after the news emerged of Stompie's killing. And he had done so despite the risk to his own standing.

The ANC's behavior, as well as its choice of leaders, suggested that moderates had won the upper hand. During the course of 1990, the Congress accepted the absolute need to pacify the townships, even if that meant talking to enemies such as Chief Mangosuthu Buthelezi and the white police. In the early part of the year, such discussions had been frustrated by hard-liners like Harry Gwala, who was head of the ANC office in the Natal Midlands as well as being a communist. By the end of 1990 Gwala's influence was gone; and in January Mandela led a delegation of ANC people to meet Inkatha. Buthelezi addressed the peace conference at length. He recalled the past occasions on which he had been abused by ANC leaders. "Mr. John Nkadimeng is present here today," he said. "I ask that he quietly tells the world that he was wrong in calling me a snake that must be hit on the head." But the ANC resisted the temptation to demand a reciprocal apology from Buthelezi, and the meeting ended with a joint appeal for peace.

The talks with Inkatha were matched by a softening of the ANC's hostility toward the police. In March 1990 the police shooting of eleven black demonstrators in the township of Sebokeng had been enough for the ANC to cancel a meeting with the government. In September the army shot another eleven blacks in the same township; this time Mandela met the minister of law and order to discuss what had happened, and emerged to say that their exchange had been "extremely fruitful." Equally, in early 1990 the ANC demanded that troops leave the townships, even though their deployment in Natal in April had quickly reduced ANC-Inkatha killings by a third. By early the next year the ANC's position had changed completely. The Congress accepted that troops could play a useful role; indeed, it called upon the government to deploy more security forces in the townships, and threatened to call off talks with the government if this was not done. The ANC's pragmatists had persuaded the militants that, however imperfect the white police force, they had better work with it to minimize the slaughter. Only Winnie Mandela and a handful of communist extremists still seemed to believe that ungovernability was good.

The politicians' muddled shift toward moderation was matched by a similar movement further down. Trade union leaders were also sounding more pragmatic. The importance of this shift was hard to overestimate, because during the 1980s the unions had reinforced the politicians' militancy, calling strikes to express political grievances as much as industrial ones. Strikes frequently turned violent, and did South Africa's industry untold harm. In the second half of the 1980s the economy lost an average of 2 million man-days a year, compared with 200,000 in Pakistan (whose population is three times South Africa's) and 110,000 in Mexico (population two and a half times as big as South Africa's).[6]

In the 1980s the strikes were understandable. The government had suppressed most other black organizations, so the unions were left to carry the torch of black pride. Managers were not used to taking black workers seriously, so the unions had to shout and bang the table to make themselves heard. By the 1990s, however, many company managers had initiated an industrial reformism, analogous to the political reforms of President De Klerk. With varying boldness, they were coming to accept the need for trade unions, as well as the urgency of promoting more blacks. In industry as in politics, the question was whether blacks would respond to these concessions, or whether the culture of strikes and boycotts was too deeply rooted. Trade union leaders, and their allies in the Communist Party, were presented with a choice. They could become the leaders of indiscipline, or they could decide to instill in the ranks a spirit of compromise.

Not all the evidence was encouraging. The political turmoil of 1990 brought an increase in strikes and stayaways: 4 million man-days were lost, up from 3.1 million in 1989. In November 1991 a battle at one gold mine between strikers and those wanting to work left seventy-six dead. Yet anecdotal evidence suggested that a mood of compromise was growing; and that, given less extraordinary political circumstances, industrial ungovernability would ease. Employers reported a new rapport with union negotiators. Shop stewards occasionally advised work mates to restrain wage demands, arguing that, in times of recession, overambitious demands would backfire. At the end of 1990 the Chamber of Mines and the mining union announced the formation of a "conflict monitoring group" to control violence at the workplace. The new cooperation extended to retrenchments, which were inevitable in the hard-pressed gold mines. Managers of the Freegold South mine set aside 1 million rand to create jobs for those who were laid off. Hard times were pushing people together.

As well as inviting me to tour their operations in black Africa, the Premier Group's managers allowed me to sit in on a meeting with the unions in 1991. In the previous decade Premier had suffered its share of strikes. Managers gave warning that disruption was making the poultry division unprofitable. The unions had dismissed this as a racist ploy to deny its members decent pay. In the heady atmosphere of the mid-1980s, some union members believed that the township uprisings might overthrow the state. They were therefore undismayed by the threat of job losses: "Close the place, that's five hundred more people for the revolution," one union man declared. In the end the strikes did result in the closure of the poultry division and the loss of twelve hundred jobs.

By the time I visited Premier, attitudes had changed. The unions had come to understand that Premier's managers could not be pushed too far. The managers knew that they must take the unions seriously. Corrie Cloete, the management's chief negotiator, sat on one side of the long conference table, flanked by three colleagues, two white and one black. On the other side were seven trade unionists, one of them wearing an ANC badge. Cloete announced that he was planning a vacation in

August, so there had better not be strikes. The union men chuckled and promised to strike in July instead.

Cloete then recalled a meeting a few years ago, before the union had won recognition from Premier. He had organized it to ease the tension between workers and managers at one of Premier's factories; at first, the white managers did not want to talk to the workers at all. Cloete had reassured them that if they felt unhappy at the way the discussions were going, the managers could withdraw to talk privately among themselves. The two sides sat down. Within five minutes one of the white managers demanded an interruption; he was horrified because the unionists called each other "comrade"—"Did you hear that! These workers are communists, we should not talk to them at all." "You remember those days!" said Cloete, and the unionists across the table roared with laughter. Both sides congratulated each other lengthily on how things had improved. As the meeting continued, the discussion turned serious; neither side had forgotten the disaster of the poultry strike. But the atmosphere was always friendly. People began their comments with phrases like "As far as I can see" and finished off with "Well, at least that is how it seems."

Other companies, with similarly moderate trade unionists, still suffered from the culture of boycott and stayaway among the rank and file. In 1990 a strike at the Mercedes-Benz factory in the city of East London showed how persistent ungovernability could be among the work force. At the same time, however, the outcome of this episode proved that even supposedly hardline leaders saw the need to instill discipline rather than pander to the slogans of the past.

For most of the 1980s, Mercedes had been typical of South Africa's insensitive style of management. Four-fifths of the factory supervisors were white, although most were less educated than the top fifth of the black work force. White bosses treated black workers brusquely; black unions responded with militancy. As a result the average completed car had sixty-eight defects before inspection, compared with thirteen in Germany. With better industrial relations, however, it was evident that

South Africa's workers would be capable of excellence. After Nelson Mandela's release, they decided to work overtime to build a car to present to him; this gift had only nine defects before inspection.[7]

A new chairman, appointed in late 1988, started to improve things. He recognized the union, cultivated an understanding with the shop stewards and adopted one of the most liberal employment codes in the country. Very soon three-quarters of the supervisors were black. The shop stewards stopped calling strikes and boycotts and accepted the managers' right to manage. But their followers were nostalgic for the days of confrontation. In August 1990, therefore, two thousand workers organized a sit-in in defiance of the union leadership. Eighteen shop stewards decided they had no choice but to follow popular opinion and support the strike. Only five stewards opposed it.

Further up the ladder, however, both unions and communists firmly took the moderate side. None other than Joe Slovo, the communist leader, came down to East London, where the strikers were flying the communist flag from the company flagpole. Management, union leaders and Communist Party boss joined in urging the workers to give up; they succeeded, and Mercedes was narrowly prevented from closing the factory. The strike cost the company seven weeks' production and 500 million rand. But the episode served to tame the extremists in the work force. After the strike, the managers told Patti Waldmeir of the London *Financial Times* that production targets were being met for the first time in five years.

Ungovernability cuts across politics and the economy; it affects almost all the issues that will determine the success or failure of the post-apartheid state. In the trade unions and churches, in all the political parties, South Africa needs leaders who believe in hard work and compromise, and who are ready to stand up to hotheads who do not. No country can succeed if its people blame others for their troubles; if their expectations exceed what can possibly be delivered; or if slogans get the better of clear thought. Success in South Africa will take clear-eyed realism and a willingness to forgive the past. As this book goes to press, the tentative evidence from the first eighteen months of South Africa's transition is that realism will win.

Perhaps the last word should go to Paul Mashatile. He had been through a lot for a man in his late twenties, and half of what he had been through would have been enough to make most people hard. In the uprising of the mid-1980s, when ungovernability became the goal of the African National Congress, he was president of the Youth Congress in Alexandra, one of Johannesburg's satellite townships. The police detained him for seven months, released him and arrested him again. The second detention lasted three years and ended only when Mashatile went on a hunger strike. By the time of his release Mashatile was thin and exhausted; yet he returned directly to politics in Alexandra, not even pausing to visit his family first. After the ANC's unbanning in 1990, Mashatile was elected to the executive of the Congress's Alexandra branch. He was also a member of the Communist Party. And when I visited him in 1991, Alexandra was in the middle of the kind of violence that would turn anyone sour.

Townships are not comforting places for uninitiated whites. There are no street signs or maps, and even if they did exist they would rapidly cease to match the pattern of proliferating shacks. The ANC office in Alexandra is off a street lined with refuse and scavenging animals: dogs, chickens, cows and goats. Market stalls make the roads still narrower, and cars have in any case to proceed slowly because of the potholes and ruts.

Thousands of Alexandra's people live in cardboard and corrugated-iron structures. In some places you can still see the Coca-Cola logo on the packing cases that make up these shelters; elsewhere enterprising residents have written, SHOEMAKER or PROFISIONAL HAIRCUT on the walls. Grim brick fortresses stick out above the cardboard settlements: these are the single-sex hostels, where migrant workers from Natal's Zulu villages sleep on concrete bunks. That month, March 1991, fights had broken out between the Zulu hostel residents and people from the rest of Alex: it was another bout of bloodletting that fit more or less under the heading of the feud between Inkatha and the ANC. To keep the two sides apart, the police had ringed the hostels with razor wire, making them look even more like prisons. People sat about on street corners, some of them talking, some of them just sitting about. If they happened to turn angry, the white motorist fumbling over the potholes would not stand a chance.

Paul Mashatile therefore suggested we meet at Alexandra clinic, a smart setup on the edge of the township that is safe and easily found. Its manicured lawns are intersected by neat brick paths, and the buildings are painted green, blue, pink and yellow, giving the clinic a playground feel. A poster proclaimed, DON'T INJECT AIDS: SHARING NEEDLES AND SYRINGES SPREADS AIDS; and then, lower down, IF YOU MUST SHARE A SET, CLEAN IT THOROUGHLY (ONE CUP HOT WATER AND TWO TABLESPOONS OF HOUSEHOLD BLEACH). Another notice, written in a spindly hand, set out the toll from a recent bout of violence:

Lacerations/stabbings etc.	40
Gunshot wounds	7
Dead on arrival	2

And a note at the bottom read: "Majority of corpses found were taken directly to the government mortuary." There could hardly have been a likelier time to hear some bitterness from Paul Mashatile, communist, hunger-striker and leader of the township youth.

A smiling, ambling man with a pen clipped neatly in his shirt pocket greeted me, apologized for being two minutes late and suggested we take my car to go to his office. This turned out to be a dingy pair of rooms off a corridor lined with bundles of blankets; the building doubled as a shelter for refugees from the recent fighting. Paul Mashatile showed me into his room. A couple of ANC posters hung on the walls; empty bottles stood in a corner; the desk was decorated with a brand-new telephone, not yet unwrapped.

Mashatile pulled out an armchair for me and kept a stool

for himself. Had the army behaved properly in controlling the recent violence in Alexandra? "Yes, it had behaved well." The police? "Yes, we have been liaising with Captain van Hysteen." How do you spell Hysteen? Mashatile opened his address book to show me the name written down. "He was one of the people who detained me before. We used to run away when we saw him. Now I pick up the phone and page him and he calls back and I say, 'Look, man, there's a problem in such-and-such an area.'" Didn't Mashatile feel angry about those three years wasted in detention? "Not really. You see, we did not waste our time. We studied political science and analyzed the strategy of the regime. So we could see that our detention was just a part of their strategy. And we played soccer, and had cultural events. When newcomers arrived, we integrated them, taught them the history of the movement. . . ."

And so it went on. The ANC saw no need to revenge itself on whites, because "those who imposed the old system were the victims of the system itself." White civil servants who held their jobs on the basis of merit would certainly keep them. The ANC would of course tolerate other parties and opinions, and would no doubt form a coalition government if the result of the first election required it. How far did this appetite for reconciliation extend? Might it even include a coalition with the National Party, with the very people he had fought so long? Mashatile laughed. "The National Party is changing. There is no principled objection to it." And he continued, "People last year talked of Comrade De Klerk. We know the past. But when things change, you have to change as well."

AFTERWORD

It is easy to be glum about the future of South Africa. The 1990s seem an age away from the high spirits of Africa's early independence celebrations, when a youthful self-confidence was in the air. "Seek ye first the political kingdom," said Kwame Nkrumah, Ghana's first president; he and his generation honestly believed that black control of the state would end black poverty as well. In Africa and Europe the 1950s and 1960s were a time of faith in politics, a time when spreading bureaucracies seldom doubted their ability to do good. The world's rich role models were nationalizing key industries and expanding welfare services. Nkrumah and his fellow Africans naturally assumed that the same policies would transform their countries too.

These days the opposite belief is tempting. South Africa is throwing off white rule at a time when the state has been discredited, both in Africa and elsewhere. In Europe the idea that politicians can command economies has collapsed along with communism. In Africa overambitious government has brought about three decades of economic disappointment; the continent has paid dearly for putting the political kingdom first. The old optimism has given way to a sad cynicism. A few Africans even pose the darkest question: is political emancipation cause for celebration after all?

Set in this age of antipolitics, South Africa's political transition could never match the youthful celebrations of thirty years ago. There was a moment of euphoria when Nelson Mandela walked out of prison, and many black South Africans certainly hoped that the coming of their savior would dissolve all their pain. But the leaders and policy-makers soon returned to brooding over problems that lie beyond the reach of politicians. They discussed demography and the price of gold, literacy rates and terms of trade. As violence has mounted in the townships, the damage wrought by these impersonal forces has grown more evident by the day.

The remorseless currents that undermined South Africa's white government seem sure to weaken a black-led one, however enlightened its policies may be. The country cannot escape the demographic shift that comes at its stage of development: medicine has reduced child mortality, but the birth rate has not yet adjusted to match. As a result, South Africa's population is growing by about 2.5 percent a year—less alarming than the 3 percent that prevails in much of Africa, but nonetheless enough to extend the already endless lines for houses and jobs. Likewise, no government can restore the price of gold to its former glory: the economy's traditional engine can no longer be relied upon to pull it along.

Other problems are more amenable to political remedies, but cannot be solved fast. Political leaders can appeal for sexual prudence and encourage open discussion of AIDS; both measures may slow but hardly stop its spread. Enlightened land reform may contain soil erosion and rural poverty, though the implementation of reform is a vast administrative task that will take years rather than months. The new government may resolve to spend more on black education; but the backlog is enormous. It is these kinds of issues—health, agriculture and schooling—that will most affect black lives in the future. None lends itself to a quick fix.

Measured against the headier expectations of impoverished South Africans, the new government is bound to fail. Its policies will not solve the crisis in schools and hospitals and housing, nor give everyone a job. Indeed a determined pessimist might bet that bigger budgets in these areas will not help the poorest citizens, for government spending tends to benefit educated people who know how to work the system well. Across Africa independence has improved the lives of a minority of towns-people, who secure jobs in the ministries and manage to get their children into the best government schools. Illiterate people often know nothing of the help they are theoretically entitled to, and are ill equipped to lobby government for a fairer share.

With its more sophisticated bureaucrats, South Africa might hope to escape this problem; yet the same misdirection of state welfare occurs even in the developed world. In the United States William Julius Wilson, an academic from the University of Chicago, has described how middle-class blacks have done well since the civil-rights reforms of the 1960s, while the black underclass has grown. The number of blacks enrolled in full-time higher education nearly doubled in the 1970s; black home ownership rose 47 percent, compared with a 30 percent increase for whites. Meanwhile poor blacks have remained likely to be born out of wedlock, to be unemployed and to go to jail. In 1959 only 15 percent of black births had been to unmarried mothers; by 1982 57 percent were.[1] While the incomes of blacks in stable families went some way toward catching up with their white counterparts, the average black man in his twenties earned steadily less.

Twenty years from now, today's pessimism may seem vindicated: if rich America has failed to cure the poverty of the underclass, there seems little chance that South Africa will. And yet there is a danger in despondency, for it may obscure much of what is good. Measured against the high spirits of Nkru-mah's generation, South Africa will indeed fail. Measured against more reasonable yardsticks, there are grounds for hope.

Black Africa provides one such yardstick. At times South Africa has seemed at risk of matching the continent's miserable post-independence record, or even of doing worse. Its troubles in some ways go deeper than those elsewhere in Africa because of the circumstances under which transition has come about. The British and French colonists left other African countries before they were forced to, before most independence leaders had resorted to armed resistance, economic sabotage and the language of revolt. The countries they bequeathed were poor; they lacked educated people; but they did at least boast stability and decent economic growth. In South Africa, by contrast, whites have hung on as long as they could. They have repressed black anger and so cultivated ungovernability. They have provoked international anger and so deprived the economy of foreign investment and loans. After its prolonged and damaging struggle for independence, South Africa is now enduring a transition that in some ways seems just as bad. Civil conflict, which in most of Africa emerged only after the independence celebrations, has raged in South Africa from the moment of Mandela's release. White extremists have threatened to add to the bloodshed. Constitutional talks, which the government once declared would start early in 1991, have been repeatedly delayed.

Yet white extremism and constitutional disagreement are easier than demography to deal with; they lie within reach of political solutions, and seem likely to be contained. This book has suggested that the threat of white backlash is much exaggerated. White policemen have undoubtedly fomented violence in the townships during 1990 and 1991, but the police force has also distinguished itself by arresting white extremists outside its own ranks. When protesting white farmers jammed the streets of Pretoria, or when members of the Afrikaner Resistance Movement demonstrated in Ventersdorp, white policemen obeyed orders to arrest white troublemakers—and, in Ventersdorp, to shoot at them as well. All the bluster of white bully-boys has so far resulted in much less violence than expected. A couple of extremist gunmen have opened fire on black pedestrians; gangs have attacked picnicking black children. Just as in Namibia and Zimbabwe, there has been no serious revolt.

This book has also suggested that, however frequently interrupted they are, constitutional talks will carry on. Neither the government nor the ANC has an alternative. President De Klerk knows that without legitimate government his country will descend into worse recession and civil conflict; the ANC knows that without its old communist allies it can hardly return to its guerrilla campaign. The negotiations assemble a bewildering array of ideologies, ranging from the confused black militants of the Pan-Africanist Congress to the dreamy white exclusionists of the far right. This tangle of opinion will make the bargaining long and quarrelsome, but will not block it forever.

The key negotiators are the government and the ANC; these groups agree on many principles, ranging from proportional representation to an independent judiciary and a bill of rights. Smaller parties will throw their weight behind the larger ones; by late 1991 the Pan-Africanist Congress had allied itself loosely with the ANC. South Africa may not arrive as quickly at its new constitution as other African countries did at independence, for in most such cases the new constitution was designed in Europe and imposed with minimum debate. But the failure of those imported constitutions suggests that the months of thrashing about at the negotiating table in South Africa will be months well spent.

Whatever document emerges, it stands a better chance of meaning something than have most African constitutions. That is not just because it will have been written locally; South Africa is less afflicted by the other weaknesses that have undermined political freedom in Africa. Admittedly it suffers from diversity and tribal tension. But its people are richer and better educated than elsewhere on the continent; no government will silence its wealth of outspoken lawyers and journalists and trade unionists, many of whom are black. There will not be perfect democracy: this scarcely exists anywhere outside the developed West. Nor will there be an autocrat who extinguishes all freedom, let alone a monster like Ethiopia's Mengistu Haile Mariam or Uganda's Idi Amin.

Besides brightening the prospects for democracy, South Africa's stock of educated people improves the chances that the nation can avoid some of the other problems discussed in this book. At the time of this writing, black nationalists' instincts clearly include those which have wrought havoc elsewhere in

Africa: they are attracted by communal land tenure; they share the disdain for traditional chiefs and medicine. Yet the lessons from the rest of Africa have a fair chance of sinking in. South Africans are energetic pupils; lecturers and managers and activists are forever writing papers and convening debates. "How can we spread discussion of future economic policy to all South Africans?" wondered an intense group of Johannesburgers at one typical conference, as if their own presence there that weekend were no achievement in itself.

There is still time for learning. Under South Africa's existing constitution, President De Klerk must call a fresh whites-only election by 1995. He says he is determined to avoid this; he must therefore negotiate at least the outline of a new constitution before then. That gives the ANC a chance to prepare itself for government, to sharpen its ideas and administrative skills. It gives De Klerk time to push through reforms that should make the last stage of the transition less of a shock.

Long before concluding the task of constitutional negotiation, the president has started to chip away at the racial imbalances in schools and housing. He has granted 2 billion rand to a special development trust, set up to tackle the backlog of black services. He has offered first-time home-buyers various grants and incentives, to speed the growth of a black property-owning class. He has opened whites-only hospitals to black patients; he has allowed white state schools to drop the color bar; he has told town councils to desegregate swimming pools and parks. He has repealed the Land Acts, allowing blacks to farm outside the homelands; he has promised to help extend to black farmers the credit, advice and training that once went to whites alone. Residential segregation, which had started to crumble before De Klerk's arrival, is now no longer law.

The president's lead has been supported by local initiatives. In May 1990 unemployed black youths in Middelburg, a drab Transvaal steel town, threatened to attack black personnel officers at the steelworks unless the company gave them jobs. The white bosses responded typically: they denounced intimidation and notified the police. The unemployed then called a rally in

252

the township soccer stadium. There was talk of attacking not only black steelworkers but white ones as well.

That provoked a change of heart among the managers. Four whites arrived at the stadium and promised the unemployed a formal meeting and a chance to put their case. When the meeting began, the black delegates refused the Coca-Cola and tea provided by the management and drank instead from a bucket of water that they had brought. But the suspicions and bitterness were gradually defeated, and the talks went well enough to lead to more. The two sides founded the Middelburg Forum: representatives of the steelworks, the unemployed, the ANC and even the right-wing white town council began to meet regularly to discuss their common problems. The steel company promised money for projects that would dent local unemployment. These proved difficult to organize. But the company and the township leaders did manage to start a small enterprise that made kitchenware out of stainless steel discarded from the factory. The new company was called Compots, short for comrades' pots.

The Forum also tackled the local electricity boycott. As in townships all across South Africa, Middelburg's black residents had ceased to pay their electricity bills. The arrears had piled steadily higher, until the white local authorities cut the township off. Thieves and murderers thrived under cover of darkness. The Middelburg Forum convened a meeting. After sixteen hours' negotiation, the company wrote a cheque for 376,000 rand to the electricity authority, canceling the township's entire debt. By this time it was the middle of the night, but the negotiators woke up the town clerk, presented him with the check and demanded that the electricity be switched on again.

This spirit of enlightened self-interest extends beyond Middelburg. Since 1991 three white councils in northern Johannesburg have held regular meetings with the leaders of Alexandra, the neighboring township; they have agreed, among other things, that white taxpayers should meet the cost of supplying water, electricity and refuse collection to their black neighbors. Other white town councils have made similar concessions;

across South Africa, white institutions are inviting black advice and participation. Companies are anxious to promote black managers and to take trade unions seriously. Schools and universities invite black speakers to lecture their white students. Even the police force has taken steps to establish liaisons with township leaders.

These initiatives, and the president's legislative changes, do more than prepare whites for yielding some of their power. They also prepare blacks for the shock of exercising it. People who have never shared in power seldom make good rulers; in South Africa blacks' exclusion has fostered ungovernability. Now, as they grow used to their new influence, blacks are starting to question the assumptions that the struggle created. They are coming to realize that power brings compromise, not instant liberation. Trade unionists see that excessive wage demands push companies to bankruptcy. Township leaders discover the practical difficulties of reducing unemployment. As constitutional talks proceed, the compromising will go further—and the spirit of pragmatism will spread.

Here too South Africa is better placed than the rest of Africa. The happy optimism at independence in the 1960s was followed by disappointment, precisely because the optimists had little experience of power and expected too much of it. They sought to modernize ambitiously, forgetting that ancient traditions are resilient. They tried to extend the colonizers' affluence to everyone, as though prosperity could be created by government decree. South Africans' pessimism, and their disillusion with politics, may save them from such folly; they may avoid self-defeating ambition in government and put their faith in individual diligence instead. Pessimism may help to create a gritty realism. "Africa is always trouble!" said Gija Nyambi, my guide in KaNgwane. "When things change, you have to change as well," said Paul Mashatile, the young leader in Alexandra. "Our futures lie in our hands," said an ANC man at the Middelburg Forum. "The government may not address our need for housing and education, but we will do it ourselves."

NOTES

1 THE STRUGGLE AGAINST STRUGGLE

1. Quoted in Martin Meredith, *In the Name of Apartheid* (London: Hamish Hamilton, 1988), p. 73.
2. Allister Sparks, *The Mind of South Africa* (London: Heinemann, 1990), p. 266.
3. Nomavenda Mathiane, *Beyond the Headlines* (Johannesburg: Southern Book Publishers, 1990), pp. 23–25.
4. J. B. Peires, *The House of Phalo* (Berkeley: University of California Press, 1981), p. 111.

2 A DRAGON FOR AFRICA

1. "Long Waits for Telephone Services Put Some Countries' Development on Hold," *World Bank News*, vol. 10, no. 6 (7 Feb. 1991), p. 2.
2. Paul Bennel, "British Industrial Investment in Sub-Saharan Africa," *Development Policy Review*, vol. 8 (1990), p. 169.
3. "Foreign Disinvestment from South Africa Slows to a Crawl," *South Africa Reporter* (Washington, D.C.: Investor Responsibility Research Center, 1990), p. 73.
4. Anthony Sampson, *Black and Gold* (London: Coronet Books, 1987), p. 16.
5. Charles Becker et al., *The Impact of Sanctions on South Africa* (Washington, D.C.: Investor Responsibility Research Center, 1990), p. 26.
6. Drew Forrest, "Ordinary Men Shafted from Their Jobs," *Weekly Mail* (28 Mar. 1991), p. 8.
7. *Gold 1991* (London: Gold Fields Mineral Services, 1991), p. 21.
8. Gavin Maasdorp et al., "External Imperatives: South Africa and the World Economy" (Economic Research Unit, University of Natal, Feb. 1991), p. 9.

9. Patti Waldmeir, "A Long Way from the Land of Milk and Honey," *Financial Times* (7 May 1991), p. ii.
10. Maasdorp et al., "External Imperatives," p. 4.
11. Sampson, *Black and Gold*, p. 40.
12. Ibid., p. 55.
13. Breyten Breytenbach, *Memory of Snow and of Dust* (London: Faber, 1989), pp. 121–22.
14. Laurence Harris, "The Economic Strategy and Policies of the African National Congress: An Interpretation," in *McGregor's Economic Alternatives*, ed. Anne McGregor (Kenwyn, South Africa: Juta, 1990), pp. 25–73.
15. Sampson, *Black and Gold*, p. 256.
16. *Standard Bank Economics Review* (Johannesburg: Standard Bank, Aug. 1990).

3   THE WHITE TRIBES

1. A. S. Cripps, quoted in J. M. Coetzee, *White Writing* (New Haven: Yale University Press, 1988), p. 165.
2. Quoted in Robert Rotberg, *The Founder* (New York: Oxford University Press, 1988), p. 38.
3. Rian Malan, *My Traitor's Heart* (London: Bodley Head, 1990), p. 344.
4. Beatrice Webb, *Our Partnership* (London: Longmans and Green, 1948), pp. 40–42.
5. See Arthur Goldstuck, *The Rabbit in the Thorn Tree* (Harmondsworth: Penguin, 1990), p. 16.
6. *Socio-political Tracking Study* (Johannesburg: Markinor, Apr. 1990).
7. Peter Krost, "It's Show-house Sunday for Black Home-hunters," *Sunday Times* (Johannesburg, 24 Mar. 1991), p. 6.
8. Quoted in Meredith, *In the Name of Apartheid*, p. 212.

4   THE QUEST FOR A CONSTITUTION

1. The pamphlet was compiled and published by Renier Schoeman, M.P., chief director of the Federal Information Service of the Nationalist Party, Cape Town.
2. Donald L. Horowitz, *A Democratic South Africa?* (Berkeley: University of California Press, 1991), p. 205.
3. Lynette Dreyer, *The Modern African Élite of South Africa* (London: Macmillan, 1989), p. 99.
4. Horowitz, *A Democratic South Africa?*, p. 62.
5. Ibid., p. 54.

6. Patti Waldmeir, "Mandela Ends Conference on Conciliatory Note," *Financial Times* (8 July 1991), p. 3.
7. Horowitz, *A Democratic South Africa?*, p. 55.
8. Ibid., pp. 50–51.
9. Brian Du Toit, ed., *Ethnicity, Neighborliness, and Friendship among Urban Africans in South Africa* (Boulder, Colo.: Westview Press, 1978), pp. 158, 153, quoted in Horowitz, *A Democratic South Africa?*, p. 66.
10. Christopher Wren, "The Chief Steps Forward," *New York Times Magazine* (17 Feb. 1991), p. 56.
11. Mike Nicol, *A Good-Looking Corpse* (London: Secker and Warburg, 1991), pp. 358–59.
12. Robert van Tonder, "A Concoction of the Devil and the British," *Frontline Magazine* (Sept. 1990), p. 27.
13. Horowitz, *A Democratic South Africa?*, p. 158.

5   THE LAND, THE SOIL, OUR WORLD

1. Wendy Davies, *We Cry for Our Land* (Oxford: Oxfam, 1990), pp. 41–42.
2. Ibid., p. vii.
3. *Race Relations Survey 1987/8* (Johannesburg: South African Institute of Race Relations, 1988), p. 162.
4. Nicholas Christodoulou and Nicholas Vink, "The Potential for Black Smallholder Farmers' Participation in the African Agriculture Economy," paper delivered at Newick Park Initiative, United Kingdom (Oct. 1990), p. 7.
5. Ibid., p. 3.
6. ANC Land Commission, "Summary Report on the ANC Land Commission Workshop" (Bellville, South Africa: Centre for Development Studies, Nov. 1990), p. 9.
7. Zola Skweyiya, "Towards a Solution to the Land Question in Post-apartheid South Africa: Problems and Models," *Columbia Human Rights Law Review*, vol. 21, no. 211 (1989), p. 232.
8. Essy M. Letsoalo, *Land Reform in South Africa: A Black Perspective* (Johannesburg: Skotaville, 1987).
9. Jennifer Seymour Whitaker, *How Can Africa Survive?* (New York: Harper and Row, 1988), p. 163.
10. Sparks, *The Mind of South Africa*, p. 140.

6   THE SHADOW OF TRADITION

1. Quoted in Rotberg, *The Founder*, p. 100.

2. Terence Ranger, "The Invention of Tradition in Colonial Africa," in *The Invention of Tradition*, ed. Eric Hobsbawn (Cambridge: Cambridge University Press, 1983), p. 226.

3. Ali Mazrui, *Soldiers and Kinsmen in Uganda: The Making of a Military Ethnocracy* (London: Sage, 1975), pp. 206–7.

4. Z. K. Matthews, *Freedom for My People* (Cape Town: David Philip, 1983), p. 54.

5. E. G. Barendse et al., "Witchcraft Accusations amongst the Black Workforce of Pick 'n' Pay" (Pretoria: Human Sciences Research Council, 1991), p. 9.

6. Goldstuck, *The Rabbit in the Thorn Tree*, pp. 72–74.

7. Mathiane, *Beyond the Headlines*, pp. 80–83.

8. Laurence Cockroft, *Africa's Way: A Journey from the Past* (London: Tauris, 1990), p. 5.

9. Ibid., pp. 80–81.

10. Quoted in Saul Dubow, *Racial Segregation and the Origins of Apartheid in South Africa 1910–36* (Basingstoke: Macmillan, 1989), p. 4.

11. Quoted in Dubow, p. 70.

12. Quoted in Dubow, p. 72.

13. Quoted in Dubow, p. 115.

14. Ranger, "The Invention of Tradition," p. 239.

15. Hobsbawn, *The Invention of Tradition*, p. 167.

16. Quoted in Meredith, *In the Name of Apartheid*, p. 73.

17. Benson Ntlemo, "Free Petrol and Bush Toilets," *Frontline Magazine* (Sept. 1990), p. 29.

18. Modikwe Dikobe, "Hey People, You've Been Bewitched by Mangope," *Weekly Mail* (30 Mar. 1990), p. 11.

19. Eddie Koch and Edwin Ritchken, "The political economy of witchcraft," *Weekly Mail* (23 Mar. 1990), p. 11.

20. All these figures come from the South African Institute of Race Relations.

7 ACROSS THE BORDER

1. *Metal and Minerals Annual Review 1991* (London: Mining Journal, 1991), p. 39; *Gold 1991*, p. 21.

2. Hans Gustafsson et al., *South African Minerals: An Analysis of Western Dependence* (Uppsala: Scandinavian Institute of African Studies, 1990), pp. 11–15.

3. *The Military Balance 1989–90* (London: International Institute for Strategic Studies, 1989), pp. 139, 144, 143.

4. *Race Relations Survey 1987/8*, p. 521.

5. Director of Central Intelligence, "South Africa: Defense Strategy in an Increasingly Hostile World" (Jan. 1980), pp. F-3, F-2.
6. "Foreign Disinvestment from South Africa," p. 73.
7. Neil van Heerden, "Developments in Southern Africa," occasional paper (Johannesburg: South African Institute of International Affairs, Dec. 1990), p. 5.
8. Quoted in John Barratt, "Current Constraints on South Africa's Foreign Policy and Diplomacy," paper delivered at Leicester University (Mar. 1991), pp. 9–10.
9. Quoted in Michael Holman, "On the Road to 'Normalisation'," *Financial Times* (7 May 1991), p. vi.
10. Richard Hall, *My Life with Tiny* (London: Faber, 1987), p. 8.
11. All these figures come from *South African Destabilization: The Economic Cost of Frontline Resistance to Apartheid* (Addis Ababa: United Nations Economic Commission for Africa, Oct. 1989).
12. Quoted in Rory Riordan, "The Great Black Shark: an Interview with Chris Hani," *Monitor* (Port Elizabeth, Dec. 1990), pp. 15–16.

8 THE TAMING OF UNGOVERNABILITY

1. Mike Muller, "Third World Role Models for South Africa in Transition: Some Pointers from Brazil," *South Africa International*, vol. 21, no. 2 (Oct. 1990), p. 69.
2. *Human Development Report 1990*, published for the United Nations Development Program (New York: Oxford University Press, 1990), p. 153.
3. See statistical annexes to *World Bank Development Report*, 1987 and 1991.
4. See, in particular, Graham Boynton, "How Bad Is Winnie Mandela?", *Vanity Fair* (Oct. 1990), pp. 228–42.
5. Allister Sparks, "Jaw-jaw Takes Over from toi-toi Dancing," *Observer* (7 July 1991), p. 20.
6. *Year Book of Labor Statistics, 1989–90* (Geneva: International Labor Office, 1990), pp. 1003–8.
7. Patti Waldmeir, "A Demonstration of the Distance Travelled," *Financial Times* (15 Feb. 1991), p. 18.

AFTERWORD

1. William Julius Wilson, *The Truly Disadvantaged* (Chicago: University of Chicago Press, 1987), p. 28.

INDEX

ABOUT THE AUTHOR

———

SEBASTIAN MALLABY, the Africa correspondent for *The Economist*, was born in 1964. He was educated at Eton and at Oxford, where he earned a first-class degree in modern history. Since joining the foreign department of *The Economist* in 1986, he has written extensively on South Africa and on a wide range of issues concerning the developing World. In 1989 and 1990 he was based in Zimbabwe and reported on East and Southern Africa, during which time he covered many stories originating in South Africa, including the release of Nelson Mandela in February 1990. In addition to his duties at *The Economist*, Mallaby also contributes occasional radio comments to American Public Radio and to the BBC. He lives in London with his wife, Katty Kay.